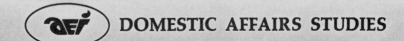 DOMESTIC AFFAIRS STUDIES

PUBLIC CLAIMS ON U.S. OUTPUT

Federal Budget Options in the Last Half of the Seventies

David J. Ott · Lawrence J. Korb
Thomas Gale Moore · Dave M. O'Neill
Attiat F. Ott · Rudolph G. Penner · Thomas Vasquez

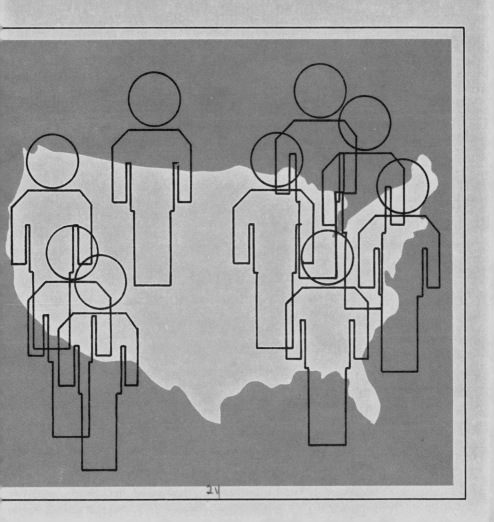

PUBLIC CLAIMS ON U.S. OUTPUT

PUBLIC CLAIMS ON
U.S. OUTPUT

Federal Budget Options in the
Last Half of the Seventies

David J. Ott · Lawrence J. Korb
Thomas Gale Moore · Dave M. O'Neill
Attiat F. Ott · Rudolph G. Penner · Thomas Vasquez

American Enterprise Institute for Public Policy Research
Washington, D. C.

This volume is the second study to result from the AEI Long Range Budget Projection Project. Contributors to this volume are DAVID J. OTT, professor of economics, Clark University; LAWRENCE J. KORB, associate professor of history and government, U.S. Coast Guard Academy; THOMAS GALE MOORE, professor of economics, Michigan State University; DAVE M. O'NEILL, director of human resources studies, American Enterprise Institute for Public Policy Research; ATTIAT E. OTT, professor of economics, Clark University; RUDOLPH G. PENNER, professor of economics, University of Rochester; and THOMAS VASQUEZ, staff member, AEI Long Range Budget Projection Project.

DAVID OTT, LAWRENCE KORB, THOMAS MOORE, ATTIAT OTT, and RUDOLPH PENNER are adjunct scholars of AEI.

ISBN 0-8447-3116-1

Domestic Affairs Study No. 18, September 1973

Library of Congress Catalog Card No. L.C. 73-88674

Printed in United States of America

CONTENTS

1

INTRODUCTION AND SUMMARY OF FINDINGS

The outlook for the federal budget over the remainder of this decade became a major issue of public policy in 1972. Considerable publicity surrounded two studies published that year, both of which concluded that the federal budget could not be balanced at full employment, at least through 1976, without substantial program cuts or tax increases.[1] The Congress and the President fought the "battle of the budget" in the fall and winter of 1972-73. The President asked Congress to pass a $250 billion ceiling on fiscal year 1973 outlays and to let him determine where the needed cuts (then estimated to be around $7 billion) should be made. When Congress refused, the President proceeded to impound funds to keep 1973 outlays to the $250 billion level. The administration's budget for fiscal 1974 proposes to hold outlays close to full employment revenues by program terminations and savings of about $12 billion, and projects another balance in the fiscal 1975 full employment budget if the proposed savings are realized.

The details of the fiscal 1974 budget and some of the issues it raises are dealt with in another AEI monograph.[2] This volume focuses on the long-term outlook for the federal budget in terms of the overall balance between outlays and receipts and, perhaps more important, the possible program options that might be considered in

---

[1] Charles L. Schultze et al., *Setting National Priorities: The 1973 Budget* (Washington, D. C.: The Brookings Institution, 1972), and David J. Ott et al., *Nixon, McGovern and the Federal Budget* (Washington, D. C.: American Enterprise Institute, 1972). The latter is the first study to be produced by the AEI Long Range Budget Projection (LRBP) Project.

[2] Murray L. Weidenbaum, Philip Marcus, and Dan Larkins, *Matching Needs and Resources: Reform of the Federal Budget* (Washington, D. C.: American Enterprise Institute, 1973).

policy planning over the long term. Chapter 2 provides an overview of the budget outlook for the last half of the 1970s. Attention is given not only to the likely outcome in terms of the full employment budget balance, but also to analysis of what the full employment balance in the federal budget *should* be if federal budget policy were to concern itself, as it should, with balancing the demand for and supply of total national output. Chapters 3 through 10 discuss possible program options within budget categories, from national defense through income security. Highlights of the findings of the study are discussed in the following sections.

It should be noted that all estimates discussed in this volume are based on the fiscal 1974 budget, and thus do not account for events that have occurred since, such as passage of the Agricultural Act of 1973, court decisions on impoundments, and so forth.

The Budget Outlook

The salient features of the outlook for the federal budget are summarized in Table 1-1. The administration has clearly succeeded, assuming its proposals are adopted, in achieving near-term (1975) balance between full employment receipts and expenditures. Indeed, if present administration programs are projected forward, and no additional new programs are launched, there is a growing full employment surplus in the federal sector (national income accounts basis) beyond 1975. The margin of receipts over expenditures is not large in 1976 (about $9 billion), but it becomes very large by 1980 (about $57 billion). Naturally, any new programs or improved benefit

Table 1-1

OUTLOOK FOR THE FEDERAL FULL EMPLOYMENT BUDGET, FISCAL YEARS 1975–80

(NIA basis, billions of current dollars)

Item	Year					
	1975	1976	1977	1978	1979	1980
Receipts	299.7	323.7	349.1	379.8	409.0	440.6
Expenditures	300.3	315.1	331.7	348.1	364.5	383.3
Surplus (+) or deficit (−)	−0.7	+8.7	+17.4	+31.7	+44.6	+57.3

Source: Table 2-2, Chapter 2, this volume.

schedules for existing programs must be assumed to occur by those years, and they would reduce this projected surplus correspondingly.

On the other hand, the *appropriate* full employment balance in the federal budget is very difficult to pinpoint. First of all, the appropriate fiscal posture depends on whether fiscal policy is viewed as the basic tool to be used to keep aggregate demand and supply in balance, or whether this function is seen as a more appropriate one for monetary policy. Using first the assumption that the budget is to be used as a stabilizing device, Chapter 2 looks at several possibilities, using the AEI budget and resource allocation model.[3] The appropriate budget posture turns out to be very sensitive to the assumptions made about the personal saving rate, the unemployment rate, and the size of the surplus run by the state and local sector.

This last variable is particularly important. As in the 1972 Long Range Budget Projection (LRBP) study, the AEI model projects large potential surpluses, on a national income accounts (NIA) basis, for the state and local sector for 1975-80—surpluses ranging from $20 to $26 billion. However, these projections assume that past trends in this sector continue—specifically, trends in the growth of per pupil expenditures on education and per person outlays for other purposes. The projections also assume that state and local taxes are raised in the future as they have been historically. However, it is possible that the state and local sector may come in with considerably smaller *actual* surpluses by *not* raising taxes as in past years or by "spending away" the surplus, or both.

In 1975, the problem is particularly acute. If the state and local sector runs a balanced budget, then in order to equate aggregate demand with aggregate output (assuming a 7 percent saving rate), the federal government should seek a balanced full employment budget. On the other hand, if the state-local sector runs surpluses, or if the saving rate is higher, then a deficit in the federal full employment budget would be required to balance demand for and supply of the nation's output. After 1975, there is an increasing margin for federal tax cuts or expenditure initiatives, whatever happens to the state and local surplus or to the saving rate.

Even if the state and local sector runs an *aggregate* surplus, individual units in the sector may still face a fiscal squeeze. For federal policy, the problem is not only to get a better "fix" on the likely size of the surpluses—because of the implications of such surpluses for the appropriate budget posture of the *whole* govern-

---

[3] Paul N. Courant et al., *AEI's Budget and Resource Allocation Projection Model* (Washington, D. C.: American Enterprise Institute, 1973).

ment sector—but also to find out which units are relatively affluent and which are not, in order better to target federal grants-in-aid. On the other hand, if monetary policy is used to balance aggregate demand and supply, then the role of budget policy is to provide an optimum use of resources, taking into account the effect of federal capital outlays and the effect of federal taxes and private saving. A sizable full employment surplus is probably appropriate for fiscal 1974 and after, though considerable conjecture is involved.

Policy Options

A major problem with past budget policy has been that new spending programs and tax cuts have been initiated without considering the long-run impact on the federal budget. Chapter 2 provides a framework for "pricing out" initiatives on either the expenditure or tax side of the budget.

At the same time, the "elbow room" above present commitments that emerges in the federal budget after 1975 or perhaps 1976 (Tables 2-2 and 2-5) should not divert attention from the need for continuous review and evaluation of existing programs and commitments. Whatever the budget margin with existing commitments, before using up that margin it is prudent to examine what it might be if existing programs were reviewed, in terms of both the desirability of their objectives and their efficiency in pursuing these objectives. This is the purpose of the analyses of program areas in Chapters 3 through 10, which are individually authored by participants in the LRBP project.[4]

Defense. The discussion of defense budget alternatives in Chapter 3 attempts to identify spending cuts that could be made without weakening the nation's ability to meet current strategic objectives. It is argued that personnel costs could be cut slightly, if "grade creep" among the military and civilian employees of the Department of Defense were reversed. More substantial savings could come from reducing support costs through closing excess bases and lengthening the average tour of duty for military personnel. Still more substantial savings could be obtained from cuts in procurement—specifically by eliminating the B-1 bomber, the AWACS warning system, and the SAM-D (anti-aircraft missile) programs, and by stretching out procurement of the Trident submarine.

---

[4] There is no "grand design" or blueprint for federal budget priorities underlying these chapters. In fact, individual participants in the study may not agree with all of the analyses and conclusions that are presented.

Agriculture. With current concern over increasing food prices, the analysis of agriculture and rural development in Chapter 4 centers on the price and income support programs. These programs are found to be inefficient in achieving their stated goals of raising the rate of return in farming and preventing agricultural poverty. Furthermore, their elimination would reduce agricultural prices by about 10 to 15 percent. As an alternative to the present programs, agricultural subsidies could be tied to the farmer, not the farm, and could be phased out over a five-year period. However, this might pose some problem of capital losses for farmers to the extent the subsidies are capitalized in land prices.

Science, Technology, and Industry. While small cuts are outlined in all program categories in the general area of commerce and transportation, the large savings are found in the area of space research and technology, water resources, and pollution control. Thus Chapter 5 examines the budgetary effects of canceling the space shuttle, initiating major cutbacks in the dam, flood control, and irrigation programs of the Corps of Engineers and Bureau of Reclamation, and replacing the existing grant program for water waste treatment plants with a pollution certificate program. Options considered in the commerce and transportation area include the abolition of maritime subsidies and federal grants for mass transit, the payment of air transportation expenses locally, and cutbacks in the highway program.

Housing. The analysis in Chapter 6 suggests that past housing policies require radical reform. Several possible new approaches to the problem are explored, but none is costed out, because reform in this area is a very long-term affair and would have little or no impact on the budget during the last half of this decade.

Education. Two program options in the education area are presented in Chapter 7: a "variable voucher" system for elementary and secondary education and a "cost-sharing plan" for financing higher education. Under the variable voucher system, a family with school-age children would receive, for each child, a voucher redeemable only for school tuition. The value of the voucher would be tied to the income tax bracket of the recipient and, thus, would be variable. Under the cost-sharing plan, the cost of higher education would be shared among the federal government, the state government, and the student. These plans are designed to improve the distribution of the "educational subsidy" and achieve a greater degree of competition in the education market.

Manpower. A major reorientation of federal manpower programs is proposed in Chapter 8. It is argued that the performance of training programs for the nondisadvantaged—particularly the MDTA program and the public employment program (PEP) has been distinctly unfavorable and they might justifiably be dropped. Evidence on other programs—WIN and the Employment Service—is less clear, and provides no basis for arguing for increases or cuts in spending in these areas. Finally, programs for the disadvantaged (the Job Corps, the National Youth Corps, and Operation Mainstream) have high success rates that justify expansion in these areas.

Health. The soaring cost of serious illnesses has become a major worry for American families. At the same time, there have been institutional constraints on the spread of private catastrophe insurance. Chapter 9, therefore, considers a government health insurance plan to replace Medicaid for the poor and to provide coverage against major illnesses for the rest of the population. In basic philosophy and resource cost this plan is similar to the administration's 1971 proposal. However, it avoids certain inequities contained in that proposal. In addition, it would be financed within the federal budget, whereas part of the administration's proposal would have forced private firms to buy employee insurance. The administration's financing device would hold down budget costs, but would place the same burden on the private sector as a tax-financed plan of the same magnitude.

Income Security. Chapter 10 examines possible changes in the social security system and the welfare system. In the rush to expand benefits and coverage under the social security system, Congress has overlooked some serious inequities in its structure. The treatment of married couples when both partners work, the significant disincentive to delayed retirement, and the inequities resulting from interrelations between the personal income tax and social security structure are a few of many areas requiring reform. However, it is enormously expensive to accomplish improvements in equity if no one is to be deprived of benefits. Since such deprivations would violate the people's trust in the system, reform must proceed very gradually. Either new entrants to the labor force must be put under a new system, in which case complete reform would not be accomplished for a generation or two, or inequities must be eliminated gradually by slowly improving the benefits of those now treated harshly by the system. In either case, it is unlikely that any major reforms can be accomplished in the decade of the 1970s and, therefore, particular alternatives are not costed out in this study.

The discussion of welfare reform notes that the administration's proposals in this area have foundered because of inconsistencies between, on the one hand, providing liberal payment levels and, on the other, keeping federal costs down, limiting eligibility to a small group, and avoiding work disincentives. It is argued that these inconsistencies could be prevented to some extent if benefits were allowed to vary with some index of the cost of living from state to state and region to region, thus making possible a lower "tax rate" on earned income of welfare recipients by cutting overall costs, and also avoiding benefits that representatives of the northern industrial states consider too low and those from southern states view as too high. An illustrative version of such a scheme is presented briefly and its costs are estimated.

An Overview of the Program Changes

Table 1-2 shows the net budget cost (including some proposed revenue changes) of these policy alternatives. Taken together they would cost some $14.5 billion in calendar 1978, comfortably below the margin of $32 billion (Table 2-1) calculated for the full employment surplus. If these programs were all adopted, there would be some margin for tax cuts or other outlay initiatives, or a combination

Table 1-2
NET BUDGET COST OF MAJOR PROGRAM CHANGES PROPOSED, CALENDAR YEAR 1978
(billions of dollars)

Category	Net Budget Cost
Defense	−7.5
Science, industry, and technology	−8.9
Agriculture	−4.4
Education	12.0
Health	18.5
Welfare reform	4.8
Total net budget cost	14.5

Source: Chapters 3 through 10, this volume. No significant budget effect would result from proposals discussed for housing or social security. The proposals discussed for manpower programs netted to zero within that category.

of both. However, as noted above, these options were not developed as part of a "package" and the specific programs and cost estimates are less important than the issues raised in the individual chapters. Others with different value judgments would suggest different program changes. But whatever proposals for program changes, terminations, initiatives, or tax cuts are made, they should be priced out in terms of a target path for the full employment surplus, preferably one which, allowing for the uncertainties involved, best budgets total output.

Since the individual discussions in Chapters 3 through 10 were not coordinated, the separate authors did not attempt to discuss the relative merits of spending more (or less) on program areas other than those for which they were responsible. While a common philosophy of priorities in federal spending might have produced a more integrated whole—a "counterbudget" of sorts—the results presented here are particularly interesting for the common threads that emerged without plan in the individual analyses.

First, taken together, the discussions of issues in health, welfare, housing, and education—the so-called social programs—have a common theme. In each of these areas, Congress has concluded that, without these programs, lower income families would consume less than they should of specific goods that are socially important (housing, health care, education, or food) or they will suffer from a general inability to consume "enough" goods and services (welfare). The basic assumption underlying these program areas is that the combined effect of the tax system and an economy based on ownership of private property and market transactions is to produce an unacceptable distribution of income, and that this effect must be corrected by general and specific forms of support, which are income-conditioned. The result is a set of programs that produce the "implicit marginal tax rate dilemma." As a family's income rises, it not only pays more federal (and state-local) income and payroll taxes, but also loses housing benefits, food stamp subsidies, and educational support, and pays more for medical insurance. The poor thus end up facing theoretically confiscatory tax rates, which act to discourage work. Moreover, specific support for various "socially good" types of consumption distorts the consumption patterns of beneficiaries.

Presumably, if the tax system and the marketplace produced the "right" distribution of income in the first place, none of these programs would be needed. Thus the root of the problems running through these program areas may lie largely in the defects in the present federal income tax system.

A second feature common to all the chapters is that the discussions of program alternatives are largely free of considerations of "political feasibility." The federal government has pursued activities in which the costs greatly exceed the benefits. But if a program's benefits are showered on a few recipients, it is in the interest of those recipients to oppose vigorously the program's termination; and if the costs are spread over the whole population, no one loses enough to warrant the expense of the political action necessary to oppose the special interest groups. By drawing attention to these programs and discussing their possible elimination, this study does not mean to imply that it will be easy to overcome the tendencies outlined above. In fact, it will be enormously difficult. However, there will be no hope at all of greater efficiency in government if studies such as this ignore wasteful programs solely because they are so firmly entrenched politically.

2

THE BUDGET OUTLOOK: AN OVERVIEW

David J. Ott

The administration's 1974 budget has brought into sharp focus some key issues of federal budget policy in general, as well as a host of issues involving specific federal programs. This chapter discusses the long-run outlook under the administration's budget and some of the general issues that the budget raises about future directions in federal budget policy. Specific program issues are dealt with in succeeding chapters.

The Budget Outlook

Projections of fiscal year 1975-81 budget outlays under the programs and initiatives proposed in the fiscal 1974 budget are shown, by major function, in Table 2-1. These estimates were built up from separate projections of individual programs, using consistent assumptions about future rates of inflation and compensation per worker.[1] The *real* rate of growth of individual programs was based on projected program caseloads and plans and policies enunciated in the budget document itself.[2] The projections also assume that the proposed savings outlined

---

[1] The rate of inflation is assumed to fall from its calendar 1972 rate of 2.6 percent (private GNP deflator) to 2.5 percent in calendar year 1974 and 1975-80. Output per man-hour in the private economy is assumed to fall from its 1972 gain of 4.2 percent to an annual rate of increase of 3.0 percent in calendar 1975-80. Compensation per man-hour is assumed to grow at 5.5 percent after 1974.

[2] More detail about these assumptions is presented for major programs in the chapters that follow. Additional information is presented in Appendix A.

A recent Brookings study projects much higher outlays after fiscal 1975 than shown in Table 2-1, viz. $308 billion in fiscal 1976, $329 billion in fiscal 1977, and $348 billion in fiscal 1978 [E. R. Fried et al., *Setting National Priorities: The 1974 Budget* (Washington, D. C.: The Brookings Institution, 1973), p. 414]. Most of the difference between the two projections reflects much higher outlays

Table 2-1

PROJECTED ADMINISTRATION BUDGET: FEDERAL OUTLAYS, BY FUNCTION, FISCAL YEARS 1975–81

(unified budget, billions of current dollars)

Function	Fiscal Year						
	1975	1976	1977	1978	1979	1980	1981
National defense	84	88	93	97	98	99	104
International affairs and finance	4	4	4	4	4	4	4
Space	3	3	4	4	4	4	4
Agriculture and rural development	7	7	7	7	8	8	8
Natural resources and environment	5	5	6	6	6	7	7
Commerce and transportation	13	14	14	14	15	15	15
Community development and housing	5	6	6	6	6	6	6
Education and manpower	10	11	11	11	12	12	13
Health	26	29	32	35	39	43	48
Income security	88	95	101	108	116	124	133
Veterans	13	13	13	13	14	14	14
Interest	25	26	27	28	29	30	31
General government	6	7	7	7	8	8	9
General revenue sharing	6	6	7	7	7	7	7
Intrabudgetary transactions	−10	−12	−12	−13	−14	−16	−17
Total outlays	288	302	317	334	349	365	385

Source: AEI Long Range Budget Project (LRBP) estimates. The assumptions used for most categories are discussed in Chapters 3 through 10 below. Appendix A summarizes the bases for the projections for international affairs and finance, veterans, interest, general government, and general revenue sharing.

in the 1974 budget are largely realized and that the four special revenue-sharing proposals contained in the 1974 budget (urban community development, education, manpower training, and law enforcement) are enacted, with outlays following the paths suggested in that document.[3] No allowance is made for possible additional expenditures for programs proposed but not priced out in the budget, for example, health insurance for the poor.

The budget document indicates that "unconstrained" outlays in fiscal 1975, assuming full employment, would have been about $312 billion without the outlay savings proposed in the fiscal 1974 budget. This is some $11 billion *above* the AEI LRBP estimate published in September 1972[4] and the estimate in the Brookings study of May 1972.[5] By the end of the 1972 session of Congress, the administration's goal of maintaining a balance between full employment revenues and outlays, even in the near term, required considerably more restraint on outlays than when these studies were published.

Converting the outlay projections to a national income accounts basis and to calendar years (1975–80) yields NIA federal sector expenditures, which are shown, by NIA category, in Table 2-2. These figures exclude purely financial transactions and other aberrations that occasionally distort the unified budget outlay numbers and thus they provide a better measure of the economic impact of the federal budget.[6] Table 2-2 also shows NIA federal sector full employment receipts for 1975–80, as generated with the AEI LRBP model,[7] and the resultant full employment surplus in the federal sector.[8]

Table 2-2 shows that the administration budget, if implemented, meets the administration's goal of a virtual balance between expenditures and full employment receipts in calendar 1975; it also provides

---

projected by the Brookings group for "defense, space, and foreign affairs." They project outlays in this category to be $107 billion in fiscal 1977, and $113 billion in fiscal 1978, while this study projects such outlays to be $101 billion and $105 billion in these respective years. The difference in the defense projection is discussed in Chapter 3. The difference in projected outlays in other categories is no doubt due to different assumptions about workloads, inflation rates, and so forth. However, the assumptions behind the projections of the Brookings group are not precisely spelled out, and their categories differ from those used here and in the *Fiscal 1974 Budget*, so a detailed comparison is not possible.

[3] *The Budget of the United States Government, Fiscal Year 1974* (Washington, D. C.: U.S. Government Printing Office, 1973), pp. 50–57.

[4] Ott et al., *Nixon, McGovern and the Federal Budget*, p. 4.

[5] Schultze et al., *Setting National Priorities: The 1973 Budget*, p. 418.

[6] See the Technical Note to this chapter for an explanation of the NIA conversion.

[7] Courant et al., *AEI Budget Projection Model*.

[8] The revenue estimates allow for a $.4 billion revenue loss for the administration's proposals for tuition credits for certain children in private schools.

Table 2-2

PROJECTED ADMINISTRATION BUDGET: FEDERAL RECEIPTS, EXPENDITURES, AND SURPLUS OR DEFICIT, FULL EMPLOYMENT BASIS, 1975–80

(NIA basis, billions of current dollars)

Item	1975	1976	1977	1978	1979	1980
Receipts						
Personal income taxes	128.3	139.7	152.2	165.0	179.1	194.2
Contributions for social insurance	93.5	106.5	107.2	118.7	127.1	136.1
Corporate income tax	53.5	57.4	61.9	66.6	71.4	76.7
Indirect business taxes	24.4	26.0	27.8	29.5	31.5	33.5
Total receipts	299.7	323.7	349.1	379.8	409.0	440.6
Expenditures						
Total purchases	120.7	124.5	130.1	135.0	138.6	143.7
Defense	78.7	82.4	86.3	88.6	89.5	92.0
Other	42.1	42.1	43.9	46.4	49.1	51.7
Total transfers	113.7	122.6	131.1	140.6	151.1	162.3
To persons	110.4	119.0	127.2	136.6	146.8	157.7
To foreigners	3.3	3.5	3.8	4.0	4.3	4.6
Grants to state and local governments	44.5	46.7	49.6	52.0	54.6	57.4
Subsidies, less surplus of government enterprises	5.9	6.1	6.0	5.9	5.9	5.9
Net interest paid	15.5	15.2	14.9	14.6	14.3	13.9
Total expenditures	300.3	315.1	331.7	348.1	364.5	383.3
Full employment, surplus (+) or deficit (−)	−0.7	+8.7	+17.4	+31.7	+44.6	+57.3

Note: Details may not add to totals because of rounding.
Source: LRBP estimates.

a surplus of about $9 billion in 1976, which rises to around $57 billion by 1980. In short, to the extent that the administration is able to realize its proposed budget savings, or match increases in expenditures above those proposed with cuts elsewhere, a small margin for tax reduction or for new program initiatives appears in calendar 1976. Much more "elbow room" appears in the following years of the 1970s.

The Budget Outlook for the State and Local Government Sector

Since 1971, the state and local sector *as a whole* has shown a rather remarkable improvement in its budget, as pictured in the national income accounts. From 1929-69 (excluding World War II years), the balance between receipts and expenditures for the state and local sector in the NIA accounts showed no trend. In nineteen of those thirty-seven years, the sector showed a surplus, and in eighteen years it ran deficits. In only one year (1958) did the deficit or surplus exceed $2 billion. In general, the trust funds (mostly state and local employee retirement funds) showed a steadily growing surplus. On the other hand, there was a growing deficit on general account, which, however, fluctuated from year to year rather than growing steadily. The net result was an overall deficit or surplus in a narrow range of plus or minus $2 billion, with the ups and downs reflecting a behavior of the balance on general account. This picture is summarized in Figure 2-1.

However, since 1969, the state and local government sector has shown a rather remarkable increase in its NIA surplus—from $1.8 billion in 1970 to $4.0 billion in 1971, to $13.1 billion in 1972.

Figure 2-1

STATE AND LOCAL SECTOR: ANNUAL SURPLUS OR DEFICIT
IN TRUST FUNDS, OTHER ACCOUNTS, AND OVERALL
SURPLUS OR DEFICIT, 1929-41 AND 1946-69
(NIA basis, millions of current dollars)

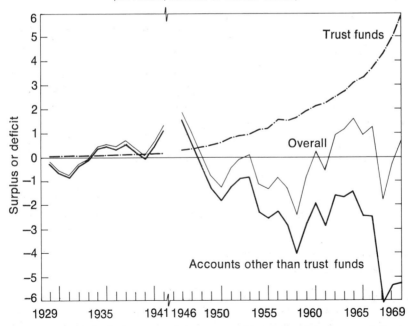

Source: U.S. Department of Commerce, *The National Income and Product Accounts of the United States,* 1929, pp. 54-55 and 58-59, and *Survey of Current Business,* various July issues, 1968-72.

Preliminary figures show a surplus of $14.0 billion (at a seasonally adjusted annual rate) for the first quarter of 1973. More significant, the increase in the overall surplus of the state and local sector reflected not only a continuation of the increase in the surplus of the trust funds, but a sharp fall in the deficit on general account. In fact, between 1971 and 1972, the general account swung from a $3.4 billion deficit to a surplus of about $4 billion.

Table 2-3 shows projections of receipts, expenditures, and the surplus of the state and local sector, as generated by the AEI budget projection and resource allocation model using the projections of grants-in-aid from the federal sector under the administration budget.[9] Essentially, these projections show what the yearly surpluses for the

Table 2-3

PROJECTED RECEIPTS, EXPENDITURES, AND SURPLUS IN THE STATE AND LOCAL SECTOR UNDER THE ADMINISTRATION BUDGET, 1975–80

(NIA basis, billions of current dollars)

Item	1975	1976	1977	1978	1979	1980
Receipts						
Personal tax and nontax receipts	46.2	51.9	58.4	65.6	73.6	82.5
Indirect business taxes	128.7	116.3	124.5	132.9	142.0	151.7
Corporate taxes	6.0	6.5	7.1	7.6	8.3	8.9
Contributions for social insurance	12.3	13.3	14.3	15.4	16.5	17.8
Grants	44.5	46.7	49.6	52.0	54.6	57.4
Total receipts	217.7	234.7	253.9	273.4	294.9	318.3
Expenditures						
Purchases	185.6	200.8	217.0	234.8	254.1	275.2
Transfers	17.5	19.0	20.4	21.7	23.2	24.7
Net interest paid	0.4	0.4	0.4	0.4	0.4	0.4
Subsidies, less surplus of government enterprises	5.6	6.0	6.5	6.9	7.4	8.0
Total expenditures	197.9	214.1	231.3	249.9	270.3	292.3
Surplus	19.8	20.6	22.6	23.5	24.7	26.0

Note: Details may not add to totals because of rounding.
Source: LRBP estimates.

[9] An AEI LRBP projection for this sector was presented for the Nixon budget as it looked in September 1972 in Ott et al., *Nixon, McGovern and the Federal Budget*, p. 23. For a description of how the AEI model generates the projected budget for this sector, see Courant et al., *AEI Budget Projection Model*, Chapter 3.

state and local sector as a whole would be (1) if tax receipts of states and local governments responded to increases in the tax base (personal taxable income, corporate profits, consumption) as they have historically (that is, if tax rate increases and the rise in receipts brought about by the growth of the tax base occurred at past rates, and (2) if expenditures of state and local governments rose so as not only to maintain *real* expenditures per pupil (in education) or per person (for other functions) but also to allow for the historical rate of growth in the "quality" (real expenditures) of state and local spending per pupil or person.

The results indicate that, even after allowing for a "quality adjustment," the growth in total state and local spending will slow down enough in the last half of the 1970s so that a continuation of tax increases at past rates would produce substantial surpluses—on the order of $20 billion in 1975 and perhaps $26 billion by 1980. This largely reflects demographic trends. Enrollment is already declining in elementary and secondary education, and the rate of growth in higher education enrollment will probably drop to less than half its present rate (about 4 percent in 1972) by the end of the decade. About 40 percent of state and local expenditures go for education,[10] so that these trends in school age population can hardly help but ease the pressure for growth in state and local outlays. Furthermore, the Census Bureau has reported recent fertility rates below those on which this study's population projections are based, and they continue to show a downward trend.[11] If anything, the projections of population and number of students used here is probably too high.

While there is strong evidence that the rate of growth of state and local expenditures may lessen in the last half of the decade, it is not clear that the projected surpluses shown in Table 2-3 will materialize at the levels suggested. Faced with reduced spending pressures, taxpayers may succeed in slowing down the rate of growth of state and local taxes, so that receipts and the surplus will follow a lower path than shown. One possible path might be that the overall surplus will roughly equal the surplus in state and local trust funds.[12] This

---

[10] U.S. Department of Commerce, *Survey of Current Business*, July 1972, pp. 29 and 33.

[11] U.S. Bureau of the Census, *Current Population Reports*, Series P-20, No. 248, "Birth Expectations and Fertility: June 1972" (Washington, D. C.: U.S. Government Printing Office, April 1973).

[12] The AEI model projects state and local contributions for social insurance (SCSI) at $12.3 billion in 1975. If the growth in the benefits paid out by the trust funds were to continue at its trend measured rate of 11.4 percent per year from 1960-71 and investment income grew at its trend rate of 15 percent a year, the trust fund surplus would be running at a level of around $10 billion in 1975.

would imply a balanced budget on general account, that is, no net increase in the liabilities of the sector as a whole. Another possible path is one where state and local governments run an overall surplus that reflects not only the surplus in the retirement funds, but also a surplus on general account, as was the case in World War II. In other words, reduced pressure for services might allow the sector to reduce its total indebtedness. Units might still carry out capital expenditure programs and issue new debt, but the retirement of maturing state and local bonds would exceed new issues. Still another scenario might be a surge of state and local outlays for new or different purposes—school equalization costs, pollution control, mass transit, or other programs—which could materially reduce the projected surplus, conceivably even to its historical level of near zero.

In short, while the state and local sector as a whole will face much less pressure for spending on its traditional functions, the implications of this for the sector's budget balance as a whole are not clear. Yet, as will be evident shortly, what the state and local governments in fact do with potential surpluses is critical to the appropriate posture for the federal budget.

Finally, it should be stressed that a brighter outlook for the state and local government sector as a whole does not imply a bright budget outlook for every unit in the sector. Significant numbers of individual units may face a continued budget squeeze due to population shifts, loss of tax base, special problems, et cetera.[13] Indeed, one of the most pressing needs is for research into the outlook for different units in the sector as well as the outlook for the sector as a whole. Which are the "wealthy" state and local units? Which units face continued budget stringency and why? The results of such a study would do much to aid the federal government in shaping its future policies in regard to the type and allocation of grants-in-aid to state and local governments. It makes little sense to structure federal grants so that fiscal relief is extended on a large scale to the relatively affluent members of the state and local sector. Means should be found to target federal aid where it is most needed, and this requires firm evidence of where the need actually lies.

The Federal Budget and Claims on GNP

In choosing a particular budget posture, the federal government is not only choosing a balance between full employment outlays and

---

[13] This was noted in our previous discussion of the state and local budget outlook. See Ott et al., *Nixon, McGovern and the Federal Budget*, pp. 24-25.

receipts but, given a path for monetary policy, it is "budgeting" the balance between total output and total demand as well. To put it another way, if fiscal policy is to be used for stabilization purposes, an important consideration in the choice of a budget posture is the implication it has for the balance of aggregate demand and aggregate output. If a full employment path is to be achieved through the use of monetary policy, then the fiscal posture of the federal government is still important in terms of the best allocation of resources. However, from either viewpoint the "optimal" full employment surplus is difficult to estimate.

Consider first the optimal full employment budget surplus path from the point of view of stabilizing the economy via fiscal policy. Given a path for monetary policy, the AEI budget projection and resource allocation model allows the user to ascertain the implications of alternative federal budget policies for the balance between aggregate demand and supply.[14] The administration's budget was examined from this viewpoint, with alternative assumptions about the personal saving rate and the unemployment rate.[15] Table 2-4 shows the GNP path and the path of total final demand for GNP under the administration's budget projections (in current dollars), assuming that the unemployment rate is 4 percent, the personal saving rate is 7 percent, and the projected state and local sector surpluses are realized. The unemployment rate is consistent with that used by the administration in defining full employment receipts. A 7 percent saving rate, while somewhat above the experience of 1960-66, is below the ratio observed for 1967-71 and very close to the 1972 saving rate of 6.9 percent.

As Table 2-4 shows, this combination of assumptions produces a comfortable margin between total GNP and total claims on GNP; the "gap" is negative—that is, final demand is less than gross national product—by some $17 billion in 1975. This excess of output over claims on it rises rapidly to some $42 billion in 1977 and to more than $90 billion in 1980. Taken at face value, the results indicate that the appropriate posture for the federal budget in 1975 would be a full employment *deficit* instead of the administration's goal of a balanced full employment budget; a full employment *deficit* of $17 billion

---

[14] See Courant et al., *AEI Budget Projection Model*, Chapters 1 and 2, for a detailed discussion of how the AEI model is structured for this purpose.

[15] Other assumptions built into the AEI model are explained in ibid., Chapters 1 and 2. Note in particular that net exports are projected to be zero over the period 1975-80. The recent currency realignments and "float" of European currencies might call for assuming some positive swing in net exports. Note also that the private GNP deflator is assumed to rise at 2.5 percent per year in all projections, whether this is in fact consistent with the other assumptions or not.

Table 2-4

PROJECTED ADMINISTRATION BUDGET: GROSS NATIONAL PRODUCT, FINAL DEMAND, AND THE GAP, 4 PERCENT UNEMPLOYMENT RATE AND 7 PERCENT SAVINGS RATE

(NIA basis, billions of current dollars)

Item	1975	1976	1977	1978	1979	1980
Gross national product	1,435.8	1,541.3	1,655.2	1,774.9	1,902.6	2,038.8
Consumption	871.9	930.1	992.2	1,054.1	1,123.3	1,196.6
Business fixed investment	163.5	175.6	188.5	202.0	216.4	231.7
Inventory investment	15.9	17.0	18.3	19.6	20.9	22.4
Residential construction	60.9	62.7	67.3	69.3	74.3	76.5
Net exports	0.0	0.0	0.0	0.0	0.0	0.0
Federal purchases	120.7	124.5	130.1	135.0	138.6	143.7
Defense	78.7	82.4	86.3	88.6	89.5	92.0
Other	42.1	42.1	43.9	46.4	49.1	51.7
State and local purchases	185.6	200.8	217.0	234.8	254.1	275.2
Final demand	1,418.5	1,510.7	1,613.4	1,714.8	1,827.7	1,946.1
GAP (excess of final demand over GNP)	−17.3	−30.6	−41.8	−60.1	−74.9	−92.7

Note: Details may not add to totals because of rounding.
Source: LRBP estimates.

would be consistent with balancing aggregate demand and supply,[16] at a 4 percent unemployment rate. However, the assumptions are certainly tenuous. There is no assurance that the state and local sector will run the projected surpluses. If it were to use up the 1975 surplus of some $20 billion by increased outlays, this would more than use up the $17 billion of "unused" GNP. Also, a 1 percentage point fall in the savings rate would sharply increase final demand: with disposable personal income of some $964 billion in 1975, this would raise consumption and final demand by almost $10 billion. On the other side of the coin, a higher savings rate or larger realized state and local surpluses could make the shortfall of final demand even larger. Table 2-5 shows, for different combinations of savings rates and state and local surpluses, the addition to total demand via tax reduction or increased federal expenditure that would just use up the remaining GNP, assuming a 4 percent unemployment rate.[17] At one extreme, an 8 percent savings rate with the projected $20 billion of state and local surplus would justify additional stimulus

Table 2-5

GNP MINUS FINAL DEMAND FOR DIFFERENT COMBINATIONS OF SAVINGS RATES AND STATE AND LOCAL SURPLUSES, 1975

(NIA basis, billions of current dollars)

	State and Local Surplus (4 percent unemployment)				
Savings Rate	$20	$15	$10	$5	0
6%	8.2	4.0	− .2	− 4.4	− 8.6
7	17.3	13.1	8.9	4.7	0.5
8	26.5	22.3	18.1	13.9	9.7

Source: LRBP estimates.

[16] The effect on final demand and GNP of a change in federal budget outlays or in full employment receipts depends on *what* is changed. Federal *purchases* could be $17 billion higher because they have a "dollar for dollar" effect on final demand. On the other hand, personal taxes could be cut some $21 billion, because a dollar reduction in taxes raises final demand by less than a dollar. For a more detailed discussion, see "A Note on Interpretation of the GAP Shown in the Output," ibid., pp. 77-78.

[17] State and local surpluses less than the $20 billion projected are assumed to fall because the sector reduces taxes. Thus, the effect of a fall in the state and local surplus of, say, $1 billion is to raise final demand by less than $1 billion (roughly $836 million), ibid., p. 77.

of about $26 billion over that projected under the administration budget. At the other extreme, a 6 percent savings rate and a zero balance in the budget of the state and local sector would signal a need to *reduce* federal purchases or *raise* taxes $8 to $9 billion from their projected levels.[18] On balance, though, Table 2-5 suggests that some margin for reduced taxes or increased federal spending would probably exist under all but extreme values for the savings rate and the state and local surplus, if the unemployment rate is 4 percent. For a $10 to $15 billion state and local surplus and a 6.5 percent savings rate in 1975, the margin for tax cuts or increased federal expenditures is about $4 to $8 billion. Beyond 1975, there is increasing room for expenditure growth or tax cuts.

As noted in the description of the AEI model,[19] an unemployment rate of 4 percent may not be consistent, even in the long run, with the 2.5 percent rate of increase in the private GNP deflator used in the budget projection. Thus, it is instructive to look more explicitly at the balance between GNP and claims on GNP for alternative (higher) unemployment rates.[20] This is shown, again for 1975-80, in Table 2-6. With an unemployment rate of 4.5 percent, there is a much smaller gap between final demand and GNP. In 1975, for example, GNP falls by some $23 billion and final demand also falls. But the decrease in final demand is smaller than the decrease in GNP for two reasons: First, government expenditures remain at virtually the same level as in Table 2-4; second, a $1 decrease in GNP induces a decline in private spending of less than $1 due to the usual "leakages." Clearly, if a 4.5 percent unemployment rate is more consistent with reasonably full employment, then the budget posture projected from the fiscal year 1974 budget brings demand for output produced and productive capability well within tolerances for 1975. After 1975, there is again the prospect of expenditure growth or tax cuts to balance claims on GNP against GNP, although the path of the gap between output and

---

[18] Spending increases in the form of transfers, grants, or subsidies, or equivalent tax *reductions* could be larger than expenditure changes on purchases, since the effect on final demand is less than "dollar for dollar," as noted in footnote 16 above.

[19] Courant et al., *AEI Budget Projection Model*, Chapter 2.

[20] The full employment budget balance is unaffected if a 4 percent unemployment rate is used as the benchmark for calculating revenues and outlays even though the actual rate stays at a higher level. While an adjustment is necessary to reduce unemployment benefits to what they would be at 4 percent unemployment, a similar adjustment to receipts is necessary, since a "steady-state" higher unemployment rate will cause unemployment trust fund receipts to be increased to meet the higher level of benefits, and these receipts should not be included in projecting a budget for 4 percent unemployment.

final demand is lower because the GNP path is lower, given the higher unemployment rate assumption.

The assumption of a 5 percent unemployment rate as reasonably full employment would further reduce the excess of output over final demand throughout the projection period.

If it is assumed that monetary policy is used to preserve full employment, then, as Bailey shows,[21] the optimal full employment surplus is one which (1) allows for loan finance of a portion of investment-type *civilian* expenditures and (2) allows for government savings (a surplus) to offset the reduction in private savings caused by the federal income tax. Following Bailey, assuming that 90 percent of the $37 billion of fiscal 1974 investment outlays of civil programs have diffused benefits and that depreciation and obsolescence on existing federal assets are half of capital outlays, then a full employment deficit of $16.6 billion would be needed to match the uncertainty of the benefits from such spending with uncertain costs (that is, to avoid the fall in private spending that would be caused if such expenditures were tax-financed). On the other hand, with total personal savings running at about $60 billion, then, following Bailey's calculation,[22] the additional federal savings required to offset the effects of the federal tax system on private savings would be on the order of $22-32 billion. Thus, even with stabilization policy not a factor, a full employment surplus of $6-16 billion might be warranted to produce the correct federal fiscal posture to allocate resources properly. Since both federal civil investment outlays and personal savings would grow over the period 1975-80, the size of the optimal full employment surplus would depend on the relative rates of growth of the two. On the assumptions above, however, a monetarist approach to stabilization policy provides a case for running, at least in the near term, a sizable full employment surplus rather than a balanced budget at full employment.

Conclusions

The thrust of this overview of the budget outlook is that the proposed budget for fiscal 1974 does come to grips with the problem of long-run balance of federal expenditures and receipts. The administration has, in fact, proposed a budget posture which restrains outlay growth enough in fiscal years 1974 and 1975 to keep the budget on the track of full employment balance.

---

[21] Martin J. Bailey, "The Optimal Full-Employment Surplus," *Journal of Political Economy*, vol. 80, no. 4 (July/August 1972), pp. 649-61.

[22] Ibid., p. 659.

Table 2-6

PROJECTED ADMINISTRATION BUDGET: GROSS NATIONAL PRODUCT AND FINAL DEMAND, AT 4.5 AND 5 PERCENT UNEMPLOYMENT RATES AND 7 PERCENT SAVINGS RATES

(NIA basis, billions of current dollars)

Item	1975	1976	1977	1978	1979	1980
			At 4.5 percent unemployment			
Gross national product	1,412.7	1,516.5	1,628.6	1,746.3	1,872.0	2,005.9
Consumption	859.7	917.0	978.1	1,039.1	1,107.2	1,179.4
Business fixed investment	160.7	172.6	185.2	198.5	212.6	227.6
Inventory investment	15.6	16.7	17.9	19.2	20.6	22.0
Residential construction	60.9	62.7	67.4	69.4	74.4	76.6
Net exports	0.0	0.0	0.0	0.0	0.0	0.0
Federal purchases	120.8	124.6	130.3	135.1	138.8	143.9
Defense	78.7	82.5	86.4	88.7	89.6	92.1
Other	42.1	42.2	43.9	46.5	49.1	51.8
State and local purchases	185.6	200.8	217.0	234.7	254.1	275.2
Final demand	1,403.3	1,494.4	1,595.9	1,696.0	1,807.6	1,924.6
GAP (excess of final demand over GNP)	−9.5	−22.2	−32.7	−50.3	−64.3	−81.3

	. . . . At 5 percent unemployment					
Gross national product	1,389.8	1,491.9	1,602.1	1,717.9	1,841.5	1,973.3
Consumption	847.4	903.9	964.1	1,024.1	1,091.2	1,162.2
Business fixed investment	157.9	169.5	181.9	195.0	208.8	223.6
Inventory investment	15.3	16.4	17.6	18.9	20.2	21.6
Residential construction	61.0	62.8	67.4	69.4	74.5	76.7
Net exports	0.0	0.0	0.0	0.0	0.0	0.0
Federal purchases	121.0	124.8	130.4	135.3	138.9	144.1
Defense	78.8	82.5	86.5	88.8	89.7	92.2
Other	42.1	42.2	44.0	46.5	49.2	51.8
State and local purchases	185.6	200.8	217.0	234.7	254.1	275.1
Final demand	1,388.1	1,478.1	1,578.5	1,677.4	1,787.7	1,903.3
GAP (excess of final demand over GNP)	−1.7	−13.8	−23.6	−40.5	−53.8	−70.0

Note: Details may not add to totals because of rounding.
Source: LRBP estimates.

At the same time, it is not clear what balance in the federal budget (measured at full employment) is in fact necessary, by 1975, if the objective is to budget national output rather than full employment receipts or to achieve an optimal allocation of resources. Looking at budget policy from the viewpoint of stabilizing the economy, the unemployment rate that is consistent with reasonably full employment and the behavior of the state and local sector are critical factors in determining the appropriate stance to take in federal budget policy. Realization of large projected state and local surpluses makes possible larger deficits in the federal budget. If the state and local sector reduces taxes or "spends away" its surplus, more restraint in the federal budget is called for. After 1975, there will be an increasing margin for tax reduction or outlay initiatives at the federal level. From the point of view of resource allocation, a sizable full employment surplus may be needed, if monetary policy is used to preserve full employment.

Technical Note on the Conversion from the Unified to the NIA Budget

Unified budget outlays were converted to national income accounts expenditures for each fiscal year for use in the AEI LRBP model. This was accomplished as explained below by projecting, for fiscal years 1975-81, the components of the adjustment.

Grossing for Retirement. The NIA accounts add to the outlays in the unified budget an amount equal to the federal government's contribution, as an employer, to the civil service retirement fund and to the OASDI fund. Contributions to the civil service fund consist of those matching employee contributions and a special payment to amortize the unfunded liability of the fund, which changes when pay increases are given to civil service employees. The NIA adjustment was estimated using the projected path of federal civilian employment (FECIV) and the assumption that annual compensation per worker rises at 5.5 percent per year. A separate calculation was made for the unfunded liability contribution and then added to the previous calculation to get total "grossing for retirement." On the receipts side, these same amounts were included in OASDI contributions (COASDI) or in "other" contributions for social insurance (FCSIO).

Financial Transactions in the Expenditure Account. The NIA accounts exclude certain expenditures in the unified budget because they represent purely financial transactions. Examples are Commodity Credit Corporation (CCC) nonrecourse loans and capital contributions to international financial institutions. The adjustment to outlays for such transactions in fiscal 1974 was −$1.7 billion. This adjustment was simply extrapolated forward, since it is impossible to project every component. The adjustment was assumed to become absolutely smaller over time as CCC lending declines and other financial transactions are taken out of the budget.

Other Netting and Grossing. This adjustment is mainly for proprietary receipts that are netted in the budget against outlays but treated as receipts (indirect business taxes) in the NIA accounts. This adjustment was also estimated using a trend.

Other Adjustments. Separate adjustments were made for "grossing up" receipts from offshore oil leases and for postal service capital outlays financed outside the budget.

The sum of the NIA adjustments to unified budget outlays was then subtracted, for each fiscal year, from budget *expenditures* (that is, outlays less net lending) to obtain total NIA expenditures. Total NIA expenditures for each fiscal year were then broken down into the NIA components—purchases, transfer payments, grants, and subsidies less surpluses of government enterprises. Transfer payments and grants were estimated separately for each program by the LRBP staff and then summed. Subsidies less surpluses of government enterprises were estimated separately for the largest components of this category—the CCC, the postal service, and housing. This provided a base for obtaining a total for this category, since for all other programs the net is virtually zero. Federal purchases were then obtained as a residual by subtracting grants, transfers, and subsidies less surpluses from total NIA expenditures. This was further divided into defense and nondefense purchases by estimating defense purchases and treating nondefense purchases as a residual.

3

NATIONAL DEFENSE

Lawrence J. Korb

The fiscal 1974 defense budget projects a slight rise (5.6 percent) in total expenditures, provides for declining levels of military manpower, contains funds for the procurement of several controversial and costly weapon systems, and foresees a drop in the level of spending for Southeast Asia. Since the administration has also presented an expenditure figure for fiscal 1975, which is about 5.6 percent above the fiscal 1974 level, it appears that the remaining three defense budgets of the second Nixon administration will also follow these patterns.

Like its four predecessors, the fiscal 1974 budget has stimulated considerable controversy and debate. Because of the reductions in many social programs in the overall fiscal 1974 budget, this year's debate is especially bitter. Congress seems to agree with the President that total federal spending must be kept down, but many congressmen argue that the reductions should come from the defense area rather than from social programs. Many critics feel that a rise in defense outlays, however slight, is unthinkable when social programs are being cut. They reason that, if we can no longer afford guns and butter, then we must eliminate some guns.

Defenders of the Nixon defense budget point out the $3.2 billion, or 76 percent of the increase in Department of Defense (DOD) outlays for fiscal 1974, is accounted for by military, civilian, and retired pay increases, and that the remaining $1 billion of the rise is largely attributable to inflation in the cost of materials and services purchased by the department. Administration spokesmen also note that, as a percentage of total federal outlays and the GNP, defense expenditures are at their lowest level since pre-Korean War days. Furthermore, "when adjusted for pay and price increases, defense spending in 1974 will be about the same as in 1973 and about one-third *below* 1968." [1] Even then secretary of defense, Elliot Richardson, who many felt would reduce some areas of the defense budget, stated at a news conference on March 5, 1973, that he could find no "pockets of fat" in the fiscal 1974 budget. [2]

Opponents of the level of defense expenditures in this budget call attention to the fact that even though defense outlays, as a percentage of the total federal budget and the GNP, are declining slightly, the Pentagon still takes a comparatively high percentage of both. Moreover, they add that if one examines the fiscal 1974 budget closely, the real increase is not $4.2 billion but nearly twice that amount. For this budget provides for 55,000 fewer military men and contains 53 percent less money for Southeast Asian operations than the fiscal 1973 budget. [3] The savings are $.6 billion from the manpower reduction and $3.3 billion from Southeast Asia so that the actual increase in the fiscal 1974 budget is $8.1 billion.

Although this chapter does not discuss the question of priorities in the federal budget, it may contribute to the dialogue between the proponents and opponents of the present level of defense expenditures. The first part of the chapter projects defense expenditures through 1980 based upon the trends and patterns established in the fiscal 1974 budget. This is followed by estimates of savings which may be achieved in this same period by possible reductions in certain areas of the defense budget.

The Budget Outlook

For purpose of analysis, defense expenditures may be broken down into the following categories: (1) personnel, (2) procurement, (3) operations and maintenance, (4) construction, (5) research, development, test and evaluation (R, D, T&E), and (6) military assistance. These are the categories or titles under which the Armed Services and Appropriations Committees authorize and appropriate outlays for national defense, and they include all defense expenditures except those paid by DOD to the Atomic Energy Commission (AEC) for nuclear warheads. (These expenditures are discussed in Chapter 5.)

Two major assumptions affect the Nixon budget projections in each of these categories. First, no funds are included for the incre-

---

[1] "Budget Message of the President," *Fiscal 1974 Budget*, p. 15.

[2] Transcript of the news conference supplied by the Department of Defense.

[3] Unless otherwise indicated, all the figures in this chapter come from the *Fiscal 1974 Budget*.

mental costs of Southeast Asia activities. For fiscal 1974 these costs are estimated to be $2.9 billion—$1.9 billion for military assistance to South Vietnam and Laos, and $1.0 billion for support of U.S. naval and air forces in the area. Expenses in the post-1974 period will depend primarily upon the cost of rebuilding North and South Vietnam, which is presently estimated by some to be about $7.5 billion. However, the administration has not yet decided on the total amount or the pace of rebuilding or whether funds for it will come from the DOD budget. At a press conference on March 2, 1973, President Nixon stated that funds for rebuilding North Vietnam will come from the national security budget, which includes both the defense and foreign aid budgets. Three days later, Secretary of Defense Elliot Richardson said that funds for aid to North Vietnam might be made available from the $2.9 billion allocated to Southeast Asia.[4]

Second, no significant incremental funds are included for the all-volunteer force (AVF). It is assumed that the $4.6 billion expended through fiscal 1973 has raised pay and living conditions to a level sufficiently high to attract the AVF,[5] and that only pay increases in step with the private sector and bonuses for certain skills (for example, for enlistment in combat arms) will be needed from now on. In fiscal 1974, allowances for the AVF are only $140 million and these projections include similar amounts for the rest of the decade.

Personnel. Table 3-1 projects the costs of personnel in the defense budget for the period from fiscal 1975 through 1981. Under the assumptions discussed in this section, costs in this area should rise by 43 percent by the end of the decade.

Personnel expenditures will consume 56 percent of the total DOD budget in fiscal 1974 and amount to about $44 billion. Ten years ago, expenditures in this category were only $22 billion or 43 percent of the defense budget. This tremendous increase in personnel costs is attributable to three factors: inflation, the move toward the AVF, and efforts to keep government salaries in line with rising productivity in the private sector. Personnel outlays consist of pay and allowances for four categories of personnel (military active, civil service, military reserve, and military retired) and housing costs. Table 3-1 summarizes the LRBP projection of personnel expenditures in defense.

For fiscal 1974, the Nixon administration is projecting an average active military strength of 2.233 million. This represents a decrease

---

[4] Transcripts supplied by the Department of Defense.

[5] An AVF composed of 2.2 million active duty military personnel and 1 million drilling reservists.

Table 3-1

DEFENSE PERSONNEL COSTS, FISCAL YEARS 1975–81

(billions of current dollars) [a]

Category	1975	1976	1977	1978	1979	1980	1981
Military personnel [b]	25.2	26.6	28.0	29.6	31.2	32.9	34.7
Civil service	14.0	14.8	15.6	16.5	17.4	18.4	19.3
Military retired [c]	5.3	5.8	6.3	6.6	7.0	7.6	8.2
Housing [d]	.7	.8	.8	.8	.8	.8	.8
Total	45.2	48.0	50.7	53.5	56.4	59.7	63.0

[a] Includes both inflation and productivity increases.
[b] Includes reserves.
[c] Without recomputation.
[d] Excludes pay.
Source: LRBP estimates.

of 1.270 million men, or 36 percent, since fiscal 1968, and will bring military manpower to 414,000 below pre-Vietnam levels and to its lowest level since prior to the Korean War (that is, fiscal 1950), when military manpower was 1.460 million.

Despite the reduction in the military forces, personnel costs have continued to rise. During the past ten years outlays for active military personnel have risen by over $11 billion. Ten years ago the average salary in the armed services was $3,100. Today it is $8,200. This represents an increase of 165 percent in a decade. A Senate Armed Services Committee study has estimated that the cost of maintaining a member of the armed services on active duty has risen from $3,443 in fiscal 1950 to $12,448 in fiscal 1974, an increase of 262 percent.[6]

DOD spokesmen have stated that manpower levels have bottomed out, and they predict no further significant reductions in force levels in the foreseeable future.[7] However, Congress usually makes some personnel cuts, and the projections here allow for a reduction of 33,000 personnel by fiscal 1975 and a level force of 2.2 million for the rest of the decade. The cost of this force in current dollars will rise from $23.0 billion in fiscal 1974 to $26.0 billion in fiscal 1977 and to $32.2 billion by fiscal 1981.

[6] *Navy Times*, May 2, 1973.
[7] Melvin Laird, *Final Report to the Congress*, January 8, 1973, p. 14; Robert C. Moot, *Department of Defense FY 1974 Budget Briefing*, January 27, 1973, p. 22; and Richard Nixon, *U.S. Foreign Policy for the 1970's: Shaping a Durable Peace*, May 3, 1973, p. 189.

The civil service picture is quite similar to that of the military. Fiscal 1974 civilian employment in DOD will be 32,000 below pre-Vietnam levels and yet the cost of the civil service payroll has risen from $7.3 billion in fiscal 1964 to $13.5 billion in fiscal 1974. This represents an increase of 85 percent in a decade and has brought the average annual cost of each civilian in DOD to $13,300.

Present civil service strength in DOD is 1.013 million. The analysis here allows for a drop of 13,000 by fiscal 1975 and projects a level of 1 million for the remainder of the decade. Costs for these personnel in current dollars will rise from $13.5 billion in fiscal 1974 to $15.6 billion in fiscal 1977 and to $19.3 billion in fiscal 1981.

The number of reservists and national guardsmen who will draw drill pay in fiscal 1974 will be about 1 million, at a cost of $1.7 billion. Because the Nixon administration's "total force" concept considers the drill pay reservists as an integral part of the nation's defense force and because of the decline in the number of active duty personnel, the analysis projects that the number of reservists will remain at the present level. The cost of these citizen soldiers will rise to $2.0 billion in current dollars in fiscal 1977 and to $2.5 billion by the end of the decade.

The situation with respect to military retirees is dramatically different from that of active personnel. While active duty strength has been declining rapidly, the number of retired personnel has been increasing dramatically and will continue to do so. In fiscal 1974 the number of former military personnel drawing military retirement pay will be 1.017 million. Two years ago it was .867 million and by fiscal 1981 more than 1.2 million people will be on the retired rolls.

Since the military retirement system is unfunded (the system presently has a liability of $196 billion), it will present an increasing burden on DOD. Whereas outlays for military retirement in fiscal 1964 were $1.2 billion, in fiscal 1974 they will be $4.7 billion. By fiscal 1977 outlays are projected here to be $6.3 billion and by fiscal 1981 about $8.2 billion. Between now and the end of the century, DOD will have to pay out at least $340 billion in retired pay.[8]

In addition to the increase in the number of retirees, there is an additional factor threatening to increase the costs of military retirement. This is the demand for recomputation of the base by those who retired before the large increases in active duty pay. In both the 1968 and 1972 presidential campaigns, the major presidential candidates

---

[8] The present military retirement system reform proposal, which is supposed to be presented to Congress this year, will reduce costs by 7 percent over the next twenty-seven years, but will not have any real impact in this decade.

pledged themselves to support recomputation, and in fiscal 1973 the administration actually provided $.3 billion in the defense budget for partial recomputation.

The Senate passed a recomputation bill in the summer of 1972, but it died in conference. During the fall and winter of 1972, a House subcommittee studied the question in great detail and recommended that recomputation not be considered because of its prohibitive costs. The committee estimated that the Nixon proposal would have a cumulative cost of $17 billion and full recomputation would have an eventual price tag of $137 billion.[9]

Nevertheless, the Nixon administration again provided $.3 billion for recomputation in the fiscal 1974 budget. This analysis does not include any funds for recomputation. The leaders of the military committees in Congress are opposed to it and the Pentagon is not actively supporting it. In his first press conference as Secretary of Defense, Secretary Richardson said that the $360 million for recomputation was a good example of an area where Congress might profitably cut the fiscal 1974 budget.[10]

Outlays for housing, excluding pay, will reach $725 million in fiscal 1974. This represents an increase of $329 million or 83 percent since fiscal 1968. For the following reasons, the projections assume that outlays will remain at this high level for the remainder of the decade. First, surveys have shown that adequate housing is an essential ingredient for attracting and maintaining an effective AVF. Second, there is still an acute shortage of housing—for example, the Navy maintains that, at the present rate of expenditures, it will take ten years to provide adequate housing for enlisted bachelors and twenty-two years to provide sufficient housing for bachelor officers.[11] Third, in fiscal 1974, budget authority for housing is 19 percent above outlays. Outlays for housing thus are assumed to rise to $773 million by fiscal 1977 and to $836 million by fiscal 1981.

Procurement. DOD is currently developing 116 weapon systems with a total estimated cost of $153 billion. Through fiscal 1973, Congress has appropriated only $63 billion of this total.[12] Thus, within the

---

[9] U.S. Congress, House Armed Services Committee, *Recomputation and Other Retirement Legislation*, 92nd Congress, 2nd session, December 29, 1972, pp. 17626 and 17627.

[10] *Washington Post*, February 1, 1973.

[11] U.S. Senate, *Report 92-1249*, September 30, 1972, p. 4.

[12] Comptroller General of the United States, *Cost Growth in Major Weapon Systems*, March 26, 1973, p. 1. Procurement estimates allow for inflation. This is an innovation of Melvin Laird.

next five years Congress must appropriate at least an additional $90 billion if these weapon systems are to be completed. Although many of them are controversial and very expensive and have generated a great deal of debate in Congress and among the informed public, Congress has not yet canceled any of them. Table 3-2 contains a list of the major weapon systems with their cost data up through the President's fiscal 1974 budget request.

Outlays for procurement requested in fiscal 1974 are projected to be $16.5 million. As indicated in Table 3-2, about 50 percent of these outlays will go to these major ongoing programs. Very few new programs were initiated in the fiscal 1974 budget. The only ones of any consequence are the proposed Submarine Launched Cruise

Table 3-2

NIXON BUDGET: MAJOR PROCUREMENT PROGRAMS
(billions of dollars)

Program	Total Cost	Unit Cost[a]	Authorized Through FY 1973	Requested in FY 1974	Remaining
MIRV	8.5	N/A	4.7	.8	3.0
Trident	12.8	1.0B	1.1	1.7	10.0
AWACS	2.7	64M	.2	.2	2.3
SAM-D	5.2	N/A	.5	.2	4.5
B-1	12.7	52M	1.1	.5	11.1
F-15	7.8	10M	1.9	1.1	4.8
F-14	5.2[b]	17M	3.4	.6	1.2
S-3A	3.2	16M	1.3	.5	1.4
P-3C	2.5	12M	1.2	.2	1.1
CVN[c]	4.0	1.0B	.3	.6	3.0
SSN[d]	10.9	186M	3.1	.9	3.0
DD-963	2.8	90M	1.1	.6	1.1
AX (A-10)	1.6	3M	.2	.1	1.3
	79.9		20.1	8.0	51.6

[a] B = billions, M = millions, N/A = not available.

[b] On March 8, 1972, the Navy announced that it was planning to buy only thirty-four planes for $3.46 billion, or $25.8 million per plane.

[c] Assumes that one CVN will be funded every other year.

[d] Assumes that six SSNs will be funded annually.

Sources: Various authorization and appropriations hearings and reports on the DOD budgets for FY 1972 and 1973; Comptroller General of the United States, *Acquisition of Major Weapon Systems: Report to the Congress, B-16058,* July 17, 1972, pp. 63-65; Department of Defense, *Program Acquisition Costs by Weapon System,* January 29, 1973; Comptroller General of the United States, *Cost Growth in Major Weapon Systems,* p. 60.

Missile (Harpoon), for which only $15.3 million was requested, and a mobile ICBM program, for which only $6 million was asked.

Based upon the amount of the unexpended balance for the weapon systems currently being developed and the fact that budget authority for fiscal 1974 is 14 percent above outlays, procurement expenditures are projected to rise through fiscal 1978 to $19.6 billion in current dollars. After that, outlays for procurement should fall as the proposed weapon systems are completed, if no major new programs are undertaken in the interim. By fiscal 1981 we estimate that procurement outlays will fall to about $15.5 billion.

Our projections in this area are based upon completion of these major programs and assume that, if cost overruns exceed the anticipated inflation by a large amount, DOD will either procure fewer units or stretch out the program. Such practices have become common in recent years. For example, when the F-14 program experienced a cost overrun of nearly 100 percent, the Pentagon reduced the program by half; and when S-3A costs rose, the purchase of thirteen planes was transferred from fiscal 1973 to fiscal 1974.

Projections in the procurement area are fraught with great uncertainty. Should real progress toward disarmament be made in the upcoming SALT II negotiations or the European Security Conference, major weapon systems might be shelved. However, should the spirit of SALT I not continue (for example, if the Soviets should seek to exploit their newly acquired MIRV capability), dramatic increases could occur. President Nixon estimated that if the SALT I negotiations had not been successful, procurement funds would have had to increase substantially.[13] Full-scale development of the mobile ICBM mentioned above would be one example of an expensive new program; development of "hard target" weapons would be another.

Operations and Maintenance. Operations and maintenance (O&M) costs include ship and aircraft fuel, transportation and travel, overhaul of ships, aircraft and other weapons, and medical supplies and services. For fiscal 1974 the nonpersonnel costs for these items should amount to about $11.5 billion. Total O&M costs, including those of civil service personnel, will be $22.3 billion.[14]

---

[13] *Washington Post*, June 30, 1972. The President stated that procurement costs would rise about $15 billion annually without SALT I, but there does not appear to be any real basis for this figure. It was probably meant to impress Congress with the necessity of ratifying SALT I.

[14] Although this analysis discusses civil service personnel costs separately in the personnel category, Congress considers them in the areas affected. The majority of civil service personnel costs occur in the O&M category. Small amounts are found in the construction, R, D, T & E, and housing accounts.

Projections in this area are based upon three assumptions: (1) the cost of these goods and services will rise at the same rate as prices in general; (2) the major weapon systems to which the administration is committed will be completed and they will be phased into the active forces on time and in the projected numbers (significant slippage in the delivery schedule of the new weapon systems will cause a rise in O&M costs of keeping the present systems in operation beyond their useful life); and (3) the number of carriers will decline from fifteen to twelve because during the remaining years of this decade only one carrier will become operational and four will be retired as they reach the end of their thirty-year useful life period.

On the basis of these assumptions, total O&M costs are projected to rise to $24.8 billion in fiscal 1977 and to over $30.5 billion by fiscal 1981. Nonpersonnel O&M costs will be $12.9 billion and $15.8 billion, respectively.

Construction. Military construction projects are tied primarily to the procurement area. For example, the Trident program will necessitate the construction of a new base at Bangor, Washington, at a cost of about $550 million. Therefore, the projections in this area are similar to those in procurement. Construction costs are projected to increase from $1.3 billion in fiscal 1974 to $1.8 billion by fiscal 1978 and then to decline slightly, if no new major projects are launched.

Research, Development, Test and Evaluation (RDT&E). Outlays in this area for fiscal 1974 are projected to be $8.1 billion. Comptroller Robert C. Moot has stated that there will be no real increase in the R&D accounts for the next five years.[15] Therefore, the projections allow only for inflation. It should be noted that, despite official statements, expenditures in this area might increase in real terms should international agreements slow down the procurement of new weapons. For example, after the SALT I agreements about $.2 billion was transferred from procurement to R&D.

Military Assistance. Outlays for military assistance in fiscal 1974 are estimated to be $800 million. (The amount funded in this portion of the DOD budget includes only a small part of the total cost of military assistance. Total military assistance, funded in all parts of the federal budget, is about $10 billion.) The projections here foresee no real increase in this category for the remainder of the decade.

---

[15] Moot, *DOD 1974 Budget Briefing*, p. 8.

In principle, outlays for military assistance should rise as total troop strength and overseas forces decline. However, this area is very vulnerable to congressional reductions. Military assistance has no real constituency and congressmen are free to make reductions in this area with impunity. In the past five years, Congress has reduced administration requests in this area by about 25 percent, and did not complete action on the fiscal 1973 request until the end of the fiscal year.[16]

Summary. Table 3-3 summarizes our projections by category. If the assumptions developed here are correct, outlays for defense purposes will rise by $23 billion or 29 percent between now and the end of the decade. This is an average annual increase of $3.2 billion or 4.1 percent (a real increase of only 1.6 percent). About $17.8 billion of the increase will be caused by rising personnel costs. Indeed, after

Table 3-3
DEFENSE OUTLAYS BY APPROPRIATION TITLE, FISCAL YEARS 1975–81
(billions of current dollars)

Appropriation Title	1975	1976	1977	1978	1979	1980	1981
Military personnel [a]	25.2	26.6	28.0	29.6	31.2	32.9	34.7
Military retired	5.3	5.8	6.3	6.6	7.0	7.6	8.2
O&M [b]	22.7	23.8	24.8	26.3	27.6	29.1	30.5
Procurement [b]	16.7	17.8	19.1	19.6	17.5	15.1	15.5
R&D [b]	8.3	8.5	8.7	8.9	9.1	9.3	9.5
Construction [b]	1.3	1.6	1.7	1.8	1.7	1.6	1.8
Other [c]	.5	.5	.5	.5	.5	.5	.5
Military assistance	.8	.8	.9	.9	.9	.9	.9
Total	80.8	85.4	90.0	94.2	95.5	97.0	101.6

[a] Includes reserves.

[b] Includes the cost of civilian personnel.

[c] Includes housing, civil defense, special foreign currency, and revolving and management funds.

Source: LRBP estimates.

[16] Outlays in this account might rise if expenditures for military assistance to Southeast Asia, which are currently funded in the service budgets, are transferred to it. Prior to 1966, military assistance to Southeast Asia was funded in this account.

fiscal 1978 outlays for investment (procurement, RDT&E, and construction) will decrease in real terms.

The projection for fiscal 1975 is $2.2 billion less than the administration's figure of $83.0 billion. This difference is due to the fact that no funds for Southeast Asia or recomputation are available in the administration's budget projection. If these funds ($3.2 billion) are subtracted from the administration's fiscal 1975 budget projection, then the projected budget here is actually $1 billion higher.[17]

Possible Savings in Defense

If one is looking for ways to reduce federal outlays, an obvious place to begin is the defense budget. Not only are DOD expenditures quite large (28.4 percent of total federal outlays and 6 percent of GNP), but defense outlays represent 69.5 percent of the controllable expenditures in the federal budget.

However, before examining areas of possible savings in the DOD budget, certain facts ought to be made clear. As a percentage of the total budget and GNP respectively, defense outlays are at their lowest level since 1950 when DOD accounted for 26.6 percent of the federal budget and 6.6 percent of the GNP. As recently as fiscal 1968, DOD expenditures represented 42.5 percent of the federal budget and 9.4 percent of the GNP. Moreover, only $52.3 billion or 66 percent of the DOD budget itself is "controllable." Finally, defense spending in real terms has not risen since fiscal 1968, and has actually decreased in real terms by about 10 percent since fiscal 1964.

Nevertheless, there are at least three areas in which many experts believe defense spending can perhaps be reduced without undue risks to security, although there may be some impact upon the AVF. They are personnel, support, and procurement.

Personnel. Any attempt to find possible places to reduce defense spending should focus initially on the personnel area for two reasons.

---

[17] Projections for defense outlays in fiscal years 1975-80, made by the Brookings group, are also somewhat higher than our projections (Fried et al., *Setting National Priorities: The 1974 Budget*, pp. 334-335). There are four reasons for this. First, the Brookings group uses a higher rate of inflation to calculate pay and price increases—over 4 percent in many categories. Second, the group makes allowances for real cost growth over and above official administration cost estimates. Third, it included funds for unspecified new initiatives. And fourth, it added $1 billion annually to outlays in order to close the gap between total obligational authority and expenditures. The Brookings group admits that as a prediction of what will happen their defense projections are probably on the high side.

First, personnel costs now represent 56 percent of total outlays for defense. Second, personnel reductions are the quickest way to reduce defense spending. Payments to laid-off personnel stop almost immediately. Indeed, the National Urban Coalition's alternative defense budget for fiscal 1974 achieves a large part of its suggested $5.1 billion reduction by recommending an additional cut of 300,000 active duty military personnel.[18]

Nevertheless, for three reasons it does not seem probable that there will be any attempts on the part of Congress to make significant reductions in manpower levels at this time without any changes in U.S. commitments or strategy. First, since taking office, the Nixon administration has already reduced military and civilian manpower in DOD by about one-third, that is, from 4.8 million to just above 3.2 million. Second, the present manpower level is the lowest that the total DOD labor force has been since June 1950, just prior to the outbreak of the Korean War, and lower than at any time during the Eisenhower, Kennedy, and Johnson administrations. Third, the projections discussed above already allow for a reduction of 46,000 additional military and civilian personnel between now and the end of fiscal 1975.

However, it is obvious that the armed services will make significant efforts to search for ways to economize on labor. Under the draft, manpower was underpriced and hence profligately used. Future weapon systems should be designed with a view to replacing manpower with mechanization. Moreover, DOD should continue to attempt to civilianize those military jobs which can be done more cheaply by civilians (for example, the Pentagon civilianized 31,000 military positions within the last year).

But, even within this comparatively small labor force, there is one area which is likely to be seized upon by those interested in reducing defense expenditures, that is, a reduction in the proportion of high-level military and civilian personnel. From fiscal 1964, the last pre-Vietnam year, to fiscal 1973, there has been an 11 percent decrease in military personnel. (Senator Walter Mondale, D.-Minn., has already introduced legislation to bring this about.) Despite this reduction in total personnel, the number of flag officers has increased by 25, the number of colonels and lieutenant colonels (captains and commanders in the Navy) has increased by 2,552, and the number

---

[18] The National Urban Coalition, *An Alternative Budget for Fiscal Year 1974*, March 27, 1973, p. 1. This is also true of the $14 billion reduction in the fiscal year 1974 defense budget proposed by the Project on Budget Priorities in its *Military Policy and Budget Priorities*.

of high-level enlisted men (E-7, E-8, and E-9) has increased by 36,853. The House Appropriations Committee has estimated that this increase in grade level, or "grade creep," cost about $1.3 billion in fiscal 1973.[19]

In the fiscal 1974 budget, the services have made some efforts to reduce this grade creep. They have reduced the percentage of officers from 14.4 percent to 14 percent and the percentage of enlisted personnel in the top six grades (E-4 to E-9) from 66.1 percent to 63.5 percent,[20] and they have lengthened the time in grade requirements for promotions. However, these changes have been relatively small. For example, the Navy has increased the number of junior officers (grades 01 to 03) by only .3 percent and decreased the number of senior officers (grades 04 to 06) by only 3 percent, while leaving the number of admirals unchanged. These actions will save only about $.2 billion in fiscal 1974.

The civil service situation is somewhat less severe. Programs enacted in 1970 by OMB have succeeded in reducing the average grade level for civilians in the fiscal 1973 budget. But, within DOD the number of supergrade civilians has remained virtually unchanged at 1,625 since fiscal 1968, despite a reduction in the civilian work force from 1,287,000 to 1,031,000, or almost 21.3 percent. Maintaining these additional supergrade civilians costs about $30 million a year.

If the Pentagon could reduce the number of high-level positions and restore the grade distribution pattern of fiscal 1964, personnel costs in fiscal 1974 would be about $1.1 billion lower. However, such a step is neither practical nor legal since these personnel have certain tenure rights. A more vigorous effort on the part of the Pentagon to forcibly retire high-level personnel who have reached the minimum legal age and length of service requirements for retirement could be undertaken with a saving of $.3 billion in fiscal 1974. Many congressmen would like to see these high-level reductions take place in the command/headquarters category, where the Senate Armed Services Committee has concluded that a 25 percent reduction could be made without an adverse impact on defense capability.[21]

---

[19] U.S. Congress, House Appropriations Committee, *Report 92-1389*, September 11, 1972, pp. 24-25. "Grade bulge," which has occurred after every war, might be a more accurate term than "grade creep."

[20] Moot, *DOD 1974 Budget Briefing*, p. 5.

[21] *Report 92-1398*, p. 63. Congress is currently considering a Defense Department plan for the overhaul of official promotion and tenure laws. New laws might make it possible to reduce the grade bulge even more. The new Urban Coalition estimates that half the process of restoring the fiscal 1964 grade distribution would save $600 million annually.

Support.[22] Indirect support costs in the defense budget include such items as recruit and specialized training, pilot training, personnel assignment, depot-level maintenance function, headquarters operations, and base operations.

As indicated in Table 3-4, indirect support costs in the fiscal 1974 budget account for 27 percent of the total outlays. Although this represents a slight decrease from fiscal 1973, this level is still higher than either the pre-Vietnam level or that attained at the height of the Vietnam war. The average support cost per military man for fiscal 1974 will be $1,030,[23] while ten years ago it was only $425. Because of this high level of support costs, many have proposed savings in this area.

DOD spokesmen themselves have suggested that the largest waste in the support area results from the operation of "excess" bases. Former Deputy Secretary of Defense David Packard estimated that about $1 billion a year could be saved by closing unnecessary bases in the continental United States (CONUS),[24] and Admiral Elmo R.

Table 3-4

INDIRECT DEFENSE SUPPORT COSTS,[a]
SELECTED FISCAL YEARS
(billions of current dollars)

Category	1964	1968	1970	1973	1974
Training medical and general personnel [b]	5.7	10.1	10.9	12.0	12.9
Central supply and maintenance	4.6	8.4	9.1	8.7	8.4
Administration	1.1	1.2	1.5	1.7	1.7
Total	11.4	19.7	21.5	22.4	23.0
Total, percent of defense	23%	26%	28%	28%	27%

[a] Obligational authority.

[b] Excludes retired pay.

Sources: Figures for 1964, 1968 and 1970 are from Binkin, *Support Costs in the Defense Budget*, p. 10. Figures for 1973 and 1974 are from Department of Defense news release, January 29, 1973.

[22] The ideas for savings in this area owe their origin to Martin Binkin's excellent work, *Support Costs in the Defense Budget: The Submerged One-Third* (Washington, D. C.: The Brookings Institution, 1972).

[23] This figure does not include allowances for housing, incentive pay, or bonuses.

[24] *New York Times*, December 14, 1971.

Zumwalt, the chief of naval operations, conjectured that if the Navy could close all the bases it ought to close, a quarter of a billion dollars per year could be saved by his service alone.[25] Yet from mid-1970 to mid-1973 there were no major CONUS base closings and the average base population decreased by 27 percent in that period.[26]

Although on April 17, 1973, Elliot Richardson did announce the details of 274 specific actions to consolidate, reduce, realign, or close military bases in CONUS and Puerto Rico during fiscal 1974, the savings will not be as great as those projected by Packard and Zumwalt. The then secretary of defense estimated that the annual savings from these actions would be only $350 million and admitted that "we've got to push harder" in the area of base closings.[27] Moreover, James Schlesinger, the present secretary of defense, has directed the services to send him a list of expendable installations by December 1973.

Another support item that many view as wasteful is the number of personnel transfers. The House Appropriations Committee has referred to the current rotation policies of the armed services as unrealistic and feels that the armed services are spending too much money in this area.[28] Personnel transfers are expensive for two reasons. First, there is the cost of the move itself. For example, in fiscal 1973 each rotational move cost about $1,400, while each operational transfer amounted to $800.[29] Second, there is the cost of additional personnel who are unable to perform a military mission because they are in a transient status. In fiscal 1972 there were 97,000 such transients.

At present the average tour length for a member of the armed forces is 10.4 months. In fiscal 1964 the average tour length was 13.0 months. The savings for each additional month that an average tour is extended have been estimated at $.2 billion.[30]

While the "one year" policy for personnel assigned to Vietnam was responsible for shortening the average tour length, the decrease

25 *U.S. News and World Report*, September 13, 1971, p. 77.

26 Fiscal 1970 figures from Binkin, *Support Costs in the Defense Budget*, p. 27. Present figures from Department of Defense news release, January 29, 1973.

27 Department of Defense news release, April 17, 1973, and *Navy Times*, May 2, 1973.

28 *Report 92-1389*, pp. 72-73.

29 Ibid., p. 73. One indication of the escalation of personnel transfer costs is that the Navy overspent its permanent change of station accounts in each of the last three fiscal years. The total overrun was $125 million.

30 Binkin, *Support Costs in the Defense Budget*, p. 22.

in the number of personnel transfers has not kept pace with the reduced U.S. presence in Southeast Asia. Hence the Senate Armed Services Committee has recommended a reduction of 12,000 man-years of transient personnel for fiscal 1973 at estimated savings of about $.1 billion.[31] If the services begin now to extend tour lengths, there is no reason why they cannot be increased to fiscal 1964 levels by fiscal 1975. Such an increase would result in annual savings of about $.5 billion in fiscal 1973 dollars.

Thus, closing bases and increasing tour lengths to thirteen months would result in annual savings of at least $1.5 billion.[32] Congressional committees have pointed out that additional, but smaller, savings could be achieved by such actions as doing away with reenlistment bonuses to personnel with over fourteen years of service, bringing pilot training into line with operational needs,[33] increasing the reliance upon on-the-job training, and decreasing the cost of maintenance per flying and steaming hour.[34] The total of these smaller savings would be about $.5 billion [35] and thus the total annual savings in the support area could be about $2 billion in fiscal 1974 dollars.

Procurement. Congressional reductions in procurement requests in the first four Nixon defense budgets have been quite extensive. Congress has reduced the new obligational authority requests in the budgets from fiscal 1970 to fiscal 1973 by $16.0 billion, for an average reduction of $4.0 billion or 5.3 percent. Of all the areas in the DOD budget, procurement has fared the worst during the legislative cycle. Reductions in this area alone have totaled $9.6 billion or 11.95 percent annually. The fiscal 1973 procurement reduction was nearly 16 percent. Table 3-5 contains a summary of congressional impact on the Nixon administration's defense budgets.

All indications are that a similar pattern of congressional activity will persist for the foreseeable future. Senator John L. McClellan,

---

[31] *Report 92-1389*, p. 62.

[32] The $350 million savings resulting from the announced base closings were not taken into account in the first part of this analysis or by the administration in its projected fiscal 1975 budget.

[33] In fiscal 1974 the Air Force will train 3,425 pilots for 8,313 active aircraft (Department of Defense news release, April 17, 1973). Ten years ago they trained only 1,675 pilots for 15,380 active aircraft. Binkin, *Support Costs in the Defense Budget*, p. 20.

[34] In fiscal 1972, the Navy "saved" $108 million from its ship overhaul programs and reallocated it to other accounts. *Report 92-1389*, p. 105.

[35] Amounts are estimated from *Report 92-1389*, pp. 60-81, and Binkin, *Support Costs in the Defense Budget*, pp. 16-29.

Table 3-5

CONGRESSIONAL REDUCTIONS IN THE NIXON DEFENSE BUDGETS, BY MAJOR APPROPRIATION CATEGORIES, FISCAL YEARS 1970–73

(in percentages)

Category	1970	1971	1972	1973	1970-73
Personnel	3.31	1.23	1.06	1.88	1.87
O&M	4.28	0.78	1.68	2.42	2.29
Procurement	14.58	7.65	9.67	15.91	11.95
R, D, T&E	10.37	4.99	5.41	9.22	7.50
Overall Defense	7.49	3.13	4.02	6.56	5.30

Source: Department of Defense, Office of the Assistant Secretary of Defense (Comptroller) and Lawrence J. Korb, "Congressional Impact on Defense Spending, 1962-1973," Paper presented at the 1973 meeting of the American Political Science Association, p. 16.

chairman of the Senate Appropriations Committee, had already recommended that Congress reduce the fiscal 1974 defense budget by $5 billion, and many analysts are anticipating a reduction of at least $3 billion for fiscal 1974.[36] If this pattern persists, severe reductions in the procurement area can be expected for the remainder of the decade.

Before discussing which weapon systems are likely to experience the most difficulty in receiving funding from the Congress, two things ought to be pointed out. First, outlays for procurement have declined markedly since fiscal 1964, both in real terms and as a percentage of the overall defense budget. In fiscal 1964 actual outlays for procurement were $15.3 billion. In fiscal 1973 the actual outlays will only be $15.6 billion or $10.4 billion in fiscal 1964 dollars. Ten years ago procurement outlays represented 31 percent of the total outlays. Today they represent only 21 percent.

Second, when discussing whether or not to build certain weapon systems, one enters a realm filled with biases and value judgments. Unfortunately, one cannot quantify all aspects of a weapon system, nor can one accurately predict the future of the international environment. Obviously, canceling any weapon system may entail certain risks. But since future defense funds, especially those for invest-

---

[36] For example, see Murray L. Weidenbaum et al., *Matching Needs and Resources* (Washington, D. C.: American Enterprise Institute, 1973, p. 21. The armed services committees already have reduced the fiscal 1974 procurement and R, D, T & E budgets by about $2 billion.

ment, are limited,[37] every current weapon system must be examined carefully to see if real savings can be brought about without presenting unacceptable risks to our national security.

At this time there are several controversial and expensive weapon systems at various stages of development. Experts within DOD and outside of the department have challenged the rationale for building many of these weapon systems, and in the 1972 presidential campaign, Senator George McGovern proposed the cancellation of no less than fourteen major weapon systems. At the present time, most of the controversy revolves around the F-14 and F-15 fighter aircraft, the S-3A anti-submarine warfare (ASW) aircraft, the B-1 supersonic strategic bomber, the SAM-D and AWACS air defense systems, the Trident submarine program and the nuclear aircraft carrier program.

Whatever the validity of the arguments for developing and producing the F-14, F-15 and S-3A, by 1975 these programs will have advanced so far that no real savings could be effected by canceling them. Indeed, when cancellation costs are included, it might be more expensive not to build them.[38] Therefore, these programs will not be discussed in this analysis. The same situation does not prevail with the B-1, SAM-D, AWACS, Trident, and nuclear carrier programs, all of which are in an early stage of development.

SAM-D and AWACS. SAM-D and AWACS are designed primarily to protect our cities against Soviet bombers. But many military experts point out the Soviet Union has only 140 long-range bombers with 250 nuclear warheads, and in SALT I, the U.S. has agreed to forego nationwide defenses of our population against 1,618 Soviet ICBMs with about 2,000 warheads.[39] Therefore, these experts feel, it is not very logical to build expensive defensive weapon systems against the least likely and least effective Soviet threat.

On the other hand, it can be argued that the reason the Soviet Union has not developed a strong long-range bomber force is that

---

[37] For example, see Lawrence J. Korb, "The $100 Billion Threshold: Its Implications upon the Future of the Department of Defense," *Naval War College Review*, May-June 1973, pp. 2-11.

[38] In addition to the cancellation cost, there is the cost of building an alternative weapon system, for example, substituting the F-4J, which costs $4.5 million, for the F-14 and F-15. It should also be noted that savings discussed here also spill over into the R, D, T & E area.

[39] Department of State, *Peace, National Security and the Salt Agreements*, August 1, 1972, pp. 7-8. Also, the number of bombers is not expected to increase by 1977.

the U.S. has always had a strong air defense system, and that failure to build the SAM-D and AWACS systems will tempt the Soviets to build a strong bomber force, especially since bombers are not covered by SALT I. While such psychological arguments are impossible to refute, many critics point out that if the Russians do develop and enlarge their bomber force substantially we would not be any more vulnerable than we are now, because our greatest vulnerability would still be to the Soviet missile force, which, by 1977, will have 3,700 warheads.[40] Moreover, we already would have the technology to modernize the air defense system should we so desire. If these arguments are valid, canceling these systems and limiting our air defenses to a surveillance role against unauthorized penetration of U.S. air space and defense against light attacks could save $2.2 billion annually in fiscal 1973 dollars.[41]

B-1. Opponents of the B-1 raise two interrelated questions about this weapon system. Does the U.S. still need the triad? Are 244 B-1s, at a cost of $52 million each, or $12.7 billion, a necessary component of the triad?

The existing nuclear force of the U.S. is based on a triad. We have about 1,000 land-based ICBMs, 656 submarine-launched ballistic missiles (SLBMs), and 498 strategic aircraft. As indicated in Figure 3-1, this force is capable currently of launching about 6,000 strategic nuclear warheads and by 1977 it will have the capability to launch almost 10,000. Today the ICBM and SLBM can deliver 3,500 strategic nuclear weapons and by 1977 they will be able to deliver nearly 6,000.

The advocates of the triad concede that the bomber force is its most vulnerable part. Both the bombers' launch time and time enroute are much longer than those of either the ICBM or SLBM.[42] Moreover, since SALT I limits the anti-ballistic missile defenses of the Soviet Union, but does not affect its already well-developed air defenses (SAMs or fighter aircraft), the bomber is more vulnerable than the ballistic missiles. At the present time the SLBMs are nearly invul-

---

[40] Department of State, *Peace, National Security and the Salt Agreements,* p. 8.
[41] Alton Quanbeck and Barry Blechman, "The Arms Accords: Everyone Gains," *Washington Post,* June 4, 1972, pp. B1-B4. There are indications that subsequent to the presentation of the fiscal 1974 budget the administration has accepted this position and that plans to buy SAM-D for CONUS have been dropped. See Edward Fried et al., *Setting National Priorities: The 1974 Budget* (Washington, D. C.: The Brooking Institution, 1973), p. 343.
[42] The B-1 will take an average of 8 hours to reach the USSR. An ICBM takes 30 minutes and an SLBM 15 minutes.

Figure 3-1

U.S. STRATEGIC NUCLEAR WARHEADS, BY CALENDAR YEAR
(estimated in thousands)

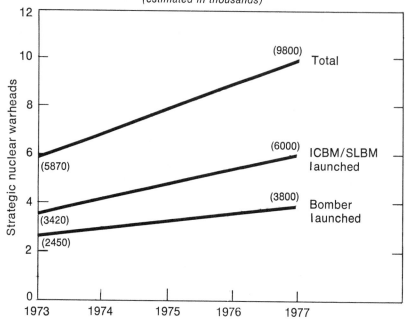

Sources: U.S. Department of State, *Peace, National Security and the SALT Agreements*, August 1, 1972, pp. 7-8; Center for Defense Information, *The Defense Monitor*, July 1972, pp. 6-8; Elliot Richardson, *Annual Defense Department Report, FY 1974*, April 10, 1973, p. 53; William Rogers, *U.S. Foreign Policy 1972: A Report of the Secretary of State*, April 19, 1973, pp. 74 and 82.

nerable, and the ICBMs are vulnerable to the SS-9s only if they are hit while in their silos.[43]

The advocates of keeping and modernizing the bomber portion of the triad base their argument principally on the proposition that the existence of a strategic bomber force makes the defensive and offensive job of the Soviets much more difficult. The Soviets cannot put all their eggs in one basket, but must concentrate their limited energies and defense funds upon defending themselves against both missiles and bombers.

If the triad position is accepted, another question remains. Does the U.S. strategic bomber fleet need the B-1 or is what the B-1 will add to the bomber force worth the cost? At present the U.S. has about 500 strategic bombers, composed of about 300 B-52 G/H, 130

---

[43] The limitations on ABMs in SALT I practically guarantee that all of the missiles will get through once they are launched.

B-52 D/F, and 70 FB-111.[44] By 1975 the U.S. will have a fleet of about 450 strategic bombers composed of 80 B-52 D/F, 300 B-52 G/H, and 70 FB-111. These bombers will be capable of carrying nearly 2,000 nuclear weapons. By 1980, before the introduction of the B-1, and with the introduction of SRAM, these planes will be capable of carrying about 5,000 strategic nuclear weapons.

The B-52 D/F will be operational until about 1980, because of a $200 million modification program which was begun in fiscal 1973. The B-52 G/H will be operational until at least 1990[45] as will the FB-111. Replacing the B-52 D/F on a one-to-one basis with the B-1, beginning in 1981, will give the U.S. bomber fleet about 9,000 strategic nuclear weapons by 1990. Without the B-1, the B-52 G/H and FB-111 would have about 7,000 warheads. Therefore, for the next 15 years, without the B-1, the U.S. will have the bomber component of the triad, capable of delivering from 2,000 to 7,000 strategic nuclear weapons.

If these arguments are accepted and the B-1 program is canceled after the production of its prototypes in April 1974, about $1.7 billion can be saved annually between fiscal 1975 and fiscal 1981.[46]

Trident. At present the most invulnerable part of the U.S. strategic forces are the SLBMs. By the fall of 1975 the SLBM force will be composed of ten Polaris-equipped submarines and thirty-one submarines converted to carry the multiple warhead Poseidon missile.[47] The average range of the Polaris/Poseidon missiles is about 2,000 miles.

Development of the Trident submarine will initially double and then triple the range of part of the SLBM force. Plans now call for the construction of ten Trident submarines, each equipped with twenty-four missiles. The Trident I missile will have a range of about 4,000 miles and the Trident II about 6,000 miles.

As discussed above, U.S. bombers are vulnerable on the ground and enroute to the target. The Minuteman ICBM force is also vul-

---

[44] Figures on the bomber force are processed from Elliot Richardson, *Annual Defense Department Report FY 1974*, April 10, 1973, pp. 53, 58-59, and Center for Defense Information, *Defense Monitor*, January 22, 1973, pp. 1-8.

[45] A total of $6 billion will eventually be spent in modernizing the B-52 fleet. *The Defense Monitor*, January 22, 1973, p. 5.

[46] A less expensive alternative, should the need for a new bomber prove compelling, would be conversion of a number of already existing air force C-5As or commercial Boeing 747s to stand-off bombers equipped with long-range cruise missiles.

[47] Figures on the SLBM force are taken from Richardson, *Defense Department Report*, pp. 54-57.

nerable to the Soviet SS-9 ICBM if the Minutemen are attacked while in their silos. But because of the present primitive state of anti-submarine warfare (ASW), our SLBM force is invulnerable. However, the Soviets are making great efforts in the ASW area and should they make a breakthrough, then each of the components of the triad would become vulnerable.

At a cost of $12.8 billion, the Trident program is designed as a hedge against a Soviet breakthrough in ASW technology.[48] Because of its longer range, it can operate in millions of more square miles of ocean than the Polaris/Poseidon boats. Moreover, it will be faster and quieter than our present fleet ballistic missile submarines. Thus the job of locating a Trident submarine will be much more difficult.

Initially, the Trident submarines were scheduled to begin to go into service in the early 1980s, but last year the program was accelerated and now Trident is scheduled to become operational in 1978. For at least two reasons, several experts argue against this crash program. First, there is no imminent danger of a giant Soviet breakthrough in ASW. Second, the SALT I agreement has already been signed and there is a possibility of SALT II within the next few years. If the Trident program is slowed down to its previous schedule, DOD can save about $1 billion annually[49] and can avoid the inefficiencies that will most surely result from the simultaneous development and production of a weapon system. A recent General Accounting Office study has found that 45 percent of the cost overruns of weapon systems are caused by trying to develop a weapon system too rapidly.[50]

Aircraft Carrier Program. In deciding whether or not the U.S. should fund three additional carriers[51] during the fiscal 1975-81 period, four factors must be weighed. First, the maximum useful life of a Navy ship is generally considered to be thirty years. Second, the U.S. presently plans to maintain four carriers continually on station, two in the Mediterreanean and two in the Pacific.[52] Third, in order to

---

[48] The Polaris program cost about $10 billion and while many, for example, the RAND Corporation, initially attacked its cost effectiveness, no one argues now that it was not a good investment.

[49] Quanbeck and Blechman, *The Arms Accord*, p. B-4.

[50] *Cost Growth in Major Weapon Systems*, p. 26.

[51] In addition to CVN-70, which was funded in fiscal year 1973 and 1974.

[52] Whether or not this is a good policy will not be considered here, but it is by no means a self-evident proposition. It should be noted, however, that Senator McGovern, who was not a great proponent of the value of aircraft carriers or overseas deployment, admitted that it was necessary to keep three carriers on station.

keep one carrier continuously on station and at the same time to provide for contingencies, training, maintenance, and sufficient time at home for the crew, three carriers are necessary.[53] Fourth, past experience has shown that it takes about eight years from the initial funding of a carrier until it becomes operational.

With the decommissioning of the carrier *Intrepid* this past spring, the Navy now has a force of fifteen carriers. As indicated in Table 3-6, five carriers were commissioned in each of the last three decades. According to the thirty year rule, the five carriers commissioned in the 1940s, that is, the *Hancock*, the *Oriskany*, and the three Midway class carriers, should be ready for retirement before the end of this decade. During this period CVN-68 (the *Nimitz*), and CVN-69 (the *Eisenhower*) should join the fleet. Therefore, by the end of the decade the Navy should have 12 carriers under thirty years of age.

Table 3-6

U.S. AIRCRAFT CARRIERS [a]

Calendar Year Commissioned	1940s	1950s	1960s	1970s	1980s
0		1			CVN-70 [b]
1			3		
2					
3					
4	2			CVN-68 [b]	
5	2	1	1		
6		1			
7	1	1		CVN-69 [b]	
8			1		
9		1			
Total	5	5	5	2	5 [b]

[a] Twelve of the fifteen aircraft carriers are strictly attack carriers; three are dual purpose, that is, they carry attack and ASW planes.

[b] Estimated.

Source: Elliot Richardson, *Annual Defense Department Report FY 1974*, April 10, 1973, pp. 82-83; Arnold Kuzmack, *Naval Force Levels and Modernization* (Washington, D. C.: The Brookings Institution, 1971), p. 45.

[53] For a complete discussion of this point, see David Ott et al., *Nixon, McGovern and the Federal Budget* (Washington, D. C.: American Enterprise Institute, 1972), p. 37.

CVN-70, which was initially funded in the fiscal 1973 budget, should become operational in 1980. It will replace the first of the Forrestal class carriers, which was commissioned in 1950. If the Navy is to replace the other four Forrestal class carriers commissioned in the 1950s before they are thirty years old, at least three carriers will have to be funded by DOD before the end of this decade.

Thus, if the U.S. intends to maintain four carriers continuously on station during the 1980s, a program of funding a carrier in the alternate years from fiscal 1975 to fiscal 1981 will need to be carried out.

Total Procurement Savings. If all the reductions envisioned here are found to be consistent with existing security objectives, total savings in the procurement area could be $4.9 billion annually: $3.9 from canceling the B-1, SAM-D, and AWACS systems and $1.0 billion from stretching out the Trident program.

A Summary of Possible Savings in Defense. As indicated in Table 3-7, if the savings discussed in this chapter in the areas of personnel, support and procurement are effected, about $7.3 billion could be cut from the FY 1975 budget. Because of inflation these savings will rise gradually to $7.6 billion in FY 1981.

Table 3-7

POSSIBLE SAVINGS IN DEFENSE, FISCAL YEARS 1975–81
(billions of dollars)

Category	1975	1976	1977	1978	1979	1980	1981
Personnel	.3	.3	.3	.3	.3	.3	.4
Support	2.1	2.1	2.2	2.2	2.3	2.3	2.3
Procurement	4.9	4.9	4.9	4.9	4.9	4.9	4.9
Total	7.3	7.3	7.4	7.4	7.5	7.5	7.6

4

AGRICULTURE

Thomas Vasquez and *David J. Ott*

Perhaps no area of federal policy is of greater current interest than that affecting food prices, especially prices of meat. In the face of rising consumer discontent, reflected in the consumer boycott of meat in the first week of April, President Nixon imposed ceiling prices on meat extending back to the packer level but not including meat products themselves. A review of federal programs affecting agriculture and agricultural prices is thus most timely.

In this chapter, the budget outlook for agriculture is considered first. This is followed by an analysis of program alternatives in the most important area in this category and the one relevant to the concern over food prices—farm price and income stabilization programs.

The FY 1974 Budget

Two major program changes are proposed for agriculture in the fiscal 1974 budget. Direct loans made at a 2 percent interest rate by the Rural Electrification Administration (REA) to electric companies serving rural areas are to be replaced by guaranteed loans at 5 percent. This will permit increased loan levels at lower federal cost. The Rural Environmental Assistance Program (REAP) is completely eliminated in the fiscal 1974 budget. This conservation program, where the federal government shares the cost of watershed construction, reforestation and other conservation activities, is being eliminated on grounds that normal conservation activities no longer require a subsidy.

The largest agricultural activity—the price and income stabilization programs—is currently under legislative review and may be

53

changed by 1975. In fiscal 1974 the price and income stabilization programs authorized by the Agriculture Act of 1970 are in effect.

The Budget Outlook

Table 4-1 summarizes the projections of outlays for agriculture and rural development for fiscal 1975-81.

Activities other than income stabilization programs were projected on the basis of population growth and inflation rates consistent with the basic assumptions of the AEI Long Range Budget Projection Model. No change in program content or scope was assumed for these activities, with the exception of REAP and REA. REAP was assumed to have been eliminated along with the direct, subsidized loans under REA.

The outlay projections for income stabilization programs require a knowledge of demand and supply conditions for each specific crop for each year of the projection period. Fortunately the Department of Agriculture recently published a study[1] which estimated supply

Table 4-1

AGRICULTURE AND RURAL DEVELOPMENT: PROJECTED OUTLAYS BY MAJOR PROGRAM, FISCAL YEARS 1975–81

(unified budget, billions of dollars)

Program	Fiscal Year						
	1975	1976	1977	1978	1979	1980	1981
Farm income stabilization	4.9	5.0	5.1	5.2	5.4	5.7	5.8
CCC price support	3.9	4.0	4.1	4.2	4.3	4.6	4.8
Other residual	1.0	1.0	1.0	1.0	1.1	1.1	1.0
Rural housing & public facilities	.5	.4	.4	.4	.4	.4	.5
Agricultural land & water resources	.2	.2	.3	.3	.3	.3	.3
Research & other	1.0	1.1	1.2	1.3	1.4	1.5	1.6
Total outlays	6.7	6.8	6.9	7.2	7.5	7.9	8.1

Source: LRBP estimates.

[1] David Culver and J. C. Chai, *A View of Food and Agriculture in 1980*, Economic Research Service, U.S. Department of Agriculture, vol. 22, no. 3 (July 1970).

and demand parameters in 1980. The supply parameters were used without adjustments; but, given lower current estimates of birth rates and a lower base population figure as reported in the 1970 census, the demand estimates were lowered.[2]

The supply and demand estimates were then used to estimate all required parameters—prices received by farmers, prices paid by farmers, parity prices and acres to be set aside. Formulas presently used to calculate payment levels were assumed to hold for the entire projection period and based on these formulas yearly budget costs were estimated for each of the crops covered under the stabilization programs.

Program Issues: Farm Income Stabilization. In terms of budget size, the major program in agriculture and rural development is the income stabilization program. The rest of this chapter discusses program alternatives in this category.

The revenue and expenditure sides of the federal budget have long contained provisions for preferential treatment to selected industries and socioeconomic groups. For example, policies to provide investment incentives and subsidies to housing have become widely accepted. Various supports for agriculture are among the oldest of such programs. Understanding the rationale for the preferences accorded this sector requires an understanding of the "farm problem."

The "Farm Problem." The demand for agricultural products grows relatively slowly. It is a well-documented fact that the overall income elasticity of demand for agricultural products is considerably less than unity. A 10 percent increase in per capita income, for example, will increase the demand for the product of this sector by perhaps 2 percent.[3] Thus, as per capita income rises in the U.S., a smaller and smaller proportion is spent on agricultural products.

In addition, the agricultural sector has shown the highest rate of productivity increase of any sector in the U.S. economy. For example, over the period from 1940 to 1960, output per unit of input

---

[2] Demand estimates were also adjusted to reflect increased exports (especially the Soviet trade agreement).

[3] Hendrik S. Houthakker, *Economic Policy for the Farm Sector* (Washington, D. C.: American Enterprise Institute for Public Policy Research, 1967), p. 6. It is possible that the very high income elasticity of demand for beef raises the derived income elasticity of other farm products, for example, feed grains. Of course, the income elasticity of demand differs from product to product.

rose 50 percent in agriculture compared to 23 percent for the economy as a whole.[4]

These two characteristics of the agricultural sector combined to depress agricultural prices and incomes, which in turn induce individuals to leave farming. If this were a one-time occurrence, the market would serve to keep the rate of return, for the marginal producer, equal to what it would be in alternative occupations. But since it is a continuous process and since resources do not move easily out of agriculture, incomes continue to be depressed relative to earnings elsewhere. In economists' terms, the low income elasticity of demand in agriculture causes the demand curve to "shift to the right" slowly as incomes rise; but at the same time the rapid increase in agricultural productivity shifts the supply curve to the right much faster. Thus, there is a tendency for prices and the rate of return to fall in agriculture relative to other sectors. Over time, this is reflected in an exodus of marginal farmers into other occupations. The market solution to the farm problem may mean persistent low income for a large number of farmers.

Basis for Government Intervention. The federal government has intervened for almost forty years in agriculture because of political pressures arising from this farm problem.[5] The market solution to the problem requires difficult adjustments by individual farmers. There is resistance by those whose incomes fall so low as to justify a shift to other occupations on economic grounds. They may like farming and the farm way of life. They may be too old to learn new skills and hence have few alternatives. They may live in regions where *local* alternatives are not good. Hence, they resist and, being voters, they seek to have the government provide programs that will obviate the need for them to get out of agriculture.

This, then, is the real basis for federal intervention. As with imports of foreign goods, the adjustment dictated by the marketplace seems harsh and cruel as it affects particular individuals. So a program is created to spread the transition costs to the public at large. Funda-

---

[4] Edward F. Denison, *The Sources of Economic Growth* (Washington, D. C.: Committee for Economic Development, paper no. 13, 1962), p. 146, Table 17; and U.S. Department of Commerce, *Statistical Abstract, 1972* (Washington, D.C.: U.S. Government Printing Office, 1972), p. 603, Table 999.

[5] Another basis for intervention would be to smooth out sharp fluctuations around a trend in farm prices and incomes caused by the vagaries of weather, et cetera. This often is confusedly mixed with the rationale which fixes the *level* of prices instead of allowing the trend to develop. Since this is conceptually separate, it is not discussed here.

mentally, this is what the farm income stabilization programs have done.

The *stated* goal of these programs is to provide a return from resources in agriculture equal to the return obtained from the other sectors of the economy. As noted above, the market mechanism itself would have—and has—induced a reduction of investment in agriculture, thus tending to keep the rate of return more in line with the nonfarm sectors. The effect of the income stabilization programs, then, insofar as they have been successful, has been to slow the shift of farmers out of agriculture and prolong the adjustment process. That the adjustment process has been prolonged, and not completely subverted, is indicated by what has happened to the number of farms. From 6.4 million in 1940, the number of farms fell to 5.6 million in 1950 and 2.8 million in 1971. The number of persons living on farms has fallen from 23 million or 15 percent of the population in 1950, to 9 million or 5 percent of the population in 1971. At the same time, the average size of a farm has risen 85 percent from 1950 to 1971, so that the reduction in the amount of land in farms has been small— about 7 percent.[6]

More recently, the program has been rationalized as an anti-poverty program. Since per family income of farm families is roughly half that of nonfarm families,[7] the argument is made that the program serves the goal of reducing this disparity.

Methods to Raise Farm Income. The mechanisms used to help raise *relative* farm income have varied over the years, but they have generally reflected various combinations of two elements: (1) restrictions on farm output and (2) direct payments to farmers.[8] Restrictions on output have their basis in the *price* elasticity of demand for farm products. Since the price elasticity of demand for farm products is generally low, an increase in price reduces the amount demanded proportionately less. Therefore, if output is reduced, causing prices to rise, the *percentage* rise in prices exceeds the *percentage* fall in output. Thus the *value* of total sales of farm products is increased. Likewise, the *net* income of farmers rises, since their costs of production fall with reduced output.

---

[6] U.S. Department of Commerce, *Statistical Abstract*, 1972, pp. 584-586. The Bureau of the Census defines a farm as a place satisfying one of the following criteria: sales of at least $250 if less than ten acres, or sales of at least $50 if greater than ten acres.

[7] See D. Gale Johnson, *Farm Commodity Programs: An Opportunity for Change* (Washington, D. C.: American Enterprise Institute, 1973), p. 2.

[8] Ibid., p. 30ff.

The gain in income for the farmer is increased when the govern-ment also *pays* him to reduce his production, as it has in the past decade. This payment is calculated on base yields and acreage allot-ments with target support prices, and has been enough to compensate for income foregone for not producing (or sometimes even more). (For example, if output was reduced by ten units at the "old" price of, say, $1 per unit, the payment would be $10.) Thus, the farmer receives a higher income both because consumers pay more for fewer units and because the government pays the farmer to reduce output.

Distribution of Benefits. As has been widely noted, farm output is concentrated in relatively few farms. In 1971, farms with sales of over $40,000 accounted for 3 percent of all farms but the sales of this class accounted for 59 percent of all sales of farm products (see Table 4-2). Since both elements in the subsidy to agriculture—the "price support" and the direct payments—are directly or closely re-lated to sales, the distribution of the income generated through the subsidy programs follows the same pattern as sales. The bulk of subsidy, whether in the form of higher prices or direct payments, accrues to relatively few large farmers.

Table 4-3 shows that the distributional pattern of direct govern-ment payments is concentrated in the larger sales classes; 60 percent of direct payments in 1971 went to only 8.6 percent of all farms

Table 4-2

DISTRIBUTION OF TOTAL FARMS, FARM SALES, AND REALIZED NET FARM INCOME, BY SALES CLASS, 1971

	Percent Distribution of:		
Sales Class	Farms	Sales	Realized net income [a]
$40,000 and over	2.9	59.4	18.3
$20,000–$39,999	5.7	19.2	16.7
$10,000–$19,999	12.5	10.8	22.7
$ 5,000–$ 9,999	16.7	5.5	18.6
$ 2,500–$ 4,999	15.6	3.0	10.3
Less than $2,500	46.6	2.1	13.4
All farms	100.0	100.0	100.0

[a] Includes government payments but excludes nonfarm income.
Source: Calculated from U.S. Department of Agriculture, *Farm Income Situation*, July 1972, Tables 1D through 6D, pp. 68–73.

Table 4-3

GOVERNMENT PAYMENTS: TOTAL, AVERAGE PER FARM AND PERCENT DISTRIBUTION BY SALES CLASS, 1971

Sales Class	Total Payments	Average Payments Per Farm	Distribution of Total Payments
$40,000 and over	$1,085,000	$4,289	34.5%
$20,000–$39,999	781,000	2,140	24.8
$10,000–$19,999	569,000	1,452	18.1
$ 5,000–$ 9,999	297,000	771	9.5
$ 2,500–$ 4,999	204,000	499	6.5
Less than $2,500	209,000	195	6.6
All farms	$3,145,000	$1,093	100.0%

Source: USDA, *Farm Income Situation*, Table 6D, p. 73.

(those with sales of $20,000 or more). The average payment was $1,093, with only 35 percent of the farms receiving at least this average. Farms with sales of over $40,000 received an average payment of $4,289 while farms with sales of less than $2,500 received only $195.

Charles L. Schultze has shown that the distribution of the benefits of price raising (or output restriction)—those resulting from higher prices under the farm program—is even more concentrated in favor of larger farms than is the distribution of direct payments.[9] Of the total increase in income due to this element in the program, some 53 percent goes to farms with sales over $40,000 and only 2 percent to farms with sales of less than $2,500. His measure of the percent distribution of *total* benefits indicates that some 40.3 percent went to the "over $40,000" sales class. In effect, then, the price support programs distribute benefits in much the same pattern as direct government payments.

Distribution of Costs. Under the farm income stabilization program, the direct payment element is financed through general revenues. However, a large portion of the price support program is financed by consumers because production restrictions artificially increase the prices of farm products. These higher prices are in fact a form of regressive taxation—the equivalent of a sales tax on food. It is well

[9] Charles L. Schultze, *The Distribution of Farms Subsidies* (Washington, D. C.: The Brookings Institution, 1971), Table 8, p. 30.

documented that families with lower incomes spend a larger proportion of their incomes on food. Thus, as a percent of their *total* income, they pay more for the price support programs than those with higher incomes.

Effects on Farm Incomes and the Prices of Farm Products. How large an income effect has resulted from the price and income support program? To what extent has the increase in farm income resulted from higher prices paid by consumers for farm products?

In 1960, two studies examined the effect that elimination of price support programs would have on farm income and prices.[10] Both studies compared the income levels of farmers in the late 1950s with the estimated levels that would be obtained in 1965, assuming that price support programs were eliminated. Both studies indicated that elimination of the support programs would have caused income reductions of about 40 percent.

However, more recent studies indicate a much smaller decrease. An econometric model developed at the Iowa State University Center for Agricultural and Rural Development has been used to estimate that the income reduction would have been less than 25 percent in 1965.[11] (In 1960 the reduction would have been only about 10 percent.) Table 4-4 shows these estimates for selected years from 1924 to 1965.

Finally, two economists from the Department of Agriculture[12] updated an earlier study conducted by the Center for Agricultural and Economic Development[13] to estimate the income effects of the agricultural program in 1970. Table 4-5 shows these estimates for 1970 by source of income and expense. Column (1) shows the actual income levels recorded by the Department of Agriculture in 1970,

---

[10] W. Wilcox et al., *Economic Policies for Agriculture in the 1960s: Implications of Four Selected Programs* (Washington, D. C.: U.S. Government Printing Office, 1960); U.S. Congress, Senate Document No. 77, *Farm Price and Income Projections, 1960-65*, a report from the U.S. Department of Agriculture and statement from the Land Grant Colleges IRM-1 Advisory Committee, 86th Congress, 2nd session, 1960.

[11] E. Heady, L. Mayer, and H. Madsen, *Future Farm Programs*, Iowa State Center for Agricultural and Rural Development (Ames, Iowa: Iowa State University Press, 1972).

[12] R. Reinsel and R. Krenz, *Capitalization of Farm Program Benefits into Land Values*, U.S. Department of Agriculture, Economic Research Service, ERS-506, October 1972.

[13] L. Mayer, E. Heady, and H. Madsen, *Farm Programs for the 1970s*, Center for Agricultural and Economic Development, Report no. 32 (Ames, Iowa: Iowa State University Press, October 1968).

Table 4-4

FARM INCOME WITH AND WITHOUT FARM PROGRAMS, 1924–65

(millions of dollars)

	Net Income	
Year	With farm programs	Without farm programs
1924	10,854	10,854
1940	10,209	9,479
1950	15,193	13,768
1960	13,772	12,504
1965	13,853	10,599

Source: Heady, Mayer, and Madsen, *Future Farm Programs,* Table 9.17, p. 381.

Table 4-5

FARM INCOME BY SOURCE, WITH AND WITHOUT FARM PROGRAMS, 1970

(millions of dollars)

		Projected	
Source	Actual (1)	Short-run adjustment (2)	Long-run adjustment (3)
Crop receipts	19,636	15,192	16,968
Livestock receipts	29,595	28,280	26,911
Government payments	3,717	401	401
Total receipts	52,948	43,873	44,280
Less cash expenses	33,949	32,053	30,100
Net receipts	18,999	11,820	14,180
Less depreciation	6,198	6,600	6,200
Actual cash income	12,081	5,220	7,980
Plus farm perquisites	3,632	3,859	3,859
Plus inventory change	226	332	332
Net farm income	15,939	9,411	12,171

Source: Mayer, Heady, and Madsen, *Farm Programs for the 1970s,* p. 3.

while columns (2) and (3) show the estimated income levels under two different conditions. Column (2), calculated under the assumption that farm programs were eliminated at the beginning of 1970, indicates the short-run effect of eliminating the farm program. It is recognized that the farm sector will experience a period of adjustment. Until resources leave agriculture, output will rise sharply relative to demand, which will lower prices and, given the inelastic demand for farm products, decrease farm receipts. In the long run, column (3), farm receipts and net income will rise somewhat above the short-run level but will remain below the levels experienced under the farm programs. Comparing columns (1) and (3), total receipts would decrease by $8.6 billion, with $3.3 billion of the reduction caused by the elimination of direct government payments. The decreased consumer cost would be about $5.3 billion, a reduction of about 10 percent.

While it was indicated earlier that the studies conducted in 1960 estimated much higher income reductions than those calculated by Mayer et al., column (2) of Table 4-5 shows that the estimates were actually fairly close. The 1960 studies were basically short-run estimates, since they assumed that resources would not leave the farm sector over the projection period. Their estimate of a 40 percent reduction in net income is approximately equivalent to the short-run estimates shown in Table 4-5. The most interesting conclusion from the most recent study is that direct government payments have had a larger effect on income than have price supports. Direct payments would account for about 90 percent of the reduction in net farm income were the program to be dropped. *Higher prices paid by consumers contribute very little to net farm income but rather are translated into higher production expenses.* Of the additional $5.3 billion paid by consumers in 1970, $3.8 billion was lost to higher expenses rather than being added to net income. The higher expenses are primarily a result of the inflated feed costs induced by the farm program.

As indicated above, consumers have paid higher prices for farm products as a consequence of the farm programs. How much higher depends upon the extent to which farm programs have succeeded in restricting output. Price support programs restrict output by requiring that farmers "set aside" some percent of their total acreage to obtain CCC loans. The percent to be set aside is determined by the secretary of agriculture and is based on estimates of demand-and-supply conditions. On their remaining acres, farmers are allowed to grow any crop they desire. This output restriction method is inefficient for three major reasons:

(1) The use of variable inputs such as fertilizers enables farmers to increase dramatically their yields per acre. Without acreage controls, farmers would substitute additional land for the use of expensive variable inputs. Thus, a reduction in yields per acre would partially offset the additional acres farmers would then be able to plant.

(2) Since farm payments are based on historical yields for each farm, farmers have an incentive to incur higher variable costs to increase yields.

(3) Since the programs are crop-oriented, they stabilize and raise crop prices and they set aside (waste) land that in a market-oriented situation would be used for forage production for livestock. Livestock prices are not supported and are highly variable, which is a disincentive to raise livestock. This inefficiency has become seriously apparent in the past year. Per capita consumption of animal products in the first quarter of 1973 was only 1 percent higher than in 1967, while meat prices have risen sharply.

For these reasons, it is reasonable to assume that if the programs are eliminated and planting is allowed on the large number of acres set aside under the present program, a commensurately large increase in output will not occur.

The complexity of farm programs and of the agricultural production process makes it difficult to determine the price effects of the supply management phase of farm programs. However, a few of the studies mentioned above attempt to provide such estimates. Mayer, Heady, and Madsen [14] estimated that the total output reduction caused by the farm programs was only about 2 percent. For the major crops covered under the price support program—wheat, cotton, and feed grains—the estimated output reduction was about 5.3 per cent. Given a low price elasticity of demand for farm products—in the range of about $-.2$ to $-.3$, the resulting price increase for the major crops would be about 20 percent. Needless to say, these estimates are extremely tenuous. However, given the knowledge concerning critical demand elasticities in agriculture, a reasonable estimate is that eliminating the farm program would reduce prices of agricultural products by between 10 percent and 15 percent. Thus, since

---

[14] Ibid.

about 40 percent of food costs are from farm products, if this component fell by 10 percent, the retail cost of food would fall by 4 percent, assuming middlemen did not absorb any of the decreased cost of farm products.

However, this estimate of the percentage reduction in food costs applies to prices determined in a stable economic setting. That is, beef and other farm products would have been higher than usual in early 1973 if there had been no farm program all along, but not as high as they were. Recent world crop failures would have produced higher beef prices, but in the absence of the farm programs the increase would have been from a lower initial level of prices.

Program Alternatives. As noted above, two rationales are offered for the farm price and income support programs:

(1) The programs slow the trend toward fewer farms, thus providing relief for farmers who would otherwise be forced out of agriculture without attractive alternative choices. In other words, the programs spread the transitional costs of market adjustments in this sector to the public at large.

(2) Average income per farm family is far below that for nonfarm families. The stabilization programs thus serve as an income redistribution or antipoverty program to raise the incomes of farm families to the level of nonfarm families.

How well does the program perform these functions? Are the objectives themselves desirable?

Consider first the argument that the long-run pressures toward fewer farms should be slowed in the interest of marginal farmers. Subsidies for the agricultural sector, either through direct payments or price supports, cause a welfare loss to society—the difference between the value of output that "marginal" resources thus kept in agriculture could produce elsewhere and what they actually produce in agriculture. Society would clearly be better off if the resources were shifted and if the gain was more than enough to compensate the farmers who lost. However, there is no way of knowing whether the gain would, in fact, be. large enough. If the alternative uses of the "extra" resources kept in agriculture via the subsidy incentives have low yields—if the resources truly have limited alternative uses—then the stabilization program might be an improvement over a world without it.

However, even if the objective of protecting marginal farmers is accepted, the structure of the stabilization program is not efficient for this purpose. As noted earlier, the bulk of the subsidy goes where it is not needed—to the large efficient producers who could survive without subsidy. Clearly the incomes of marginal farmers do not benefit much from the program. Furthermore, a large portion of the subsidy is financed through what amounts to a regressive tax.

The argument that the farm income stabilization program serves the objective of combating rural poverty is largely refuted by the evidence discussed earlier. If anything, the program helps the affluent farmer, not the poor one. More important, a government program of income redistribution should be universal in nature, not based upon the classification of individuals by production. Why should it concern policy makers whether a poor person is a farmer, a carpenter, or a scientist?

Given these shortcomings in the program, there is a strong case for eliminating the subsidy and replacing it with an unconditional grant, tied to the person, not the land. These grants could be phased out over, say, a five-year period. This would provide transitional income for those who would leave farming (indeed, the unconditional grants would provide an incentive for them to leave), and let the market mechanisms handle resource allocation.[15] In addition, it would provide some welcome relief from high food prices, at least temporarily.

If the programs were replaced by grants to farmers (not farms) and these were phased out over five years, the savings by 1978 would be about $4 billion annually.

---

[15] One difficulty with this proposal would be the capital losses suffered by farmers who have bought farm land at prices which reflect the subsidies. Johnson (Farm Commodity Programs) estimates this as perhaps 22 percent of the total value of farmland in 1972. As he notes, however, a third of these capital gains goes to owners who are not farmers. In addition, the tax system provides partial relief for any capital losses suffered. The certain payment for five years would itself provide an additional offset to any capital losses.

5

SCIENCE, TECHNOLOGY, AND INDUSTRY

Thomas Gale Moore

This chapter examines the budget outlook and program alternatives in (1) atomic energy, (2) space research and technology, (3) natural resources and the environment, and (4) commerce and transportation. The programs involved in these areas cover a wide variety of activities, from the highly secret atomic energy program, through the run-of-the-mill data-collection efforts of the Census Bureau, to the rigid and legalistic activities of the regulatory commissions. While only small sums are spent in each of these areas—at least compared with defense, health, and housing—they add up to the considerable total of some $20 billion. More important, because of their relatively small size, the programs tend to be scrutinized less carefully than other federal activities with the result that considerable waste can develop.

This chapter first examines each of the program categories in the general area of science, technology, and industry and explains the basis on which the budget figures for these programs have been projected. This is followed by a discussion, again by program category, of possible budget savings or program improvements.

Budget Projections

Table 5-1 summarizes the LRBP budget projections for each category under science, technology and industry. The basis for the projection in each category is discussed below.

Atomic Energy. The estimates for atomic energy are built up from projections of expenditures for individual program categories: production and material management, national security, energy and development, research, and all others. Of these categories only the

Table 5-1

SCIENCE, TECHNOLOGY, AND INDUSTRY: BUDGET PROJECTIONS FOR FISCAL YEARS 1975–81

(unified budget, billions of dollars)

Category	1975	1976	1977	1978	1979	1980	1981
Atomic energy	2.7	2.5	2.5	2.6	2.5	2.4	2.4
Space research and technology	3.4	3.4	3.5	3.6	3.7	3.8	3.9
Natural resources and the environment							
Water resources	3.2	3.2	3.3	3.4	3.5	3.6	3.7
Land management	1.0	1.1	1.1	1.2	1.3	1.4	1.5
Mineral resources	0.1	0.1	0.2	0.2	0.2	0.2	0.2
Pollution control and abatement	2.7	2.9	3.0	3.1	3.3	3.5	3.6
Recreational resources	1.0	1.0	1.1	1.3	1.4	1.6	1.7
Other natural resource programs	0.2	0.2	0.3	0.3	0.3	0.4	0.4
Proprietary receipts	−3.5	−3.2	−3.3	−3.5	−3.7	−4.0	−4.3
Total, natural resources and the environment	4.8	5.4	5.7	6.0	6.3	6.5	6.9

Commerce and transportation							
Air transportation	2.0	2.2	2.3	2.4	2.6	2.8	3.0
Coast Guard	0.8	0.8	0.8	0.9	0.9	0.9	1.0
Water transportation	0.8	0.8	0.9	0.9	0.9	1.0	1.0
Ground transportation	6.6	6.8	7.0	7.2	7.4	7.6	7.8
Postal Service	1.3	1.3	1.2	1.2	1.2	1.2	1.1
Advancement of business	0.6	0.7	0.7	0.8	0.8	0.9	0.9
Area and regional development	1.0	0.9	0.9	0.8	0.9	0.9	0.9
Regulation of business	0.2	0.2	0.2	0.2	0.2	0.2	0.2
Proprietary receipts	− 0.2	− 0.2	− 0.2	− 0.2	− 0.3	− 0.3	− 0.3
Total, commerce and transportation	13.1	13.4	13.7	14.2	14.7	15.1	15.7
Grand total, science, technology and industry	24.0	24.7	25.4	26.4	27.2	27.8	28.9

Source: LRBP estimates.

69

first, production and material management, is forecast by the Atomic Energy Commission (AEC) to grow in the period from fiscal 1973 to fiscal 1977. It will grow because of the increase in production of nuclear fuels, but the expenditure increase will be more than offset by an increase in revenue from the sale of enriched uranium. The revenue increase was projected on the basis of the AEC forecast of sales through fiscal 1981, assuming a real price of $32 per kilogram. The projection for the AEC budget assumes that any additional uranium enriching facilities will be constructed by private industry. This assumption reflects President Nixon's stated goal and AEC plans.

The cuts proposed in the 1974 budget eliminate about $36 million from AEC outlays in fiscal 1974 and $67 million in fiscal 1975. It is assumed that the cuts, primarily in the space program, are continued throughout the period.

Space Research and Technology. The space budget projections in Table 5-1 assume that current programs, such as the space shuttle, the Mars orbiter and lander, and the outer planet explorative programs, are continued as scheduled. No major new projects are included, but provision is made for use of the space shuttle when it is developed. It is assumed that the current budget ceiling of $3.2 billion is maintained, permitting some modest program revisions and additions.

Natural Resources and the Environment. Six of the major activities in this category are summarized below.

Water resources. The fiscal 1974 budget reduced the Army Corps of Engineers budget by $471 million and projected a saving of $650 million in fiscal 1975. It also cut the Bureau of Reclamation budget by $123 million for fiscal 1974 and $113 million for fiscal 1975. These cuts imply major eliminations or slowdowns of many projects. The announced savings for fiscal 1975 imply a funding level of around $1.7 billion for Corps of Engineer projects and around $650 million for Department of the Interior outlays, which include, besides those of the Bureau of Reclamation, a number of power projects. The projections assume that these real expenditure levels are maintained throughout the rest of the decade and that Department of Agriculture water projects level out at about $150 million. These fixed real expenditure levels imply a stringent limit on outlays for public works. Only an administration with considerable determination to hold down spending will succeed in keeping real outlays from rising.

Land management. Two programs, those of the Forest Service and the Bureau of Land Management, account for virtually all of the outlays under land management. The proposed 1974 budget forecasts savings in Forest Service outlays of $94 million and $106 million for fiscal 1974 and 1975, due in the main to shifting the construction of forest roads to timber purchasers. Since timber purchasers will not be willing to pay as much for timber rights if they must build roads, much of these savings are illusory. With growing demand for timber and grazing land, it is forecast that this area will grow with real GNP, or about 4.2 percent annually.

Pollution control. Last year the administration recommended a three-year $6 billion program of matching 50/50 grants for water waste treatment plants. Congress finally passed, over a presidential veto, a $24 billion program of which $18 billion was for waste treatment on a 75/25 matching basis. Under the Water Pollution Control Act Amendments of 1972, the government is committed to an expensive grant program, not only for constructing waste treatment plants but also for replacing combined storm and sanitary sewers. The administration has refused to incur obligations of that magnitude. It is projecting $727 million for fiscal 1973 and instead of $5 billion it is planning on $1.6 billion in 1974 for the 75 percent federal share, instead of $6 billion.

On the basis of the administration's past proposals to keep grants for water treatment plants to $2 billion, the projection assumes that contract authority will be limited to this amount throughout the rest of this decade. Given the need for more information on the environment and pollution, research and development is projected to grow at a 10 percent rate through fiscal 1981.

Recreational resources. The Office of Management and Budget and the administration are expecting that grants by the Bureau of Outdoor Recreation will level out at $300 million but that grants by the Park Service and the Bureau of Sports Fisheries will grow rapidly. The latter are forecast to expand at a real rate of 13.3 percent per year, their historical average rate of growth. Purchases by these agencies to improve and expand recreational facilities are also expected to grow rapidly, about 10 percent per year—which is considerably slower than their rate of increase from 1965 to 1973.

The fiscal 1974 budget forecasts outlay savings of $61 million in fiscal 1974 and $46 million in fiscal 1975. The projection used here assumes that the level of outlays on recreational resources has been permanently reduced by about $50 million, of which $40 million is in the form of reduced grants.

71

Other natural resource programs. Expenditures on other natural resource programs, mainly geological surveys, investigations, and research, have been growing at the real rate of 8 percent per year from 1965 to 1973. These expenditures are small and are mainly for data and information collections. It has been assumed that the 8 percent rate of increase continues.

Proprietary receipts. Proprietary receipts consist mainly of revenues from outer continental shelf leases and royalties, sales of timber, sales of power, and other mineral leases. The Geological Survey projected the revenues from outer continental shelf leasing through 1978. These estimates were extrapolated here on the assumption that the revenues would grow in real terms at an average annual rate of 4 percent through 1981. Revenues from other proprietary receipts were forecast to grow with GNP, or 4.2 percent in real terms, from the fiscal 1974 budget estimates.

Commerce and Transportation. The nine activities in this category are summarized below.

Air transportation. The Federal Aviation Administration (FAA) has projected revenues from the airport/airways trust fund, expenditures on various aviation programs, and FAA total budget authority through 1980. The budget authority has been adjusted for inflation, with the exception of the airport grants component, which has been held constant at the $295 million ceiling set by Congress. The projection assumes that National and Dulles airports will be sold and that Congress will not appropriate the growing surplus in the trust fund.

Coast Guard. In the middle of fiscal 1973, the Coast Guard was directed to reduce its projected outlays for that fiscal year by $92 million or 11 percent, thus reducing expenditures to about $750 million. The administration's budget for fiscal 1974 contains only a 3 percent increase in outlays for the nation's oldest sea service. Since the Coast Guard's budget authority for fiscal 1974 is 2.7 percent below its anticipated outlays, and since its acquisition authority is almost 50 percent below that of fiscal 1973, this analysis projects a number of lean years ahead for the service and foresees its outlays remaining below $1 billion for the remainder of the decade.

The projection for Coast Guard outlays assumes a level of 37,000 active military and 6,000 permanent full-time civilian employees and an expansion of its maritime safety and environmental protection programs, particularly in the area of detecting, containing, and cleaning up oil spills. Retirement pay costs will rise substantially

—by over 15 percent in the fiscal 1975-81 period—as the number of retirees increases. A slight decrease in the number of selected reservists to 10,000 is foreseen, and no funds are provided for state boating safety assistance after June 1, 1976, when the current legislation expires.

To offset the greatest portion of maritime safety and environmental protection, and of the rising costs of personnel, both active and retired, expansion, construction and research projects will be reduced, efficiency will be improved, and drastic cuts will take place in other areas of Coast Guard responsibility. At least three ocean stations in the Atlantic and one in the Pacific will be phased out, at least fifteen coastal rescue stations will be closed, at least thirteen high endurance cutters and four buoy tenders will be decommissioned, and several overseas and domestic Loran A stations and light stations will be shut down.

Water transportation. The merchant marine program actually has two elements: ship construction subsidies and operating subsidies. The first of these is based on a program of multiple ship construction that is intended to reduce costs and subsidies. The maximum allowable subsidy is scheduled to fall from 41 percent in fiscal 1973 to 35 percent by fiscal 1976. With increases in the cost of ship construction, it has been assumed that the real value of the ship construction subsidy will rise to about $400 million in 1975 and then level out at $450 million for the rest of this decade. This assumes a constant dollar subsidy of about $15 million per ship for the 30 ships per year to be built. The ship operation subsidy is forecast to grow at the slow real rate of 2 percent per year.

Ground transportation. The administration has requested that $800 million of the highway trust fund be made available to urban areas to be spent either on urban highways or mass transit facilities. Another $625 million from the fund is allocated for a rural transportation program, which could conceivably be used for rural mass transit but more likely will be spent on arterial noninterstate routes. Some $2.6 billion is planned for the interstate system.

The projection used here assumes that further receipts of the highway trust fund will be spent, either on highways or mass transit. This has not been the pattern in recent years. Counting 1974 receipts, the trust fund will grow to over $11 billion by the end of fiscal 1974. With a $4.4 billion appropriation in 1974, the backlog of unappropriated monies will be about $6.7 million by then, up from about $2 billion at the end of fiscal 1970. It has been assumed here, though, that no further buildup in unexpended balances will be permitted.

For AMTRAK it is assumed that the annual federal subsidy will continue to run at about $50 million. Another $60 million per year is projected for railroad research and other railroad projects.

Postal Service. For the postal service, it is assumed that the "public-needs-service" subsidy will decline as projected in the legislation establishing the corporation. A declining transitional subsidy for fiscal 1975 and 1976 is also assumed. Together, these subsidies are projected on a current basis. In addition, the subsidy to the blind is estimated to grow at the real rate at which outlays have increased for the post office from fiscal 1965 to 1971—about 4.7 percent.

Advancement of business. Programs for the advancement of business have been growing rapidly since 1965. These programs include statistical and census services, international trade and travel, minority business, Patent Office, National Oceanic and Atmospheric Administration, National Bureau of Standards, Small Business Administration, and Federal Deposit Insurance Corporation (FDIC). With the exception of FDIC expenses and receipts, these outlays have been growing at an average annual rate of about 4.2 percent in real terms and are projected to continue at this rate of growth.

Area and regional development administration. The administration proposes to phase out the Economic Development Administration. While no exact timetable has been announced, it appears from the data that this program will have run out by 1978. The administration also proposes to eliminate federal funding of regional commissions on the ground that states should bear that cost. It has been projected that all funding for that program will be eliminated by fiscal 1976.

The Appalachia program has been reasonably constant in recent years and seems likely to continue that way. The Bureau of Indian Affairs has also shown little growth. Therefore, both these programs were projected to remain roughly constant in real terms.

Regulation of business. Outlays for the regulation of business have grown modestly since 1965, primarily due to a rise in government salaries. It is forecast that these outlays will continue to grow at a real annual rate of 2.6 percent per year.

Proprietary receipts. These small receipts from numerous programs have been forecast to grow with real GNP, or about 4.2 percent per year.

Program Alternatives and Possible Budget Savings

The sections that follow discuss possible program changes and budget savings in the area of science, technology, and industry.

Alternatives have been developed for those programs which benefit special groups, for those programs which might more appropriately be handled by state or local governments, and for those cases where it appears that the program's stated objective either cannot be, or is not being, met. The changes outlined will, of course, be controversial; no one can be expected to agree with all of them. However, it is hoped that this discussion will help the public and decision makers to think through the implications of continuing these programs.

Table 5-2 summarizes the impact that adoption of program changes would have on budget outlays. The net savings would be substantial—about $7 to $9 billion between fiscal 1975 and 1981.

Atomic Energy. The AEC estimates that by fiscal 1977 it will be spending over $1.3 billion on national security, nearly half of it for weapons production and surveillance. Given the large stockpile of nuclear weapons, these expenditures seem excessive. Without examining highly classified data on the extent of the stockpile and the purpose of the new weapons production, a firm judgment on specific program improvements or cuts cannot be made. It does seem desirable, however, for the President to look to this area for substantial savings.

One possible means of generating a more informed nuclear weapons program would be to alter the procurement process. Currently, the AEC builds all atomic weapons at its own expense and makes them available to the Defense Department at virtually no cost. As William Niskanen has suggested,[1] requiring the Defense Department to purchase any nuclear weapons and to pay for its existing inventory would create a more efficient use of resources and possibly lead to considerable savings.

Space Research and Technology. As with most basic research, it is impossible to forecast all the eventual benefits from the space program. Whatever benefits that result will lie in the area of new technology and greater understanding of the laws of nature and the universe. However, most but possibly not all of these benefits can be secured by an unmanned space program. Thus, the role of man in space is undecided, with advocates of manned space activity pointing to the much greater flexibility of man over machine and the advocates of unmanned space probes pointing to lower costs. The

---

[1] *Structural Reform of the Federal Budget Process* (Washington, D. C.: American Enterprise Institute, 1973).

Table 5-2

SCIENCE, TECHNOLOGY, AND INDUSTRY: POSSIBLE NET SAVINGS IN OUTLAYS FOR SELECTED PROGRAMS

(billions of current dollars)

Category	1975	1976	1977	1978	1979	1980	1981
Space research and technology	1.3	1.5	1.5	1.1	0.1	−0.7	−1.3
Natural resources and the environment							
Water resources	1.4	2.1	2.4	2.8	2.9	3.0	3.1
Pollution control	2.1	2.2	2.2	2.2	2.3	2.4	2.4
Total, natural resources and the environment	3.5	4.3	4.6	5.0	5.2	5.4	5.5
Commerce and transportation							
Air transportation	0.6	0.5	0.6	0.5	0.5	0.5	0.5
Water transportation	0.7	0.8	0.8	0.9	0.9	0.9	0.9
Ground transportation[a]	—	—	—	—	—	—	—
Postal Service	0.3	0.5	0.7	1.0	1.2	1.2	1.1
Advancement of business	0.2	0.3	0.3	0.3	0.3	0.3	0.4
Area and regional development	0.1	0.1	0.1	0.3	0.3	0.3	0.3
Total, commerce and transportation	4.9	5.6	6.0	6.6	7.0	7.1	7.1
Grand total of savings	6.7	8.0	8.6	9.1	8.6	8.0	7.4

[a] There would be no *net* savings from cuts in this area as highway excise would fall by the same amount.

Source: LRBP estimates.

recent achievements of the astronauts in Skylab have pointed up the flexibility of man but have not closed the argument.

From this perspective, NASA's most costly and controversial program is the reusable space shuttle. The agency estimates the cost of research, development, and testing of this system at $5.15 billion. About $1 billion will be needed to refurbish the two initial orbiters and to procure three more. About $1.9 billion will be needed for ground facilities at Kennedy Space Center and Vandenburg Air Force Base, for development of a space tug, and for purchase of expendable rockets for high-orbit satellites before the tug is built. NASA estimates that the use of the shuttle instead of the currently used "throw-away" launch systems will save about $11.7 billion between 1979-1990 (12 years) if 581 missions are carried out.

The gains from the space shuttle depend on the number of missions, the actual cost of developing and constructing the shuttle, and the cost of using existing hardware to put payloads into orbit. For example, if there were only 500 launches (about 40 per year), which is more in line with past rates, and if a 10 percent discount rate is used, any overrun in costs of more than 7 percent would make the benefit/cost ratio less than one.

The president of the Institute for Defense Analyses in the fall of 1971 chaired a group to advise the President's science adviser, Edward E. David, Jr., on the shuttle project. His assessment of the project was negative. He wrote, "Prudent extrapolation of prior experience would indicate a 30 percent to 50 percent overrun."[2] Such a rise in costs would convert an expected cost saving for the entire project into an increase on the order of $1.3 billion to $2.3 billion.

This project is obviously important to NASA, since it provides the only means to keep a manned space program. As a consequence, NASA may be overly optimistic about the success of the program. Costs of developing the hardware are likely to be underestimated. The number of launches is likely to be overestimated; at least, it is unlikely that budget considerations will permit the expansion in launches NASA foresees in the 1980s. Even NASA agrees that the main justification for the shuttle is to keep a role for man in space. Budget officials and the President will have to decide how much it is worth to have a manned space program in the 1980s. All things considered, it seems unlikely that in the long run this program will save resources for the economy. It is more likely that the cost will be $1 to $2 billion to ensure a role for man in space.

---

[2] *National Journal*, August 12, 1972, p. 1295.

The projected budgetary savings from eliminating the shuttle project, which become negative (in other words, they become added costs) in 1980 and 1981 (since the shuttle will be unavailable), are made assuming no cost overruns and a forty-mission-a-year model for 1979, 1980, and 1981. Any cost overruns would make the savings larger in early years but this would be offset by larger administration baseline expenditures. If the number of NASA and Defense missions was larger than forty per year for the last three years (1988-1990), eliminating the shuttle system would add even more to budget outlays in 1980 and 1981.

Natural Resources and the Environment. In this area, significant savings are identified in the two categories of water resources and pollution control.

Water resources. The major agencies dealing with water resources are the Army Corps of Engineers, the Bureau of Reclamation, and various power and water authorities such as Tennessee Valley Authority (TVA), Bonneville Power, Southeastern Power, and Southwestern Power.

Any evaluation of the projects of the Corps of Engineers and the Bureau of Reclamation would require a detailed evaluation of the true economic benefits and costs of each project. In general, past studies have been strongly biased towards a favorable cost/benefit outcome through the inclusion of questionable benefits (for example, new business relocated in the area) and underestimates of the costs (especially environmental factors), as well as by the application of too low a discount factor for evaluating future benefits. Many observers believe that few, if any, of the existing projects could have been justified under an appropriate set of assumptions. However, since many of them are substantially completed, the benefits they will produce are likely to be greatly in excess of the remaining costs of completion. Thus, it would be wasteful not to complete those that are substantially finished.

Table 5-3 lists the Bureau of Reclamation programs that are sufficiently close to completion (over 40 percent) that abandoning them would probably be wasteful, though it is possible that certain parts of some could be eliminated.

The Bureau of Reclamation is projected to have outlays of approximately $437 million in fiscal 1974. By fiscal 1975, it should be possible to cut spending in half. A $250 million level in 1975 would permit funding of the projects listed below to continue ($153 million), plus nearly $100 million for continuations or phaseouts

Table 5-3

BUREAU OF RECLAMATION PROJECTS
OVER 40 PERCENT COMPLETED
(thousands of dollars)

Program	1974 Appropriation	Appropriation Required to Complete	Percent Completed, End of Fiscal 1973
Colorado riverfront work and levee system	762	9,711	76
Central Valley Project, California	46,925	864,549	61
Fryingpan-Arkansas Project	31,207	172,640	43
Chief Joseph Dam projects	7,725	5,128	47
Drainage and minor construction	3,291	39,479	96
Rehabilitation and betterment projects	5,661	25,478	55
Columbia Basin Project	31,083	1,061,989	46
Pick-Sloan Missouri Basin Program			
Transmission division	8,348	55,024	83
Drainage and minor construction	3,201	11,244	97
Upper Colorado River Storage Project			
Curecanti unit	5,925	23,975	74
Transmission division	2,777	60,762	67
Lyman-Wyoming-Utah	1,649	6,168	68
San Juan-Chama	1,737	22,151	73
Drainage and minor construction	2,602	32,625	89
Total	152,893	2,390,923	

Source: *Budget of the United States Government, Fiscal Year 1974: Appendix,* pp. 582-583, 590.

of other particularly worthwhile projects. In fiscal 1976 this sum could be reduced to $200 million and by fiscal 1977 it could be cut to the level of continuing the above projects or approximately $150 million. Further cuts to around the $125 million level should be feasible for the years 1978 through 1981.

While difficult to do politically, additional resources could be saved by selling Bonneville Power Administration. This system could be sold to a consortium of power companies, to one power firm, or to one or more public systems in the area, or set up as a new enterprise (like COMSAT). Basically, there is no economic justification for federal ownership or operation of any power system. In addition, any such system should cover its costs through revenues. Even if federal public power systems are kept in government hands, no additional federal money should be invested. Any new resources needed could be raised from the public by the authorities if Congress authorized such bond sales.

Power rates should be raised to cover costs so that in the long run these systems would not require any federal funds. From a budget efficiency point of view, therefore, the government could save all the projected outlays for Bonneville Power Administration, Alaska Power Administration, Southwestern Power Administration, Southeastern Power Administration, and the Tennessee Valley Authority.

Under current administration programs, the Corps of Engineers water resource programs were forecast to reach $1.7 billion in 1972 dollars by fiscal 1975 and remain at that level for the rest of the decade. In the 1974 budget, there are about 250 construction projects listed, of which thirty-five are for navigation, thirteen for locks and dams, nine for beach erosion control, seventy-five for flood control, eighty-five for reservoirs, and thirty-one for multipurpose projects, plus an assortment of other projects.

Like Bureau of Reclamation projects, there is no way to judge efficiently the merit of all corps programs, but there would seem to be little doubt that many of them could not have been justified under an appropriately done cost/benefit analysis. In addition, some could be paid for by the beneficiaries by levying tolls on users of navigable waterways, by requiring harbor or port authorities to cover the expenses, or by securing payments from communities and states which are the beneficiaries.

All in all, net outlays could be cut to around $300 million. This would provide funds for general investigations, general expenses, flood control for the Mississippi River and tributaries, with around $100 million left over for other worthwhile projects. However, it probably would not be economic to reduce support to this level by 1975. At current expenditure levels, about one-third of the projects could be finished in fiscal 1975 or 1976. By 1979, it should be possible to reduce costs to $300 million.

The Soil Conservation Service of the Department of Agriculture conducts river basin surveys and investigations, watershed planning, and watershed and flood prevention operations. The latter program results in the greatest outlays; the fiscal 1974 figure was projected to be about $111 million. These programs largely duplicate Corps of Engineers activities. In addition, there is little evidence that, on any properly estimated cost/benefit analysis, these programs are warranted. In the absence of such evidence, an appropriate policy would be to phase out these programs. By fiscal 1975, all river basin surveys and investigations and water planning should be able to be completed; by 1978, all watershed and flood prevention operations should also.

The Office of Water Resources Research gives grants to the states for state universities or colleges to conduct water-related research, and it also funds other water research projects. It would be more appropriate if research in this area were funded by the National Science Foundation, which could then objectively compare the value of these programs with other research projects.

Pollution control. Pollution results from the common property aspects of the environment. Since no one "owns" the atmosphere, the oceans and rivers, and even most lakes, no one has an appreciable incentive to protect their quality, and it is impossible to develop a market for them. With an almost zero cost to the polluter of disposing of wastes in a river or in the atmosphere, both public and private agencies attempt to minimize their costs by dumping unwanted by-products into the environment. As increasing amounts of wastes are imposed on the environment, the ability of the environment to process them into nonharmful form is overtaxed and pollution results.

The federal government has attempted to deal with this situation by imposing regulations on discharges and by partially financing treatment plants. This has resulted in the construction of quite a number of treatment facilities, but water quality in a number of areas continues to deteriorate. In response, Congress has authorized more money and is requiring stricter regulation.

A more efficient way to deal with the problem of water pollution would be to make public and private groups pay for disposing of wastes in rivers and lakes. One efficient scheme would be to sell "effluent certificates" that would authorize the owner to dump certain quantities of wastes into a river basin. The total amount of wastes that the certificates would authorize could be set to achieve whatever quality of water the public desired. The certificates would be auctioned off to both public and private entities. It would even be possible for a private conservation organization to purchase some of the certificates to reduce the level of wastes disposed of and thus improve water quality.

Such a plan would provide a strong incentive for communities as well as private firms to clean up their waste in order to avoid having to purchase effluent certificates. It would also mean that court suits as to the feasibility of achieving some given reduction in effluents would no longer be relevant. If a firm could not reduce its pollution, then it could simply buy a certificate, albeit at a high price.

Water pollution abatement provides external benefits. The construction of a sewage treatment plant may benefit downstream communities and water users more than people in its own area. Some sharing of the burden of constructing treatment plants seems desirable, but if the federal government shares a fixed portion of the cost, say 75 percent, then a community would invest in abatement to the point where it would save $1 on effluent certificates for the local marginal dollar in abatement. But if the community spends $1 on abatement, the federal government under this formula must spend $3. So effluent reduction worth $1 to the river basin would be achieved at a $4 total cost—a clear waste. Either the federal government should subsidize the costs of certificates and treatment facilities equally or it should subsidize neither.

All things considered, there would seem to be no more reason for subsidizing municipal treatment plants than for subsidizing a private firm's abatement activities. In either case, such a subsidy might induce the water treatment authority to substitute capital, which is subsidized, for labor, which is not. This line of reasoning suggests that, notwithstanding the externalities, all government grants for pollution facilities should be phased out as soon as existing contracts have been completed and that no new contracts should be signed.

Other programs of the Environmental Protection Agency, such as research and development, abatement and control, enforcement, et cetera, involve areas of clear federal responsibility in that there are substantial externalities in carrying out these activities. Thus, research and development in pollution control is not very profitable for either private industry or for individual states or communities.

Commerce and Transportation. Five of the major activities in this category are summarized below.

Air transportation. An appropriate air transportation policy would require that users pay the costs of the system attributable to their use. The Department of Transportation (DOT) is currently conducting a study to allocate costs among the sectors of the industry: commercial, private, and military. Until this study is completed, it will be impossible to draw firm conclusions as to the burden that should be placed on each type of user.

As it is, commercial and private users in total are expected to cover 44 percent of costs in fiscal 1975 and 65 percent in 1980. Clearly, military users which account for 21 percent of traffic handled by the Federal Aviation Administration (FAA) do not account for 56 percent of the costs, nor does it seem likely that they account for as much as 35 percent of the costs. Also, there is widespread agreement by economists and informed government executives that general aviation—or segments of general aviation—are not paying their share. In fiscal 1974, general aviation is expected to contribute about 7.5 percent of revenues going into the airports/airways trust fund, while in the past they have accounted for 17 percent of the total flights handled by the FAA.

It is argued by general aviation users that they do not require the sophisticated FAA equipment provided in most airports and contribute less to the total costs than would be indicated by a count of flights. On the other hand, general aviation planes are slower and so may take up more time under the direction of flight controllers. On net, it is not possible to make an allocation without a thorough study.

Many FAA expenditures, however, are purely subsidies to local airports. Such programs as airport grants and facilities and equipment as well as some operating expenses should appropriately be paid for at the local level. Local funds could be raised from higher landing fees, peak time fees, airport head taxes, and if necessary, local subsidies. Thus, if airport grants ($295 million) were eliminated, and facilities and equipment ($295 million) were paid for locally, some $590 million would be saved every year through 1980.

While good data are not available, it seems reasonable to assume that some segments of general aviation are not paying their share. Even though the general aviation share is unlikely to be as high as the 17 percent of the traffic they account for, it must be higher than the roughly 7.5 percent they are contributing. Assuming their share should be 50 percent higher and assuming that the military share is equal to 20 percent (approximately the proportion of traffic they account for), the local airport share in 1975 would be about $800 million or about $210 million over the sum of equipment and grants. This assumes that the only portion of the air transport system to be paid for by the general public is that portion accounted for by the military. Actually this sum, which in 1975 is estimated to be $392 million, should come out of the military budget. The rest should either be covered by higher fees and taxes on users, especially general aviation, or paid for by local airport authorities.

Water transportation. The express purpose of the merchant marine program—ship construction and operating subsidies—is to increase national security by insuring the availability of U.S. flag merchant ships manned by U.S. nationals and by guaranteeing sufficient work to U.S. shipyards to keep them in operation with trained manpower.

Consider the desirability of a U.S. merchant marine. Only about 11 percent of U.S. foreign commerce is currently handled by U.S. flag ships. In times of national emergency, the U.S. would have to depend on vessels manned with foreigners to carry our trade. During the Vietnam War, foreign ships were eager to carry our military supplies to Southeast Asia. Great Britain depends on foreign seamen to man its merchant vessels. In all, the United States would not appear to be purchasing any real security with the operating subsidy.

In 1971, there were 1,478 U.S. flag merchant vessels[3] of which an average of 187[4] were operated under subsidy. Assuming that subsidized vessels employ a proportional share of merchant marine seamen, eliminating the program would reduce employment by less than 4,000 out of a total of about 30,400. The dollar saving would be about $250 million in 1975 and about $282 million in 1981. It would not eliminate the U.S. flag merchant marine as long as the Jones Act protected intra-U.S. shipping from competition.

The other half of the merchant marine program supports the construction of merchant ships in U.S. yards. U.S. costs are about twice foreign costs, and if it were not for the subsidies and various laws restricting coastal shipping to U.S.-built and operated ships, little ship building would be carried on domestically. The need to have U.S. yards producing ships is open to question, however. For considerably less money, foreign ships could be bought—in fact, about two ships could be purchased abroad for the cost of building one here, doubling the potential merchant fleet.

The ship construction subsidy is often justified on the ground that it is necessary to keep U.S. yards operating and to keep trained workers so that in time of emergency ships can be produced to

---

[3] U.S. Department of Commerce, *Statistical Abstract of the U.S.*, 1972, Table 957, p. 577.

[4] *Fiscal 1974 Budget, Appendix*, p. 260.

augment the merchant marine. This argument is not completely convincing. It seems unlikely that any major war would last long enough to permit the construction of new ships—if they were needed. On the other hand, if the resources were used to purchase foreign-made ships, twice the number could be secured and mothballed ready for almost immediate use. Moreover, if the war situation permitted the construction of new vessels, the remaining yards could be rapidly expanded. Under the pressure of World War II, U.S. shipbuilding capacity was expanded fourteenfold from 1939 to 1943.[5]

During 1970, the construction of no more than seventeen ships was subsidized, while some forty-nine commercial vessels and 108 naval vessels were being constructed. This subsidized production was no more than 11 percent of production. Schultze[6] reported (in a discussion of the 1971 budget) that only 7,500 workers are normally employed building subsidized merchant vessels out of a labor force of 110,000. In any case, eliminating the program would reduce construction and labor by only about 10 percent, at a saving of around $400 to $450 million (in 1971 dollars) per year through 1980.

Ground transportation. Substantially all expenditures in this area except for a small but rapidly growing mass transportation program are for highways, especially the interstate system. The administration has proposed converting part of the highway program to an urban transportation grant program and another part to a rural transportation program.

Urban mass transit in most cases involves few if any nonlocal externalities. In other words, there is no economic justification for individuals not living in a metropolitan area to pay for any such program. In most cases, revenues from the completed system are expected to be considerably below costs—in some cases below operating costs.

The prime justification for constructing mass transit systems is to reduce urban traffic congestion. Here the evidence suggests that the program will be a failure as any temporary reduction in traffic congestion quickly generates sufficient new auto travel to recreate the congestion. Thus a mass transit program is likely in most cases to be a subsidy program for certain urban commuters who live within easy walking distance of a rapid transit stop. Since such individuals are likely to have higher than average incomes, the program is likely to be regressive.

---

[5] Charles Schultze et al., *Setting National Priorities: The 1971 Budget* (Washington, D. C.: The Brookings Institution, 1971), p. 176.
[6] Ibid.

The highway program is now financed by taxes levied on highway users. The justification for the trust fund approach is that the beneficiaries are paying for the program. If these sums are used to pay for other programs, then such a taxation scheme must be compared on efficiency and equity grounds to some more broadly based revenue raising program. While other excise taxes, such as those on alcohol and tobacco, are used for general revenue, their justification lies in taxing undesirable consumption that has negative externalities. Moreover, taxes on alcohol and tobacco bring in a negligible proportion of general revenue. Tax experts consider excise taxes as regressive and unfair compared to a general tax such as the income tax or a possible value-added tax. Thus there would seem to be no economic justification for taxing highway users for nonhighway purposes and any cutback in the size of the highway program should lead to a matching reduction in highway taxes.

Along with many other programs, there has been a tendency to federalize the construction of highways. While there is a valid role for the federal government to play in providing for a strong interstate system, local and state roads should primarily be a state responsibility. As a consequence, an efficient allocation of federal moneys (not necessarily a politically possible allocation) would involve a cutback in the federal highway program to a level sufficient to cover the remaining cost of the interstate highway system. At the same time, highway taxes should be reduced proportionately so that the remaining federal highway receipts just cover the cost of finishing the interstate system.

In the railroad area, the federal government should abandon its efforts to maintain uneconomic passenger transportation. The National Railroad Passenger Corporation should cut back its service or raise its prices until its revenues equal its expenses rather than depend on the general taxpayer. The highspeed ground transportation research program also seems unwarranted in that, if highspeed ground transportation were an economically viable project, private interests would do the research and development. Dropping the highspeed ground program and the federal subsidy for passenger transportation would have reduced the budget in fiscal 1974 by about $121.3 million.

Postal Service. Congress has seen fit to require the post office to maintain uneconomic rural post offices and services. For this purpose, the Congress has expressly authorized a government subsidy. An appropriation has also been authorized to enable the post office to offer subsidized services to blind individuals. Using the post office to transfer income to the blind and to rural individuals is inefficient. If such people are to be aided, direct grants are more appropriate. Moreover, any such programs, especially the public service subsidies, lead to a waste of resources and economic inefficiencies.

From an economic efficiency point of view, the post office should be run as a private corporation with at least some profits earned on its operations. To ensure an economically efficient postal service, elimination of the postal first class monopoly is essential. Only competition or the very real threat of competition can force an institution that operates under the rule of long-established custom, such as the post office, to change in a major way. Gross subsidization and bureaucratic procedures will disappear only when they cannot be maintained.

An efficient allocation of post office expenditures, therefore, would imply the elimination of all government aid and financing of the system. While it would seem dubious that this could be accomplished in a very short period of time, a gradual phaseout of government aid over a five-year period would be practical. Thus 20 percent of the subsidy has been eliminated in fiscal 1975, 40 percent in fiscal 1976, and so on. By 1979, federal aid would be entirely eliminated.

Advancement of business. The advancement of business area is made up of numerous small programs, some of which seem to have questionable merit. In many cases the government provides services to businesses that they should pay for if they want them. The disaster loan fund administered by the Small Business Administration, for example, reduces or eliminates the need for private insurance and private efforts to reduce the severity of natural disasters. By lowering the risk to individuals and firms of living or locating in disaster-prone areas, it leads to greater losses from natural occurrences.

The federal government not only sponsors and encourages small businesses but singles out for special consideration minority business in the minority business development program (costing $65.8 million in fiscal 1974). While discrimination against blacks has been very harmful in the past and many injustices have been done, the government should remain "color blind." Aid to minority business should be handled on the same basis as aid to any small business irrespective of the race, religion, or sex of the owner or entrepreneur.

The National Bureau of Standards has recently inaugurated a new program to foster technology (costing $8 million in fiscal 1974) by providing incentives to private industry. Such a program distorts resource allocation and is wasteful.

Nearly one-third of the outlays in this area are for Appalachian regional development, of which most are for the construction of highways and access roads in that area. Since, if such roads are desirable, they should be built by the state, this part of the program could be phased out. At the rate these roads have been finished or are projected to be finished in fiscal 1973 and 1974 (that is, 150 miles per year), it will take about four to five years to finish the approved projects.

Appalachian vocational education facilities should also be phased out as a special regional program, and demonstration health programs also seem questionable for this special region. Such projects are partly covered by other federal programs. To the extent that additional health benefits are provided there that are unavailable elsewhere, they should be eliminated. Supplements to federal grants-in-aid are also provided. While such supplements may be desirable for poor states, singling out Appalachia, which includes nonpoor Pennsylvania, for special help is unwarranted.

The only part of the Appalachian regional development program that seems worth keeping is that dealing with mine area restoration. This is a problem confined mainly to Appalachia, and while it could be argued that it should be dealt with at the state level, there are externalities that cross state borders. Hence, keeping this program is worthwhile although it might be folded into the programs of the Bureau of Mines.

The Bureau of Indian Affairs (BIA) is spending approximately $5,000 per Indian man, woman, and child. As is well known, however, many Indians are still living in abject poverty. Some restructuring of the Indian programs seems called for. The exact nature of such a program cannot be specified without considerable study. Therefore the BIA programs have been continued at their current level, although it may be desirable to spend more or perhaps it might be even better to give every Indian a grant of, say, $5,000, and turn title of the reservations over to the tribes while closing out BIA.

The goal of the Economic Development Administration (EDA) was to stimulate economic growth and employment in those regions lagging behind the growth of the rest of the country. Behind this goal was the notion that all sections of the country *should* grow together. But this implies no shift in resources from one point to another. Clearly, in a dynamic growing economy resources must shift to produce efficiently the goods and services the U.S. economy demands. Thus, the goal of EDA was basically to frustrate the movement of resources out of some regions into others. While there may be a need for income support programs for immobile resources, for example, older people, frustrating the movement of other resources can only reduce economic growth for the economy as a whole.

According to a study made by GAO, EDA has been singularly unsuccessful in achieving its primary goal, although it managed to find "depressed areas" with "worthwhile" projects in all fifty states and five territories. The projects included such items as county jails, community buildings, fire stations, village halls, community centers, et cetera.

This program was obviously popular since it provided money for all sections of the country. Traditionally "pork-barrel" projects involve rivers and harbors, but this program extended the possibilities to landlocked communities and permitted additional types of projects. The administration proposed in the 1974 budget to phase out this program entirely.

Federal funding of regional action planning commissions was designed to aid specific regions that cut across state boundaries. While not involved so much in traditional pork-barrel projects, the benefits of these commissions go to the local regions and should be supported by them. The 1974 budget has phased out federal funding for these commissions.

Regulation of business. It can be argued that regulatory commissions do more harm than good. However, no cuts in their budgets have been recommended. The cost of regulation in terms of budget impact is small. Consequently, if the agencies were to be abolished or significantly cut, it should be on other than budgetary grounds.

Conclusion

In the area of science, technology, and industry, adoption of the program changes discussed here could produce net savings of about $7 billion a year for the rest of the decade. Given the debate over budget priorities, such changes would seem to warrant serious consideration as a significant contribution to "freeing up" budget resources for other uses. More important, many of these changes should be adopted even if there were no budget pressure because the programs bring no identifiable public benefits. Other more efficient solutions are possible at much lower budgetary cost.

6

HOUSING AND COMMUNITY DEVELOPMENT

Rudolph G. Penner

The Congress hereby declares that the general welfare
and security of the Nation and the health and living standards of its people require housing production and related
community development sufficient to remedy the serious
housing shortage, the elimination of substandard and other
inadequate housing through the clearance of slums and
blighted areas, and the realization as soon as feasible of the
goal of a decent home and suitable living environment for
every American family, thus contributing to the development and redevelopment of communities and to the advancement of the growth, wealth, and security of the Nation.

This idealistic sentence is contained in the preamble to the Housing
Act of 1949. More than two decades later, a large portion of the
programs motivated by such sentiments are alleged to be in such
disarray that they were suspended prior to the issuance of the 1974
budget. What went wrong? Has the pursuit of a noble goal led to a
major fiasco, or has the President been too hasty in suspending
programs which face only minor difficulties?

Major program changes are also proposed for community development. The administration proposes to eliminate urban renewal,
model cities, and other programs, and fold them into a special urban
revenue-sharing program. The community action program would also
be eliminated.

This chapter deals with these major program issues in the area
of community development and housing. First, however, the budget
outlook implied by the fiscal 1974 budget is discussed.

The Budget Outlook

Table 6-1 summarizes projected outlays for community development and housing, based on the status of these programs in the fiscal 1974 budget.

Table 6-1

COMMUNITY DEVELOPMENT AND HOUSING:
PROJECTED OUTLAYS UNDER ADMINISTRATION BUDGET,
FISCAL YEARS 1975–81

(unified budget, billions of dollars)

Program	1975	1976	1977	1978	1979	1980	1981
Housing payments	2.3	2.7	2.7	2.6	2.5	2.4	2.3
Urban special revenue sharing[a]	2.4	2.4	2.3	2.3	2.3	2.3	2.3
Other	0.7	0.8	0.9	0.9	1.0	1.0	1.1

[a] Includes outlays for past commitments for programs absorbed by urban revenue sharing.
Source: LRBP estimates.

For purposes of projecting these outlays, it was assumed that housing payments programs will remain suspended through the 1970s. Outlays were assumed to peak in fiscal 1976 at a level slightly below commitments already made. After that, it is very difficult to estimate the rate at which payments will decline because of increases in the incomes of subsidy recipients. It was assumed that the payments under the Section 235 program will decline fastest because mortgage payments tend to be fixed in money terms. The rate of decline is assumed to be 10 percent annually after a peak of $430 million in fiscal 1976.

Theoretically, outlays under the rental assistance programs could rise or fall in the future since the subsidy depends both on market rent and tenant income. The former will rise with inflation and the latter will be affected both by the rise or fall in income of individual tenants and by changes in the mix of tenants when people move out and are replaced by new tenants with higher or, more likely, lower incomes. In making the projections of Table 6-1, it was optimistically assumed that tenant contributions would rise more absolutely than market rents and that after reaching a peak of $700 million in fiscal 1976, rental assistance payments would decline somewhat less than 5 percent per year. For low-rent public housing it was assumed that operating subsidies would be controlled somewhat more rigorously after fiscal 1974 and would rise only with the inflation rate.

All of these assumptions are highly tenuous and probably err in that they are too optimistic. The budget itself reflects the wide margin of possible error by stating that the cumulative value of future payments will be between $57 and $82 billion. All that can be said is that the assumptions made here are consistent with that wide range.

For revenue sharing, a constant money value of $2.3 billion is used for the long run and outlays for existing commitments for absorbed programs are assumed to disappear by fiscal 1977. For agencies that make direct loans and that buy and sell assets, it is assumed that net outlays will be zero throughout the remainder of the 1970s. Actual behavior will vary with conditions in mortgage markets and it is recognized that in particular years large inflows or outflows could occur, causing these projections to contain significant errors. For those other programs where there has been no explicit statement of policy changes on the part of the administration, outlays were allowed to grow either at the estimated rate of wage increases or at the inflation rate, whichever seemed more appropriate given the nature of the program.

Program Issues in Housing

What *did* go wrong with the housing programs? Can they be restructured to avoid the criticisms leveled at them, or is the problem more fundamental, that is, is there something inherent in subsidy programs of this type that makes success elusive?

In attempting to answer these questions, an obvious place to begin is to question the goal itself. Should the nation give a high priority to diverting resources away from the production of things like food, clothing, defense, and other items [1] and toward the production of houses? While this is a question of utmost importance, it will be reserved for later discussion. For the moment, the housing goal will be accepted and the suspended programs will be judged according to their effectiveness in equitably increasing housing investment, however wise or misguided this goal may be.

---

[1] Some might claim that otherwise unemployed resources will be used to produce homes. Even if this were true—and it is doubtful—the decision to use unemployed resources to produce houses implies foregoing the opportunity to use those resources to produce other things.

93

In this context, it is contended here that the problems with the housing programs are indeed serious, and that major reforms are required. To support this contention, each of the most important suspended programs will be examined in turn.

Suspended Housing Programs

A number of activities in this area are summarized below, ending with a discussion of possible new approaches.

Homeownership Assistance. Section 235 of the National Housing Act provides subsidies which lower mortgage, tax, and insurance payments to either 20 percent of the owner's adjusted income or to the payment necessitated by a 1 percent interest payment on the mortgage, whichever implies the lower subsidy. Income is adjusted by deducting 5 percent plus $300 for each dependent. In fiscal 1974, it is estimated that 503 thousand units will be under payment and cumulative contract authority commitments will total $444 million. Because there is a long time lag between the date that the government is committed to a contract and the date at which subsidized owners move into their dwellings, outlays for the program have not reached commitment levels and will probably continue to rise until fiscal 1976, even though the programs were suspended January 5, 1973. Since mortgages are subsidized for up to thirty years, the nation is committed to an enormous long-run financial outlay under the program. Theoretically, the burden for this one program could exceed $10 billion, but in fact, it is quite certain that the burden will be lowered significantly because subsidy levels will be reduced as the incomes of recipients rise. The Department of Housing and Urban Development (HUD) estimates that on an average, subsidies will actually be paid between eleven and fourteen years,[2] rather than the maximum of thirty years. Still, this represents an enormous commitment for a program when we have little solid knowledge about its effectiveness in increasing the supply of housing. Obviously, some of the 503,000 units now under payment would have been constructed without the subsidy, but there are no accurate estimates of what proportion.

Since families at the low end of the income scale cannot afford homeownership even with a 1 percent interest rate, the Section 235 program is primarily for people of moderate means. In the fourth

---

[2] U.S. Congress, House of Representatives, *HUD-Space-Science-Veterans Appropriations for 1973,* Hearings before a Subcommittee on the Committee on Appropriations, 92nd Congress, 2nd session, 1972, p. 111.

quarter of 1971, the median income of assisted owners was $6,309 and only 3.9 percent of assisted families had incomes less than $4,000,[3] while more than 10 percent had incomes greater than $7,000. Even families with incomes over $10,000 per year can continue to receive some sort of assistance at recent market rates of interest, but initially most of the funds must be used for individuals whose income does not exceed 135 percent of the maximum income allowed families admitted to low-rent public housing.

Since 135 percent of the income eligibility for low-rent public housing comes close to the median family income in many localities, about 40 percent of the U.S. population is technically eligible for some sort of subsidy.[4] Obviously, Congress has no intention of funding subsidies for more than a small portion of those eligible and, therefore, the subsidies have had to be rationed and allocated to a small portion of those who qualify. Consequently, a large portion of the eligible population, who are not lucky enough to receive a subsidy, find themselves paying taxes to help finance a subsidy that enables people with equal or sometimes greater income to live in houses more luxurious than the excluded population can afford.

It is this fundamental inequity which casts the most doubt on the program. It can be corrected only by a radical reform. Either funding levels would have to be increased enormously to serve the entire eligible population—an unlikely event given current budget stringency—or the basic structure of the program would have to be totally altered to focus the available funds on housing the poorest members of society.

In examining the equity of the program, it is important to note that the recipients of funds are not the only beneficiaries, nor are the taxpayers financing it the only ones injured. Recently, the Section 235 subsidies have only been available to persons purchasing new houses. The total stock of housing suitable for moderate-income families has been increased more per dollar of outlays than would be the case if subsidies were also available to purchase existing dwellings. Because of the resulting increase in the supply of homes, prices of existing houses may have been lowered from what they might otherwise have been. Consequently, moderate-income families already owning homes have suffered a capital loss while those contemplating the purchase of

---

[3] Message from the President of the United States, *Fourth Annual Report on National Housing Goals* (Washington, D. C.: U.S. Government Printing Office, 1972), p. 29.

[4] Message from the President of the United States, *Third Annual Report on National Housing Goals* (Washington, D. C.: U.S. Government Printing Office, 1971), p. 23.

an existing dwelling for the first time have benefited, even though they do not receive a subsidy directly. In short, *the distribution of the benefits and the harm done by the subsidies are very complicated indeed, and the only certain conclusion is that the result is very likely to be inequitable.*

Aside from being inequitable, the program has also been inefficient and susceptible to fraud. This problem is of a different order of magnitude from the problem of its basic inequity, because it can be ameliorated by making small changes in the program's technical structure, whereas improvements in equity require a more radical reform. The tendency toward inefficiency results, in part, from the fact that the subsidized owner pays only 20 percent of his income toward the mortgage regardless of the value of the house—unless the interest rate has been lowered to its minimum of 1 percent. Consequently, for example, a $22,000 house costs him no more than a $21,000 house, or in other words, the builder can add $1,000 to the cost of the house without any protest on the part of the buyer. The extra $1,000 may be a complete waste, in which case the collusion of a corrupt or incompetent appraiser may be necessary to defraud the government, but it can also be wasteful in a more subtle manner. The extras may actually have a $1,000 market value and thus they will be approved by the appraiser. However, the owner may have little need for the extras and would never contemplate buying them at the market price. Consequently, the government spends money presenting a gift to the owner that provides him with little utility. The tendency toward this sort of waste is limited by two factors. First, there is a maximum on the value of the house eligible for subsidy. The program as administered features varying mortgage limitations related to local levels of cost. This sets an upper boundary on the amount of waste possible in each subsidized dwelling. Second, the owner will have some incentive to economize if he thinks that his income will either rise sufficiently in the future to eliminate the subsidy or fall enough to make the 1 percent interest payment binding.

In fact, a large proportion of the owners are at the 1 percent limit, and for the poorer members of the subsidized population, mortgage insurance and tax payments can often exceed 40 percent of income. This has led to a high and rapidly increasing default rate as buyers attracted by low down payments find that they cannot really afford the monthly expenditures. It should also be noted that, while the owner at the 1 percent limit has an incentive to economize, his choice is often limited by government regulations which specify certain characteristics that the house must possess in order to qualify for a subsidy.

As noted before, the problem of waste can be reduced greatly, if not eliminated, by giving the buyer more of an incentive to economize and more of a choice in the selection of a house. The buyer's opportunity to economize is limited because he cannot specify to the builder exactly what he likes or dislikes. Moreover, there is no incentive to economize if the buyer's payment is determined solely by his income. Rather than have him pay a fixed proportion of his income, the government could offer something like a 90 percent subsidy to the eligible population for the first x dollars of the mortgage payment, 50 percent for the next y dollars, and 10 percent for the next z dollars. By choosing x, y, and z appropriately, the government could ensure that the typical buyer would be responsible for either 90 or 50 cents of each extra dollar of expenditure on the house, and then the buyer would have a much greater incentive to identify and protest wasteful expenditures. Obviously, the problem would not disappear entirely, because whenever the government pays a portion of any cost, there is some incentive for waste and some possibility for collusion between the buyer and builder to defraud the government. However, the sort of scheme suggested above would greatly reduce both the incentive for waste and the gains from corruption.

While the efficiency of the program might be improved by making relatively minor changes in its technical structure, it must be reemphasized that the equity of the program will remain in doubt as long as some of those who legally qualify cannot be served because of a lack of funding. Whenever a subsidy is rationed, there is opportunity for corruption and unwarranted favoritism on the part of those in a position to choose the few who will become the recipients of the government's largess, even if the program is otherwise structured efficiently.

Rental Assistance. Two major programs subsidize renters. The rent supplement program and the Section 236 program lower rent payments in a qualified dwelling to 25 percent of the tenant's income, the latter by subsidizing the mortgage of an owner of a multifamily dwelling. (The net mortgage interest rate cannot be lowered below 1 percent.) To qualify for the former, a tenant's income must be lower than that required to enter low-rent public housing while the latter is available to anyone earning less than 135 percent of that amount. The families served by both programs tend to be somewhat poorer than those receiving Section 235 assistance, but they also tend to have fewer children.[5] Often, the two programs are combined in a so-called piggyback arrangement. Rent supplements are thus paid to tenants living in Section 236 dwellings where otherwise a rent payment of 25 percent of their income would not be sufficient to provide for a 1 percent interest payment on the mortgage. In fiscal 1974, cumulative contract authority commitments will total $241 million under the rent supplement program and $527 million under Section 236 assistance. However, outlays will never quite reach these levels, because tenants generally end up contributing more in rents than is anticipated in the contracts.

The rental assistance programs contain the same deficiencies afflicting the homeownership program. Only a small portion of the eligible population receives subsidies and hence the programs are inequitable. They are also inefficient in that for most tenants their rent depends solely on their own income and not on the quality of the dwelling. Hence, they have no incentive to protest against wasteful construction expenditures.

In addition, the costs of multifamily subsidized construction are raised artificially by a variety of government regulations. One of the most important is the Davis-Bacon Act, which in effect forces the builder to pay union wages whether or not his work force is unionized. Another problem results from requirements that the mix of tenants display economic diversity. Since it is often hard to induce the rich to live with the poor, the economic viability of some projects has been threatened.

Low-Rent Public Housing. This type of housing is owned, or leased and operated, by local housing authorities. The federal government makes annual contributions toward servicing this debt and it will also subsidize operating costs sufficiently to lower the tenants' rent payments to 25 percent of their income. In addition, the local housing authorities are eligible for direct loans to tide them over while they are raising their own capital, and interest payments on their bonds are exempt from federal income taxes, thus allowing them to borrow at low interest rates. In fiscal 1974, cumulative contract authority committed will total $1.6 billion supporting 1.7 million dwelling units.

Aaron has commented that public housing has acquired a "vile image" over the years, but notes that low vacancy rates and long

---

[5] For a detailed analysis of the distribution of the subsidy payments, see Henry Aaron, *Shelter and Subsidies* (Washington, D. C.: The Brookings Institution, 1972), Chapter 8, especially Table 8-1.

waiting lists indicate that they provide better living conditions than the alternatives available to very low income families.[6] Given the deplorable conditions faced by persons with extremely low incomes in the slums of our largest cities, this may not be much of a compliment. However, in this case it is dangerous to generalize. Experience has varied greatly from city to city—from those in which low-rent public housing was barely habitable or actually uninhabitable to those in which fairly pleasant surroundings were provided to the poor.

The low-rent public housing program has the advantage of focusing aid on those who need it most—the desperately poor. Still, only a small portion of those eligible are actually aided (about 10 percent), and the program therefore faces the same problem of equity faced by the homeownership and rental assistance programs.

A major problem for the public housing program has resulted from the rapid growth in the operating subsidy. The subsidy has grown rapidly for two reasons. First, the Brooke Amendment limited tenant payments to 25 percent of tenant income in order to achieve comparability with the rental assistance programs. Second, the federal government covers all operating costs in excess of the resulting tenant contributions and there is, therefore, no incentive for local authorities to economize. Aaron suggests that a subsidy limited to some portion of costs would ameliorate this problem somewhat, but this would imply a cutback in federal aid to the project, which they could not recoup through rent increases because of both tenant opposition and the Brooke Amendment. Some technique for compensating authorities would have to be found. Perhaps a formula could be devised which would offer an annual lump-sum payment plus a share of the operating deficit, but it would be difficult to devise such an arrangement which both has a low budget cost and is satisfactory to the local authorities.

Other Housing Programs

While the programs discussed above were suspended in January 1973, and this suspension has considerable merit because of the serious deficiencies in their structure, a number of important housing programs were retained, even though they are, if anything, less equitable. The discussion now turns to an examination of the major programs which are still in force.

---

[6] Aaron, *Shelter and Subsidies*, p. 108.

Tax Preferences for Homeowners. The most important housing subsidy program does not appear in the budget at all. It results from the favorable tax treatment accorded to the income from investments in owner-occupied housing. If such investments were treated the same as investments in most other assets, income would be defined to include the gross return on the house, represented by the rent payments that were saved as a result of ownership, less the expenditures related to the investment (mortgage interest, maintenance, depreciation, and real estate taxes). In other words, an investment in an owner-occupied house would be treated just like an investment in a house which is rented to others.

Under the existing tax system, the return on an investment in an owner-occupied house is allowed to go tax free. This alone would favor housing over other investments, and homeowners over renters, but in addition, tax deductions are allowed for some of the expenditures related to the investment, namely mortgage interest and property taxes.

Correcting this anomaly would be difficult technically and politically. To put renters and homeowners on an equal basis, it would be necessary to estimate a rental value for each owner-occupied house and it would obviously be difficult to do this equitably.[7] At the same time, deductions would have to be allowed for expenditures related to the investment. However, a giant step forward would result from eliminating the deduction of mortgage interest and real estate taxes. This would have the effect of allowing the net return on owner-occupied housing to be tax free, whereas the present system actually causes the total return to the owner to be higher than that on a comparable tax-exempt investment.

While it is doubtful that such a reform would be contemplated by a rational politician, it is difficult to overstate the inequities in the present system. Because the value of a tax deduction depends on a person's marginal tax bracket, the housing investments of the rich are subsidized at a much higher rate than those of the poor. Put another way, the poor must pay higher taxes in order to subsidize those who live in more luxurious houses. This makes the situation even worse than that described earlier for the low and moderate income housing

---

[7] It was done in the United Kingdom for many years, but it was dropped several years ago in response to the practical difficulties which it created. It should also be noted that the U.S. tax system allows a deduction for interest paid to finance purchases of consumer durables. However, depreciation is typically a larger proportion of the cost of owning a consumer durable than it is of owning a house, and therefore the tax deduction is relatively less important to the cost of ownership.

subsidies in which there is probably a transfer from both poor and rich to that small number of low and moderate income families fortunate enough to receive explicit subsidy. Another indirect effect of the property tax deduction is that, all other things equal, the wealthy suburbs find it easier to tax and to provide a high level of public services than do the poorer central cities.

As noted previously, the tax subsidy to owner-occupied housing represents our most important housing program. Pechman and Okner estimate that at 1972 income levels tax liabilities would be increased $9.6 billion if net rent were taxed and the mortgage interest and real estate tax deductions were eliminated.[8] This compares to fiscal 1973 obligations under the low and moderate income subsidies of $1.8 billion ($2.1 billion in fiscal 1974). About three-quarters of the $9.6 billion increase in tax revenues would be payable by taxpayers earning more than $15,000 per year.[9]

If net imputed rent were not taxed but the property tax and interest deductions were eliminated, tax revenues would rise by roughly $4 billion or about 40 percent of the amount gained by also taxing imputed rent. This would still be sufficient to finance an expanded federal housing program for the poorest members of society, but the desirability of such a program will not be examined until later.[10]

Guarantee, Insurance, Lending, and Secondary Market Programs. Beginning in the 1930s, the federal government undertook a large number of programs to reduce the risk of investing in mortgages. These can be divided into two broad classes. First, there are the programs of the Veterans Administration (VA) and the Federal Housing Administration (FHA), which reduce default risk by either guaranteeing or insuring the mortgage for the lender. The govern-

---

[8] Net rent is defined as it would be for a business. See Joseph A. Pechman and Benjamin A. Okner, "Individual Income Tax Erosion by Income Classes," *The Economics of Federal Subsidy Programs*, U.S. Congress, Joint Economic Committee (Washington, D. C.: U.S. Government Printing Office, 1972), pp. 13-40. The revenue estimates assume that all of the other tax reforms advocated by Pechman and Okner were also adopted.

[9] Income is defined using the expanded tax base estimated by Pechman and Okner, ibid., p. 34.

[10] It should be noted that our total tax system also distorts investment patterns in rental properties and provides special advantages to investments in subsidized rental properties. For a more detailed discussion of this and related matters, see Aaron, *Shelter and Subsidies*, Chapter 4 and Chapter 8, pp. 140-141. Also, see Aaron, "Income Taxes and Housing," *American Economic Review*, vol. 60 (December 1970), pp. 789-806.

ment charges fees or insurance premiums for most of these programs, but the relationship between the fee and the actuarial value of possible losses varies greatly from program to program. Some imply significant subsidies while other programs have accumulated substantial reserves over the years. Aaron estimates that, on average, FHA and VA programs provided a net subsidy in 1966, the present value of which is $141 million. Of this amount, over 90 percent was received by people earning between $4,000 and $9,000 per year.[11] Since that time efforts have been made to make the FHA programs more progressive, for example, the high risk program, but these efforts have been plagued by defaults.

Second, the government has created financial intermediaries and secondary market institutions, such as the Federal National Mortgage Association (FNMA) and the Federal Home Loan Mortgage Corporation (FHLMC), to reduce the liquidity risk associated with mortgages. Nominally, these institutions are government-sponsored private institutions. Practically, this means that they are owned by private investors, but they receive a slight subsidy in the form of a line of credit from the U.S. Treasury.

Because these programs are partially financed by fees or are privately administered, they do not impose a significant budget cost on the federal government. However, they are extremely important to the allocation of resources. By making mortgages much more desirable investments, they have undoubtedly drawn significant credit flows away from other sectors of the economy.[12] Consequently, their budget costs are only a pale reflection of their gross social costs in a full employment economy, as measured by the reduction in economic activity in the sectors which have been deprived of credit as a result of the housing programs.

These programs have expanded very rapidly in recent years. The Farmers Home Administration, the FHA, and VA expect to have insured and guaranteed about $170 billion of mortgages in fiscal 1974

---

[11] Henry Aaron, "Federal Housing Subsidies" in *The Economics of Federal Subsidy Programs*, Part 5, U.S. Congress, Joint Economic Committee (Washington, D. C.: U.S. Government Printing Office, 1971), p. 585.

[12] For a discussion of the theory of these credit programs and for references to the relevant literature, see Rudolph G. Penner and William Silber, "Federal Housing Credit Programs: Costs, Benefits, and Interactions," *The Economics of Federal Subsidy Programs*, U.S. Congress, Joint Economic Committee (Washington, D. C.: U.S. Government Printing Office, 1972), pp. 660-675. It is assumed in this discussion that the savings rate remains relatively unaffected by changes in risk and the rate of return. Therefore, increased credit flows to one sector imply reduced credit flows to some other sector. If the programs do increase the savings rate, then they also draw some resources away from consumption.

as compared to $145 billion in fiscal 1972. In addition to the programs which reduce the risk of mortgage investments, there are a number of direct lending programs. The largest is the Farmers Home Administration, which is supposed to focus on low and moderate income borrowers, but more than 50 percent of the borrowers earned more than $6,000 per annum in 1970. Smaller lending programs are administered by the VA. In addition, the government exerts some influence over FNMA and FHLMC to become net purchasers or sellers of mortgages in order to stabilize housing markets. Needless to say, this can sometimes conflict with their role as secondary market institutions.

Possible New Approaches. While the old approaches to housing are clearly fraught with weaknesses, it is extremely difficult to contemplate any major reform which would not also add significantly to the federal or state and local housing budget. Although significant federal savings could be generated by eliminating the tax deductions for mortgage interest and property taxes and these could be reallocated to more sensible programs, this seems beyond the realm of political plausibility. At the same time, outlays on the suspended low and moderate income subsidies will continue to rise for several years, because of commitments to continue a high portion of these payments for several decades. In fact, projected outlays in fiscal 1981 will still exceed those made in fiscal 1974, even though new commitments were suspended in January 1973. Consequently, any federal reforms must be contemplated for the very long run unless taxes are to be raised or budget resources are diverted from other areas. For this reason, the reforms discussed are not costed out, since they would have little or no budget impact for the last half of the 1970s.

Before suggesting any specific reforms, it is appropriate to return to the question of whether or not the housing goal itself is desirable. The enabling legislation sets a goal of a "decent home and suitable living environment for every American family." The words "decent" and "suitable" are sufficiently ambiguous to allow wide latitude in making them operational, but as reflected in past policies, the major aim seems to have been to increase housing consumption generally without regard to the distributional consequences. Even where programs have focused on "low and moderate" income groups, income eligibility levels have been defined so generously as to obviate the possibility of focusing the limited budget appropriations on the very poor, who are most in need of improvements in the "decency" of their living quarters. In contrast, the rhetoric surrounding the programs has made it seem as though the goal was to give first priority to aiding the poor. Consequently, before new programs can be designed sensibly, the conflict between past actions and rhetoric will have to be resolved. It is also necessary to determine whether we are more serious about the distributional aims implied by the rhetoric or about the goal of simply adding to the housing stock, which is more consistent with our past actions.

There may be legitimate arguments for generally subsidizing housing consumption without immediate regard to the distributional consequences. For example, some believe that an investment in higher quality housing not only pays a reward to the owner but also increases the value of surrounding properties. Thus it has a social return in excess of the private return.[13] Consequently, there is room for collective action either on a large scale through government subsidy or on a smaller scale through the formation of neighborhood associations. Conversely, without collective action, there is a tendency for slums to evolve.[14] The problem of slum formation has been most severe in central cities containing older homes, probably because housing technology is such that one of the cheapest ways to house the poor is to subdivide high quality old houses and let them run down. Perhaps this tendency has been intensified by building codes which prevent the construction of low quality new housing. In any case, while allowing houses to run down and renting to the poor may represent the most profitable alternative to the owner, it may not be the most profitable alternative to society as a whole, because it is the whole neighborhood which must bear the cost of the visual blight that is created. In the 1930s and 1940s it was also popular to believe that many social problems, such as crime, alcoholism, et cetera, were *caused* by poor housing. There is little empirical evidence to support this belief, but it probably played an important role in shaping the explicit statement of goals in the Housing Act of 1949.[15]

Nevertheless, low quality housing does have a social cost which is not reflected in private costs and some collective action is war-

---

[13] It should be noted that it is extremely difficult to document this empirically, perhaps because the external effects are either highly localized or not very important.

[14] The tendency may be strengthened by individuals attempting to follow a safe gaming strategy in small group situations. See Otto A. Davis and Andrew B. Winston, "Economics of Urban Renewal," *Law and Contemporary Problems*, vol. 26 (Winter 1961), pp. 105-117.

[15] An interesting discussion of our social values with regard to housing can be found in Harold Wolman, *Politics of Federal Housing* (New York: Dodd, Mead & Co., 1971), Chapter 2.

ranted. There is a major issue whether the collective action should be federal or local. If anything has all of the characteristics of a local problem, it would seem to be housing, where the nature of the problem varies greatly from locality to locality and therefore would seem to require a purely local solution. On the other hand, there are severe institutional and economic constraints on local governments' ability to respond to such problems. Since the issues as to where responsibility can and should be are highly complex, they will not be explored here. Rather, the rest of the discussion sketches out the criteria which should be satisfied by sensible housing policies without regard to whether the policies are administered locally or federally.

Repeating the basic principle: high quality housing adds to surrounding property values while low quality housing depresses those values. The most serious problem emanates from the slums, where visual blight has the highest negative value. If this problem is to be attacked first, there may immediately be a conflict between efficiency and benefiting the poor. For example, in some areas the highest social return may result from rehabilitating slum dwellings and making them suitable for the middle class and rich. This process is currently occurring in the Capitol Hill district of Washington, D. C., and occurred earlier in Georgetown. Because of the predominance of private activity in this risky business, the expected private return must be quite high and the social return in terms of increased property values must surely add significantly to the total return. Consequently, the judicious use of government subsidies to encourage such developments may have a high payoff, but it is a payoff that accrues mainly to the affluent. The poor are undoubtedly worse off because they face a reduced supply of cheap housing. They could conceivably be compensated out of the increased property taxes accruing to the locality, but U.S. institutions are probably too rigid to accomplish such a delicate balancing act.

In other areas, the most efficient approach may be to engage in a less thorough rehabilitation program, simply upgrading the living conditions of the poor. Here, efficiency and distributional aims are happily more consistent.

In general, there are many different tools that can be used to upgrade housing, whether the upgrading is focused on the slums or more broadly applied to all consumption of housing. All or a select population of buyers of housing services can be subsidized whether existing or newly constructed dwellings are purchased or rented. The price of the housing stock will then rise, providing an incentive for new construction. Alternatively, only purchases of newly constructed housing can be subsidized. Additions to the total stock will increase and the price of existing housing will fall. The latter can accomplish the same increase in the housing stock for a lower budget cost. However, the main social cost in either case is represented by the resources used to construct new houses. The former involves a higher budget cost only because part of the outlays are transferred to the owners of existing dwellings in the form of a capital gain. It may also have a slightly higher social cost only because tax rates will be higher and this may create some inefficiencies elsewhere in the economy. Therefore, from the point of view of efficiency the subsidization of only newly constructed housing may have a slight advantage, but from the point of view of equity the issue is more complicated. The subsidization of all housing purchases benefits all buyers and sellers of both existing and newly constructed housing.[16] The subsidization of new construction benefits buyers of both existing and new houses but hurts sellers and owners of existing housing. Because buyers all benefit whether or not they are directly subsidized, this approach is known as the filter approach; that is, the benefits of the subsidy are filtered down to nonsubsidized buyers.[17] However, it seems likely that these filtered benefits will be more sporadic than if all purchases are subsidized.

Whether the subsidy applies just to newly constructed or to all housing, it should be given to the buyer or renter and not tied to the unit. This maximizes freedom of choice, does not tie the subsidy recipient to one location, and circumvents a myriad of government regulations which artificially increase the cost of subsidized units.

The tax preferences given homeowners represent a special sort of filtering strategy. They are granted to buyers of both existing and new houses. However, the rich are subsidized at a much higher rate than the poor and middle class. This may induce the rich to vacate existing housing suitable for lower income groups thus depressing the price, but it also gives them a large advantage in bidding for the materials and labor necessary for new construction. The tax preferences for homeownership may also depress the price of existing rental properties, but the discussion of these complex distributional effects should not be allowed to obscure the basic issue. That is that the poor could certainly be made better off if home-ownership preferences were eliminated and the increased tax proceeds were distributed on a per capita basis.

---

[16] It is assumed that the supply is not completely inelastic and the demand is not perfectly elastic.

[17] For a discussion, see Aaron, *Shelters and Subsidies*, pp. 160-163.

The discussion thus far has concentrated on policies whose prime purpose is to increase purchases of housing services without special regard to the distributional consequences. Many believe that the prime problem is housing the poor adequately and, therefore, they suggest policies which focus on the low income population. Most of these approaches involve some sort of housing allowance scheme.

Before describing this approach, it is necessary to emphasize an obvious point. If the desire is to help the poor, it is much more effective to give them cash rather than a gift in kind, such as a house, which imposes the same budget cost. With cash, the poor person can always purchase housing services if he wants to, but he can also use it for anything else that gives him more pleasure.

Aaron has analyzed a plan which would give the person a "housing allowance" equal to the difference between 25 percent of his income and the estimate of shelter costs for his area reported in the low-cost budget by the Bureau of Labor Statistics. In 1967, Aaron estimated that this would cost $6.2 billion if it were universal and it drove up housing costs 10 percent.[18]

The payment need not be contingent on actually spending 25 percent of his income plus the allowance on housing. In this case, it would be equivalent to a gift of cash and would not increase the demand for housing any more than a comparable cash grant. It would be a subterfuge with the noble purpose of providing maximum benefits to the poor while providing the illusion that it has something to do with housing. But note that this approach contains a danger. It immediately imposes an implicit tax on work effort because the person loses 25 cents for every extra dollar he earns. If it were supplemented by similar schemes for food allowances, health insurance allowances, et cetera, the implicit tax rate could soon become astronomical. Clearly, a carefully designed comprehensive negative income tax would be preferable to this piecemeal approach.

Proposals for housing allowance usually contain provisions ensuring that the housing allowance is actually spent on housing. This would only increase the demand for housing more than a cash grant to the extent that the person would have chosen of his own volition to spend less than this amount. If he would rather spend less, there is immediately an incentive for collusion between the landlord or house seller and the recipient of the subsidy. The seller of the housing service can testify to a higher price while making a kickback to the buyer. Again, this makes the allowance more like a cash grant. The administrators of the program can ignore such deals, thus giving

---

[18] Ibid., p. 169.

high priority to benefiting the poor, or at a large administrative cost they can try to prevent them, thus giving higher priority to increasing the consumption of housing services.

The structure described above essentially makes a lump-sum payment to the recipient, and government may or may not try to ensure that at least that lump sum is spent on housing. More of an impact on housing demand for a given budget cost could presumably be accomplished by paying a certain share of the poor person's housing cost up to some maximum rather than a lump-sum amount.[19] This would in effect reduce the relative price of housing up to the maximum. It would be difficult to administer because actual spending would have to be documented precisely and it would again create some incentive for collusion between seller and buyer.

At all cost, it is necessary to avoid any structure which would have the government pay 100 percent of the cost of housing in excess of some proportion of the recipient's income. This is the structure which helped cause so much inefficiency in the suspended low and moderate income housing program.

Currently experiments are being designed to test the effects of different allowance structures on the demand for housing and on the supply price of housing for the poor. The impact on prices is, of course, vitally important for it will largely determine the portion of the program's benefit which accrues to the poor and that which accrues to the sellers of housing services.

To summarize, it is necessary to decide what weight to give to helping the poor and what weight to give to increasing housing demand before a sensible housing program can be designed. The more closely a payment is tied to a housing purchase, the less benefit it gives the poor person for a given budget cost and the more it makes the benefit conveyed by the subsidy depend on one's taste for housing rather than on one's income level. Moreover, the more closely the payment is tied to housing, the more incentive there is for fraud.

Community Development

The most important changes in the 1974 budget with regard to community development are the elimination of the community action program of the Office of Economic Opportunity and the proposal to institute urban special revenue sharing to replace the urban renewal,

---

[19] Another form of tying involves the provision that the grant will only be paid if the recipient shows that he is living in a dwelling which meets certain standards.

model cities, water and sewer, and other less important programs. Total outlays of the programs to be absorbed by revenue sharing are equal to $1.9 billion in fiscal 1974. With urban revenue sharing, the funds available for these programs would rise to roughly $2.4 billion in fiscal 1975 and then gradually fall to $2.3 billion. In other words, there would be more than enough funds for the average community to maintain the canceled programs along with community action, if they thought them worthwhile. However, there would be no obligation for them to do so. Also, the distribution of revenue-sharing funds may not be identical to the distribution under the present system, although no community would be allowed to suffer as a result of the change.

Briefly summarized, the administration's argument for the change is as follows: A very large part of the effects of the canceled programs is purely local in character. Also, success rates vary greatly from locality to locality. Therefore, the local community is in the best position to decide whether the programs are successful enough to warrant continuation. As long as the programs are supported by federal cost sharing or block grants, the community's decision process is distorted, because they will continue any program whose benefits outweigh the local share of the costs. Since the local share of costs is quite small in many cases and since there are few benefits which accrue outside the locality, there is obviously a strong bias toward wasteful programs under the existing system of categorical grants. Consequently, the administration believes that there will be a large improvement in efficiency if the ties are broken between the local programs and the federal grant.

This does not mean that complete efficiency will be attained. Because the revenue sharing is not tied, it can be used to help finance any local government program for community development. Therefore, to some extent all community development services will be subsidized by the federal government and consequently will appear to be cheaper to the local taxpayer than they actually are. As a result, local governments will spend more than can be justified on the basis of local benefits. This could be justified if all expenditures had equal beneficial effects outside the community, but this obviously is not true and there is nothing in the new approach which favors the type of local spending with the highest beneficial spillovers.

One might ask whether any of the canceled programs are likely to be continued as the result of local initiative if federal support is eliminated. Only two of the most important programs will be examined very briefly—urban renewal and model cities.

Urban Renewal. When the urban renewal program was initiated in 1949, the emphasis was on slum clearance and improvement in the housing stock of central cities. In the 1960s, some funds were allocated to rehabilitation of existing structures and more emphasis was placed on nonresidential renewal. The justification for the program was similar to that used to justify housing subsidies, mentioned earlier in this chapter. The argument was that if blighted buildings were removed or rehabilitated land values in the whole neighborhood would rise sufficiently to make the whole program worthwhile. The improvement in the environment was also supposed to ameliorate social problems.

The program has been attacked for both its lack of efficiency and its distributional effects. Studies of the impact of specific completed projects on land values indicate that often costs significantly exceeded benefits.[20] To make the projects worthwhile one would have to attribute an enormous benefit to an improvement in social conditions, the very existence of which is in doubt.

Distributionally, the program is said to have generally hurt the poor by reducing the stock of housing available to the low income population. There was an attempt to correct this deficiency in 1969 by requiring that destroyed low income housing be replaced unit for unit. However, Weicher has argued that those benefiting from the new housing, while of low income, are still not as poor as the people who were displaced.[21]

The program has faced numerous other difficulties which cannot be considered in these few short paragraphs. On the other hand, the program has evolved through time and more recent unstudied projects may have a much higher payoff than those studied earlier. However, it is doubtful that recent successes would be sufficient to induce many communities to use revenue-sharing funds for urban renewal expenditures matching those of the recent past.

Model Cities. The model cities program was initiated in 1966. Its intent was to provide technical and financial assistance to help cities plan, develop, and carry out demonstration programs for improving urban living conditions. From its inception, the program was viewed as a means of carrying out experiments. A vast variety of projects

---

[20] For example, see Jerome Rothenburg, *Economic Evaluation of Urban Renewal* (Washington, D. C.: The Brookings Institution, 1967). For a broader review of the literature, see John C. Weicher, *Urban Renewal* (Washington, D. C.: American Enterprise Institute, 1972), Chapter 4.

[21] *Urban Renewal*, Chapter 8.

was initiated covering items as diverse as job retraining and housing. Given the diversity of projects, an overall evaluation is impossible here. Since the program was experimental it was never presumed that it would be continued in its present form for a long period of time. Consequently, it is unlikely that communities will extend its life in its present form, even though past experimentation may have discovered a few programs that are worth continuing.

7

EDUCATION

Attiat F. Ott

Introduction

In the fiscal 1974 budget, the administration states the federal objective in the area of education as "extending educational opportunity and . . . encouraging improvements in the quality of education through research, innovation and reform." [1] This is a broad mandate. In practice, however, the federal contribution to education is modest in relation to the overall size of the "industry." Federal outlays for elementary, secondary, and higher education are estimated, for fiscal 1974, to be about $6.9 billion, or 9 percent of total educational outlays by public and private institutions in that year.[2]

Although the 1974 budget reflects continuation of a limited federal role in education that has characterized past years, it represents a marked improvement over prior budgets in three respects. First, the administration has carefully detailed and justified the types of activity at which federal efforts will be directed. Second, the administration addresses itself to the question of efficiency in providing aid to education. Finally, the administration takes a stand on the controversial issue of aid to students in private schools in the form of tax credits for tuition.

---

[1] *Fiscal 1974 Budget*, p. 125.

[2] *Special Analyses: Budget of the United States Government, Fiscal Year 1974* (Washington, D. C.: U.S. Government Printing Office, 1973), p. 107. Total outlays on education made by public institutions is from Courant et al., *AEI Budget Projection Model*. Outlays of private institutions are estimated based on National Center for Educational Statistics, *Projections of Educational Statistics to 1974-80*, Office of Education, Department of Health, Education and Welfare (Washington, D. C.: U.S. Government Printing Office, 1971).

The 1974 budget reaffirms the position that the responsibility for education rests with state and local governments—federal aid to elementary and secondary education should aim at extending educational opportunity and improving the quality of education, but allocation of aid among these two functions is best determined by states and localities. As a result, thirty categorical grants are eliminated. In the area of higher education, a significant departure from the established practice of giving aid to educational institutions was made in the form of a more rational policy which channels aid directly to college students. To stimulate educational research and development, the 1974 budget commits additional resources to the newly created National Institute of Education (outlays are expected to reach $118 million in 1974, an increase of 174 percent over 1973).

Table 7-1 summarizes total federal outlays for education by major category. The 3 percent increase in 1974 outlays over 1973 levels is tiny if one looks at federal performance in the area of education in the past decade. In fiscal 1964, federal aid to education was about $1.4 billion with elementary and secondary education receiving $566 million. Four years later, aid to elementary and secondary education had increased four-and-a-half times and aid to higher education had about tripled. However, even with such high rates of growth, the outlook for the industry remained grim, both in terms of financing and quality of educational services. Most of the elementary and secondary education funds were boxed into narrow cate-

Table 7-1

FEDERAL OUTLAYS ON EDUCATION BY MAJOR PROGRAM, FISCAL YEAR 1974

(unified budget, millions of dollars)

Program	1974
Elementary and secondary education	1,738
Education revenue sharing[a]	1,693
Vocational education	308
Higher education	1,636
Other educational aids	906
General science	586
Total	6,867

[a] Excludes $244 million of basic school lunch funds under income security.
Source: *Fiscal 1974 Budget*, p. 124.

gorical grants for "purposes chosen in Washington," [3] which diluted the authority of local and state governments in allocating them according to other needs, and in some instances were completely directed (for example, impacted aid) towards the wrong end. In the area of higher education, a large share of federal aid found its way to public institutions, thus increasing the share of educational resources in public institutions, which began with state aid taking the form of a subsidy to the institutions rather than to college students.

Over the ten year period 1964-1974, federal outlays on all kinds of education increased from $1.4 billion to $6.8 billion, an average annual rate of growth of about 17 percent. Yet the financial crisis facing most private and many public schools is nowhere near its end; the quality of educational services is still in question, equality of educational opportunity is a long way off, taxpayers are voicing loud protests against additional taxes to finance education, and both educators and noneducators are debating the extent and form of subsidies to education in view of scarce evidence on the value of the nonprivate element of benefits from education. The general dissatisfaction with the educational system, specifically its form of finance and disagreement over the extent and level of federal commitment to education, clearly illustrates the need for reexamining present commitments and efforts. Education is an industry (though not a growing and perhaps a declining one) of sizable magnitude in terms of both the dollar value of resources used up in it and the human resources involved. It has a more lasting and far-reaching effect on society than any other industry, which makes it all that more important that it be subjected to continuous assessment and evaluation.

Because general education confers benefits on society at large as well as on the individuals consuming it, most people would argue for extending the supply of educational services beyond that which a private market system would generate. Unfortunately, both the social "optimum" level of education and the amount of subsidy required to achieve the "optimum"—even if such optimum could be defined— are difficult to determine. [4] And no general agreement exists on the best method to use in supplying educational services.

In this chapter, we will look at the present systems of elementary-secondary and higher education, particularly where federal efforts

---

[3] *Wall Street Journal*, February 28, 1973, p. 10.

[4] Alchian and Allen argue that because an educated person tends to displace or lower the earnings of an uneducated one, one should expect the rate of return on education to be sufficiently high to enable compensation to take place. See A. A. Alchian and W. R. Allen, *University Economics* (Belmont, Calif.: Wadsworth Publishing Co., Inc., 1972), pp. 211-12.

are involved. The federal role in these areas will be examined and federal efforts evaluated. Options to existing educational programs will be discussed, and the costs will be estimated, given assumptions about what the federal role should be in each area.

Elementary and Secondary Education

The 1974 Budget. The 1974 federal budget for elementary and secondary education provides for a limited federal role in education. Table 7-2 shows the details of the administration budget request. The major highlights are:

Request for education revenue sharing. The administration is proposing a major cutback on categorical aid to states and localities. About thirty programs will be replaced by education revenue sharing to give school districts more flexibility in allocating federal funds to meet local educational needs.

Aid to school districts is cut back to $76 million. The remaining funds are primarily to provide for the continuation of the follow-through and bilingual education programs. Aid to educationally deprived children, supplementary services, and funds for strengthening state departments of education are absorbed by special revenue sharing.

Continuation of Emergency School Assistance through 1974. This program is designed to improve the quality of education of school districts in the process of desegregation.

Continuation of support of child development programs. In addition, new legislation is introduced to help private schools head off financial crisis or collapse. The administration proposes a tax credit for tuition paid by students enrolled in parochial and private elementary and secondary schools. It proposes a tax credit equal to $200 per child with an income limit of $18,000 for a family with one child or $22,000 for a family with five children. The administration estimates the cost of the credit to be about $300 million in 1974. Since there are about 5 million students in private elementary and secondary schools, of which 4.3 million belong to families below the income limit, the cost estimate puts the average credit per student at about $70.

In total, the 1974 budget proposes outlays for elementary and secondary education of $3.4 billion, an increase of about 5.2 percent over 1973.

Table 7-2

OUTLAYS FOR ELEMENTARY AND SECONDARY EDUCATION, BY TYPE OF PROGRAM, FISCAL YEARS 1973–74

(millions of dollars)

Type of Program	Outlays		Recommended Budget Authority, 1974
	1973	1974	
Education special revenue sharing (proposed legislation):[a]	—	1,693[b]	2,527[c]
Elementary and secondary education	—	(1,191)	
Education for the handicapped	—	(16)	
School assistance in federally affected areas	—	(193)	
Vocational and adult education	—	(239)	
Child development	385	420	
Aid to school districts	2,444	774	
Emergency school assistance	59	202	
Other	373	342	
Total	3,261	3,431	

a Excludes $244 million of basic school lunch funds under income security, which will be included in a total revenue sharing program of $2.8 billion.

b Total evidently includes other programs not shown separately. Replaces programs under "Aid to School Districts" in 1973.

c Proposed Better Education Act.

Sources: *Fiscal 1974 Budget*, p. 124; *1974 Special Analyses*, p. 105.

The Budget Outlook, Fiscal Years 1975-1981. The following program assumptions were made in projecting federal outlays for elementary and secondary education:

(1) Special revenue sharing for education begins in fiscal 1974. The projection adopts the Office of Management and Budget's estimate that special revenue sharing for education outlays (excluding the school lunch program) for 1975-78 will be about $2.5 billion, of which $443 million will go to vocational and adult education. Outlays for 1979-81 are assumed to rise slightly (2.5 percent per year) as a result of inflation but to remain constant in "real" terms.

117

(2) Federal outlays for child development are expected to grow at roughly the same rate as for 1973-74. It is further assumed that school assistance in federally affected areas for category "B" students (those whose parents do not live on federal property) will be eliminated in 1974.

(3) Funds currently used for emergency school assistance will continue, perhaps under the administration's proposed Equal Education Opportunity Act.

(4) No new program initiatives are introduced during this period.

Table 7-3 shows projected outlays for elementary and secondary education, fiscal 1975-81, by major category. As shown, the growth rate of outlays for elementary and secondary education over the period is about 3 percent a year with no growth projected for 1975.

Cost of the Tuition Credit Proposal. Assuming some form of the administration's tuition credit proposal is approved by Congress in fiscal year 1974, the cost to the federal government in terms of lost tax revenue is estimated to be in the range of $.4 to $1.4 billion for the period 1975-81 depending on (1) the amount of the credit allowed, (2) the number of students who would switch from public elementary and secondary schools to private schools, (3) the income limit for eligibility, and (4) tuition costs in private schools.

Private school enrollment is projected to be around 5.3 million students during the period 1975-81. Assuming the credit is $200 per student (with no income limit set for eligibility), then the cost would be around $1.4 billion.

On the other hand, if the income limit proposed by the administration is imposed, then the cost, with no induced enrollment in private schools, would remain at $.4 billion during 1975-81.

Problems Facing Education in the 1970s. Although the elementary and secondary school system has always been the focal point of interest in communities throughout the United States, in the past few years a genuine concern and dissatisfaction with it has grown and spread from one community to another. This concern—which might have important implications for the federal budget in the years to come—has been manifested in several ways. In some communities, property tax increases to finance elementary and secondary education have been repeatedly voted down. In other communities, suits have been filed to challenge the existing system of local finance. In California, Kansas, Minnesota, Texas and New Jersey, the courts ruled

Table 7-3

PROJECTED BUDGET OUTLAYS FOR ELEMENTARY AND SECONDARY
EDUCATION, FISCAL YEARS 1975–81

(unified budget, millions of dollars)

Spending Category	1975	1976	1977	1978	1979	1980	1981
Education revenue sharing [a]	2,089	2,089	2,089	2,089	2,141	2,195	2,250
Elementary and secondary education							
Child development [b]	441	469	494	524	556	592	627
Emergency school assistance [c]	270	283	297	312	327	344	361
Aid to school districts	230	241	254	266	279	293	308
Other	345	362	380	399	419	440	462
Total outlays	3,375	3,444	3,514	3,590	3,722	3,864	4,008

[a] 1975-78 OMB estimates, *Fiscal 1974 Budget*, p. 361. It excludes about $244 million for school lunch and $443 million for vocational and adult education. For 1979-81, outlays are assumed to rise by 2.5 percent.

[b] Assumes an average rate of growth of 6 percent a year.

[c] Assumes an average rate of growth of 5 percent a year.

Note: Figures may not add to totals because of rounding.

Source: LRBP estimates.

that the existing systems of school finance violate the equal protection clause of the Fourteenth Amendment. The reasoning behind these decisions was that public education is a "fundamental interest" for which the state has the chief responsibility and that access to education should not be conditioned upon local wealth. State aid to elementary and secondary education does little to remove the disparities in per pupil school spending arising from differences in local wealth. The court found, therefore, that the existing system of local school finance "invidiously discriminates against the poor because it makes the quality of a child's education a function of the wealth of his parents and neighbors." [5]

The Supreme Court decision announced on March 21, 1973, overturned lower courts' decisions on this issue, thus removing the pressure put on state governments to comply with lower court orders. Nevertheless, dissatisfaction with the public school system and with the overall burden of local funding of school districts, as well as the dim future facing private schools in the absence of some form of federal or state aid, will undoubtedly have repercussions on national educational policy. In view of such problems, the federal role in elementary and secondary education will perhaps have to be reevaluated.

The federal government may be called upon to take a more active role in efforts to equalize spending between school districts, "bail out" private schools, or perhaps substitute federal funds for state and local funds in financing schools to improve the educational opportunities of all school-age children. Some of the issues facing the nation as a whole, as well as local and state governments, in seeking equalization of per pupil expenditures or educational opportunity can be summarized as follows:

(1) In what sense should per pupil expenditures be equalized? Some alternatives would be: to raise per pupil expenditures to the level of the highest-spending districts in the state, to choose a mean level in the state to which lower districts can be raised, or to raise per pupil expenditures to the level of the highest-spending unit in the nation or to some other national standard.

(2) Is spending on equalization a problem to be dealt with at the state level, or is it a national problem requiring federal action?

---

[5] *Serrano* v. *Priest*, 96 Cal. Rptr. 601 (1971). For more detail on this issue, see Robert Hartman and Robert D. Reischauer, "Financing Elementary and Secondary Education," in Schultze et al., *Setting National Priorities: The 1973 Budget.*

(3) If property taxes are to be removed as a source for financing the school system, what are the alternatives?

(4) If equalization of opportunities is the national objective, what is the most efficient way of achieving it and what should be the roles of the federal and state governments?

The Federal Role in Education. What role should the federal government play in financing the various levels of education—elementary-secondary, vocational, and higher education? In order to answer this question, one should first distinguish between those educational needs or problems which fall within states, on the one hand, and those which transcend state boundaries, on the other. The federal government clearly has a responsibility for the general welfare of its citizens.[6] Thus, whenever the educational efforts of all states and local governments fall short of achieving a national goal, the federal government must assume responsibility for the attainment of that goal. However, when some or all of the efforts of the various localities within a given state fall below a national *average*—as opposed to a national *goal*—it is not very clear whether the federal role should be extended to the local level. The following sections discuss the assumptions regarding the federal role in two areas—elementary-secondary and higher education—and estimate budgetary costs of alternative programs consistent with these assumptions.

Alternative Federal Programs for Elementary and Secondary Education. Concerning the federal role in elementary and secondary education, the relevant issues would seem to be those of national, rather than state and local, concern. Since many economists assume that much of the benefit from elementary and secondary education accrues to society as a whole, the financing of education should perhaps be carried by the public, rather than the private, sector. The federal role, in this case, should aim at ensuring an optimal (socially desirable) level. To achieve such a "social optimum," the total output of education should be sufficient to ensure that all school-age children have the opportunity to buy (consume) educational services. If such a role is assigned to the federal government, then clearly the budget expenditures on elementary and secondary education for fiscal 1974 must be evaluated in terms of (1) the educational opportunities avail-

---

[6] For example, the federal government assumes the responsibility of attaining a specific level of employment as a national goal regardless of state efforts in generating employment in their states.

able to all school-age children, and (2) the quality of educational services produced.

Federal aid, even with special revenue sharing and tax credits for private school tuition included, is modest in its scope in relation to total outlays and mostly directed toward the public school system. It would thus be expected to have only a small impact both on the quality of educational services and on equalizing educational opportunities for all school-age children.

To equalize educational opportunities for all school-age children and to ensure quality education would require that each student be given the opportunity to attend an educational program that meets his or her educational needs—a school of his or her (or parents') choice. Unfortunately, our educational system fails to provide the majority of school children with such an opportunity.

Under existing arrangements, children are deprived of attending the school of their choice for the following reasons: (1) lack of public financial support for those who choose to attend a private school, and (2) rigid school district boundaries within the public school system. Inequalities in wealth or income among parents of school-age children means, at the outset, inequalities in educational opportunities for all children. Wealthy parents can choose between sending their children to a private or a public school system. This option is more difficult or impossible for the less wealthy or the poor. In addition, because of the present organization of school districts, parents and their children are not permitted to select the school of their choice. Since educational opportunities are not equalized to begin with, due to inequality in wealth, organization of the public school districts aggravates the disparities in opportunity rather than promoting equalization.

To extend educational opportunity effectively the federal government should aim at reducing or offsetting to some extent differences in the ability of parents to "buy" educational services. Because school-age children vary in their intelligence, achievement levels, and family background, equalization of educational opportunities would require not only equalizing the ability to buy educational services but making available educational programs that meet differences in children's educational needs. Clearly, such an ambitious objective cannot be achieved without: (1) redistributing income to equalize ability to buy educational services, (2) identifying by some means (such as achievement tests) the educational needs of school-age children, and (3) developing programs that meet educational need differentials among children. Thus, it is perhaps more feasible, especially in terms of the cost involved and at least in the short run, for the federal government, in the spirit of extending those opportunities, to aim at achieving some level of equalization of educational opportunity for all children. This could perhaps be accomplished through instituting a nationwide "voucher" system, federal funding for interstate equalization, or a liberalized tax credit for tuition paid to private schools. These are discussed below as alternatives to present financing of elementary and secondary education.

A Variable Voucher System. Under the variable voucher system, a family with school-age children would receive a voucher for each child, redeemable only for school tuition equal to a basic sum of dollars which would be included in the parents' income for tax purposes, but not for purposes of determining welfare payments. Thus, a family with a total income below $5,000 would receive the full value of the voucher, while a family in the marginal tax bracket of 70 percent would, in effect, receive 30 percent of the value of the voucher.

Because the present federal income tax system allows for the exclusion or preferential treatment of certain income items, a safeguard must be provided against the misuse of the voucher system. Failing a complete overhaul of the individual income tax system, a simple rule could be adopted whereby any individual or a family subject to the "minimum tax" would be treated as if it were subject to the highest marginal income tax rate. Such families would, in effect, be allowed 30 percent of the full value of the voucher.

The net amount of the voucher would thus vary with the level of income of parents. This program would clearly require an increase in the federal budget commitment to financing elementary and secondary education and some form of reorganization of the existing educational system. In terms of budget outlays, the federal government's share of the total cost of such a program will depend on the distribution of school-age children by income class and per pupil cost, and the portion of the cost (per pupil expenditures) assumed by state and local governments.

For each state, maintenance of the combined state-local effort at its initial level would be required for participating in the voucher plan. Since local districts vary in their per pupil expenditures and because the federal share would be computed as the difference between the value of the student voucher less the combined state-local average per pupil expenditure, the state and local governments electing to join would have to seek some form of reorganization of school finance to eliminate some of the disparities in school district spending. The state responsibility would lie in finding ways to raise per pupil expenditures up to that level in those school districts below the state average.[7]

School districts and states where per pupil expenditures fall below the value of the national voucher would have an incentive to join the system for several reasons. First, the voucher system would increase per pupil expenditures above that permitted by their fiscal capacities and local willingness to finance the schools. Second, it would eliminate the need for additional taxes at the local or state level to finance future increases in per pupil expenditure. Finally, it would provide states and localities with additional funds needed to meet court or public pressure for equalization of school spending. States where many school districts have per pupil expenditures which exceed the value of the national voucher may opt not to join. However, some pressures will perhaps exist for these states (and the affected districts) to join, such as:

(1) The loss of federal aid to these districts. Under the voucher system, present forms of federal aid are eliminated in favor of direct aid to students (parents) in elementary and secondary schools.

(2) Pressure from property owners for tax relief or opposition to additional tax increases to finance increases in educational costs.

(3) The desire of some parents to give their children the option of choosing between the public and the private systems of education even though the national voucher falls short of their locality's level of per pupil spending on education.

Arguments for and against a voucher system. The idea that the government should provide educational services by paying parents of school-age children rather than by owning and operating schools dates back to Adam Smith's *An Inquiry into Nature and Causes of the Wealth of Nations.* In *Capitalism and Freedom,* Milton Friedman advocates the use of a voucher system to finance education with few, if any, strings attached. Others have since voiced their support for variants of such a system, with some form of regulation or modification to safeguard against its misuse. The merits of a voucher system are that it would:

(1) Increase competition in the educational market by providing viable alternatives to the public school system.

---

[7] The state average of state and local per pupil expenditure is computed net of present federal aid to elementary and secondary education.

(2) Permit the parents of school-age children to choose the school which best serves the educational needs of their children.

(3) Reduce the number of parents who send their children to public school because they cannot afford to send them elsewhere.

(4) Allow a greater mix of students from different socioeconomic backgrounds than is presently permitted by most school district arrangements.

(5) Provide more freedom in the choice of place of residence by weakening the link between school financing and the wealth of a school district. In many instances families are forced to live in suburbs rather than in the city because of the schools their children would attend.

(6) Ease the burden of states and localities in their efforts to deal with the issue of equalization of per pupil expenditures.

In addition, under the proposed variable voucher system, the educational "subsidy" would be more efficiently distributed than it is under existing arrangements. Under a "free" public education system, the distribution of educational benefits bears no relation to need or the distribution and amount of taxes paid by a family to finance it. Under the variable voucher system, the amount of the voucher depends on the level of income, thus imposing a form of user charge that rises as income or ability to buy the service rises. By tying ability to pay to the financing of education and increasing the freedom of choice, a more equitable distribution of the subsidy and a more efficient allocation of resources among various suppliers of education can be ensured. Furthermore, because the voucher scheme outlined (as a bribe to the states for its adoption) tends to shift a larger share of finance to the federal government, the relative tax burden of cities vis-à-vis suburban areas that presently exists would be greatly improved.

Proposals for a voucher system to replace existing arrangements have met tremendous opposition from organizations connected with public schools, particularly administrators and teachers, and from civil rights groups. These groups argue that a voucher system would destroy the public school system, that it would intensify segregation, that parents are not competent to judge educational techniques or the quality of a school, that voucher plans would lead to substantial diseconomies of scale with too many schools competing for students, or that the voucher system would be unconstitutional if parents opt to send their children to religious schools.

Obviously, a voucher plan without restrictions would be vulnerable to some of the above criticisms. Such a plan might, for example, encourage schools to practice discrimination, substitute gimmickry for quality education, or inhibit social mobility by raising economic, religious, or racial barriers to admission. By establishing criteria for eligibility or attaching a few strings to the plan, most of these objections could be eliminated. For example, to participate in the voucher plan a private or public school could be required to:

(1) Follow an admissions policy that did not discriminate against applicants because of race, religion, sex, or social status. For kindergarten through the eighth grade, a lottery system for selection could be instituted. For grades nine through twelve, a standardized achievement test could be used to determine eligibility to enroll.

(2) Meet current state accreditation requirements.

(3) Make available, in published form, information on its programs, facilities, teachers' qualifications, financial status, and the socioeconomic status of its enrollees.

The constitutionality question is a difficult one. A constitutional amendment may indeed be called for. Past decisions (or lack of decisions) by the Supreme Court on similar issues have been contradictory. The Court has ruled that "entanglement between government and religion" violates the constitutional "wall of separation" between church and state. This view has been enforced by recent Supreme Court rulings that state government indirect aid to parochial schools is unconstitutional. However, the Court has not ruled against charitable deductions under the personal income tax for church and religious educational institutions, on the constitutionality of the G.I. Bill (under which a number of World War II veterans used government funds to attend church-related schools), or against federally sponsored research conducted by faculty in religious institutions.

Cost of a variable voucher system. How would a variable voucher system work, how much would it cost, and what pattern of federal-state-local relations might emerge?

First, under a national voucher system, most existing federal programs for elementary and secondary education would be eliminated.[8] These programs and their estimated cost at 1974 levels are

---

[8] A number of studies has shown the ineffectiveness of these programs and their inadequacies in meeting objectives. See, for example, U.S. Congress, Senate, Committee on Labor and Public Welfare, *Proposed Federal Aid to Education: A Collection of Pro and Con Excerpts and a Bibliography*, 87th Congress, 1st session, 1961.

shown in Table 7-4. Other federal aid to elementary and secondary education, such as child development (Head Start), education of overseas dependents, social security benefits, and funds for the National Institute of Education and the National Science Foundation would not be eliminated. These programs are designed for the education of preschool children, meet specific needs not covered by the voucher plan, or are for the conduct of research.

Second, state governments would be the dispensing agencies for voucher funds. The state and local governments' share in the per pupil voucher would be equal to their "net" estimated per pupil expenditures for that year (with "no growth" in the per pupil expenditures in future years).[9] The federal share would be equal to the value of the voucher minus the state share. For example, assuming that the value of the voucher were $1,300 per student and that average state and local per pupil expenditure were $1,000, the federal share would be equal to $300 per pupil. Federal funds would be channeled to state governments in the form of grants for the purchase of education. State and local governments would arrange for the dispersal of these funds to parents and deal with problems facing school districts where per pupil expenditures fall below the state average.

Table 7-4

ESTIMATED COST OF EXISTING FEDERAL PROGRAMS FOR ELEMENTARY AND SECONDARY EDUCATION AT 1974 LEVELS

(millions of dollars)

Program	Cost
School lunch	1,234
Educationally deprived children	411
School assistance in federally affected areas	131
Emergency school assistance, general grants	149
Education special revenue sharing	1,527
Other	1,396
Total	4,848

Source: *1974 Special Analyses*, pp. 103-115.

[9] This is equal to total expenditures for elementary and secondary education of state and local governments' net of federal funds previously spent on eliminated programs divided by total enrollment in elementary and secondary schools.

Third, growth in outlays on elementary and secondary education for future years would be financed by the federal government and by users of education, depending on their ability to pay. The federal share would rise while the state and local share remained constant at the 1975 level to induce states to participate actively. Taxpayers who are users of education would increase their share through increased income taxes due to increments over the years of the value of the vouchers they receive.

Finally, the voucher plan would be voluntary. A school district or a state might elect not to join the voucher plan. In this case, total federal outlays would be reduced because of the reduction of existing expenditures on "eliminated" programs, with no corresponding increase under the voucher system.

The value of the national voucher is assumed to be 5 percent greater than the projected level of total per pupil expenditures during 1975-81.[10] The state and local government share (net of federal aid) is that projected for 1975. Per pupil expenditures by state and local government for the remainder of the period are assumed to remain at their 1975 level while the federal share of the voucher would be increased to allow for increases in the cost of education during the 1976-81 period.

Because payments under the voucher system would be made directly to parents rather than to the school, purchases of elementary and secondary education by the state and local sector would be eliminated and transfer payments to persons would be increased to reflect total voucher payments to all school-age children attending either public or private schools.

In Table 7-5, estimated total expenditures on elementary and secondary education under the present system are given. Table 7-6 shows the net value of the voucher by income class. Table 7-7 presents an estimate of the total cost of the voucher plan, and Table 7-8 shows "program cuts" and the corresponding changes in federal outlays. Finally, the changes in state and local spending under the voucher system are shown in Table 7-9. As shown in Table 7-8, column (6), the net federal cost of the variable voucher would be roughly zero for the first two years and then would rise to $8 billion in 1978 and to around $19 billion by 1981.

A Federal-State Equalization Plan. Perhaps a less controversial approach to equalization of educational opportunity than the proposed

---

[10] AEI budget model projections. The 5 percent increase is added as a "sweetener" to help meet the cost of quality education.

Table 7-5

TOTAL EXPENDITURES ON ELEMENTARY AND SECONDARY
EDUCATION BY TYPE, SCHOOL YEARS 1975–81

Item	1975	1976	1977	1978	1979	1980	1981
Total ($ billions) [a]	58.3	61.6	64.6	68.1	72.8	76.1	80.4
State and local outlays ($ billions) [b]	53.1	56.2	59.1	62.5	66.1	70.2	74.3
Private school outlays ($ billions) [c]	5.2	5.4	5.5	5.6	5.7	5.9	6.1
Per pupil expenditures in public schools ($) [d]	1,218	1,300	1,376	1,462	1,552	1,648	1,724
Per pupil expenditures in private schools ($) [e]	963	1,000	1,026	1,049	1,070	1,108	1,144

[a] Total includes public and private school outlays.
[b] AEI LRBP estimates.
[c] Based on national educational statistics.
[d] Per pupil expenditures in public schools are equal to total state and local government expenditures (including federal funds) divided by enrollment in public schools.
[e] Per pupil expenditures in private schools are equal to private school outlays divided by the number of students in private schools.

Table 7-6

"NET" AVERAGE VALUE OF THE VOUCHER UNDER A VOUCHER PLAN FOR ELEMENTARY AND SECONDARY EDUCATION, BY INCOME CLASS, SCHOOL YEARS 1975–81

Income Class	1975	1976	1977	1978	1979	1980	1981
Less than $5,000 [a]	$1,278	$1,365	$1,435	$1,535	$1,629	$1,730	$1,810
$ 5,000 to $ 7,000	1,063	1,136	1,194	1,277	1,355	1,439	1,506
$ 7,000 to $10,000	1,047	1,118	1,175	1,257	1,334	1,417	1,482
$10,000 to $15,000	1,029	1,099	1,155	1,236	1,311	1,393	1,457
$15,000 to $20,000	1,000	1,069	1,124	1,202	1,276	1,355	1,417
$20,000 to $25,000	967	1,033	1,086	1,162	1,233	1,309	1,370
$25,000 to $50,000	882	942	990	1,059	1,124	1,194	1,249
$50,000 and over	588	628	660	706	749	795	832

[a] This is the maximum value of the voucher, assumed to be equal to 1.05 times projected per pupil total expenditures in public schools. For income classes above $5,000, the after-tax voucher (net value of the voucher) is equal to 1 minus the average marginal tax rate of the n income class times the value of the voucher.

Sources: Per pupil expenditures are computed from the AEI budget projection model. Average marginal tax rate on income estimated from 1966 Treasury tax file, a sample of taxpayers' returns, projected to 1973.

Table 7-7

COST ESTIMATES OF THE VOUCHER FOR ELEMENTARY AND
SECONDARY EDUCATION AND COST DISTRIBUTION BETWEEN
FEDERAL AND STATE-LOCAL GOVERNMENTS, 1975–81

Item	1975	1976	1977	1978	1979	1980	1981
Enrollment (millions)	49.0	48.6	48.3	48.1	48.0	48.0	48.5
Total voucher cost ($ billions)	62.6	66.3	69.3	73.8	78.1	83.0	87.7
State and local government share under voucher plan ($ billions) a	49.7	49.3	49.0	48.8	48.6	48.6	49.1
Federal share ($ billions)	12.9	17.0	20.3	25.0	29.5	34.4	38.6

a Assuming all states and local governments belong to the voucher plan, estimated to be equal to net per pupil expenditure in 1975 times total enrollment in
each of the projection period years.
Source: Based on data in Tables 7-5 and 7-6 and AEI LRBP estimates.

voucher plan is a plan where the federal government supplements
state efforts in equalizing per pupil expenditures nationally. Under
this plan, each state government would undertake an equalization
program among its school districts to raise all their per pupil expenditures to the spending level enjoyed by the ninetieth percentile student
in the state. Because the average of per pupil expenditure, even with
state equalization efforts, is expected to vary from state to state,
the federal commitment to equalizing educational opportunity for all
school children would then take on the role of equalizing per pupil
spending *nationally.* That is, the federal government would have to
channel additional funds to those states whose average per pupil
expenditure, after state equalization efforts, still falls below the
national average. The national average, in this case, is defined as the
mean per pupil expenditure in all states after state equalization efforts.

Clearly, not all states would be recipients of these additional
funds. Alaska, California, and New York, for example, are states
where expenditure per pupil at the ninetieth percentile by far exceeds
the levels of Alabama, Arkansas, Delaware, and Florida. Although
educational costs do vary between southern and northern states or
the West Coast, it is reasonable to assume that these wide disparities
between, for example, Alabama and New York do reflect much more
than cost differentials. To the extent that such disparities reflect the

Table 7-8

ESTIMATED FEDERAL COST UNDER A VARIABLE VOUCHER SYSTEM FOR ELEMENTARY AND SECONDARY EDUCATION, 1975–81

(billions of dollars)

Year	Federal Cost of Voucher (1)	Reduction in Present Programs (2)	Net Increase in Federal Outlays (3)	Tax Revenue Increase Under Voucher Plan (4)	Revenue Gain from Elimination of Administration Proposed Credit for Private School Tuition (5)	Net Cost of Voucher Plan (6)
1975	12.9	−5.0	7.9	9.7	.4	− 2.2
1976	17.0	−5.1	11.9	10.3	.4	1.2
1977	20.3	−5.1	15.2	10.7	.4	4.1
1978	25.0	−5.2	19.7	11.4	.4	8.0
1979	29.5	−5.3	24.2	12.1	.4	11.7
1980	34.4	−5.5	28.9	12.8	.4	15.7
1981	38.6	−6.0	32.6	13.6	.4	18.6

Notes:

Column (1) equals total cost of the voucher less state and local government expenditures under the voucher system (from Table 7-7).

Column (2) presents administration budget reductions. Here it is assumed that elementary and secondary education is to be eliminated. OE outlays reduction is based on AEI LRBP model. Other outlays, including school lunch and child nutrition and supporting services, are assumed to be at about 1974 level of $1.6 billion.

Column (3) equals column (1) minus column (2).

Column (4) equals the increase in personal tax revenues due to inclusion of the voucher in taxable income.

Column (6) equals column (3) minus [column (4) plus column (5)].

Sources: Tables 7-3, 7-7, AEI LRBP estimates, and *1974 Special Analyses.*

Table 7-9

EFFECT OF VOUCHER SYSTEM ON STATE AND LOCAL BUDGETS, SCHOOL YEARS 1975–81

(billions of dollars)

Year	Projected State and Local Purchases of Elementary and Secondary Education (1)	State and Local Government Share Under Voucher System [a] (2)	Net Increase in Federal Grants to Students Under Voucher System (3)	Increase in State Transfer Payments (4)	Net Position (Effect on Surplus or Deficit) [b] (5)
1975	53.1	49.7	12.9	62.6	3.4
1976	56.2	49.3	17.0	66.3	6.9
1977	59.1	49.0	20.3	69.3	10.1
1978	62.5	48.8	25.0	73.8	13.7
1979	66.1	48.6	29.5	78.1	17.5
1980	70.2	48.6	34.4	83.0	21.6
1981	74.3	49.1	38.6	87.7	25.2

[a] State share of expenditures for elementary and secondary education would be in the form of transfer payments to parents with children in school. Projected state and local government purchases for elementary and secondary education, column (1), will thus be eliminated.

[b] Column (1) minus column (2).

Sources: AEI LRBP estimates and Table 7-7.

unequal educational opportunity of school-age children living, say, in Alabama vis-à-vis those in New York, limiting federal aid to those states well below national average expenditures can be justified. In Table 7-10, column (3), the additional cost to states and localities of

Table 7-10

COST OF EQUALIZING SCHOOL EXPENDITURES
BETWEEN STATES AND WITHIN STATES,
1969–70 SCHOOL YEAR
(millions of dollars)

State	Enrollment (thousands) (1)	Expenditure Per Pupil with State Equalization (2)	State Cost of Intrastate Equalization (3)	Federal Cost for Interstate Equalization (4)
Alabama	806	$ 493	$ 44	$319
Alaska	80	1,224	11	
Arizona	440	986	97	
Arkansas	464	622	41	124
California	4,633	1,101	828	
Colorado	550	826	72	35
Connecticut	662	1,095	141	
Delaware	132	1,052	35	
Dist. of Columbia		NA		
Florida	1,428	803	132	123
Georgia	1,099	761	177	140
Hawaii		904	10	
Idaho	182	830	37	11
Illinois		997	457	
Indiana	1,232	729	129	197
Iowa		1,007	94	
Kansas	512	870	76	10
Kentucky	717	700	63	136
Louisiana	843	692	61	166
Maine	245	792	26	24
Maryland		1,090	191	
Massachusetts		975	259	
Michigan		1,009	364	
Minnesota		1,014	121	
Mississippi	535	561	46	175

Table 7-10 (continued)

State	Enrollment (thousands) (1)	Expenditure Per Pupil with State Equalization (2)	State Cost of Intrastate Equalization (3)	Federal Cost for Interstate Equalization (4)
Missouri	1,039	835	126	56
Montana		1,209	69	
Nebraska	329	694	55	64
Nevada	127	836	9	7
New Hampshire	159	815	20	12
New Jersey		1,177	318	
New Mexico	282	821	27	19
New York		1,412	610	
North Carolina	1,192	689	95	238
North Dakota	147	754	20	20
Ohio		894	519	
Oklahoma	617	638	62	157
Oregon		1,022	63	
Pennsylvania		1,090	504	
Rhode Island		1,167	50	
South Carolina		922	32	
South Dakota	167	794	23	16
Tennessee	900	671	100	196
Texas	2,840	684	293	582
Utah	303	647	15	73
Vermont		1,167	24	
Virginia	1,078	826	145	68
Washington		891	121	
West Virginia	394	711	34	71
Wisconsin		977	102	
Wyoming		970	29	

Sources: Enrollment from *Historical Statistics of the U.S.,* 1971, p. 106. Average per pupil expenditures by states was obtained by dividing total expenditures, including state equalization costs, by the total number of students. The national average of per pupil expenditures (including state equalization expenditures) is equal to $889. Cost of intrastate equalization (column 3) is from R. Hartman and R. Reischauer, "Financing Elementary and Secondary Education," in Schultze et al., *Setting National Priorities: The 1973 Budget,* p. 352. Federal cost (column 4) is obtained by multiplying the excess of national average over the state per pupil average expenditure by the number of students enrolled.

equalizing intrastate disparities in per pupil spending is shown for school years 1969-70. Here it is assumed that, as a prerequisite to federal aid towards equalization, state governments have undertaken their own plans to bring about intrastate equalization.

Although state efforts are required, the federal equalization plan would be voluntary. Each state is free to carry out equalization efforts or decline to undertake them among its school districts. If equalization is undertaken, the state becomes eligible to receive the federal funds, otherwise it will not. Funding at the federal level of equalization could begin simultaneously with state efforts, and federal aid to states would be formulated in relation to the degree of equalization achieved by state governments.

The estimates shown in Table 7-10, column (4), assume that equalization efforts were undertaken at the state levels. Raising average per pupil state expenditure to the national level of $889 would have cost the federal government $3.0 billion in 1969-70 or about 8.7 percent of expenditures for public elementary and secondary education in that year. The total state-federal equalization cost would amount to $10 billion or about 29 percent of current expenditures of state and local governments in 1969-70.[11] For 1975-81, we have assumed that public expenditures in elementary and secondary education would still have to be raised 29 percent to cover the total cost of equalization, and that the federal share of that total would be the same percent of that total as estimated for the 1969-70 school year. Table 7-11 shows projected federal outlays for equalization for fiscal years 1975-81.

The federal-state equalization plan clearly benefits only those enrolled in public schools. Those students who elect an alternative system of education would be left without public support. Equality of educational opportunity would require that those who are in other than the public school system enjoy the same per student spending level as those in public schools. Students enrolled in private schools, with a per pupil expenditure level below the national average, would be entitled to receive some sort of assistance from state and federal governments. Perhaps a system of tax credits or educational supple-

---

[11] Because some states, such as California, New York, and Alaska, have higher than national average per pupil expenditures, they will not be eligible to receive federal funds for raising state averages to the national level. In this case, assuming Supreme Court or local pressure for intrastate equalization does not take place, the federal government can institute a system of "bribes" in the form of some percentage of their equalization cost to induce state governments to carry out full intrastate equalization. This will be an added outlay to that estimated in column (2), Table 7-11.

Table 7-11

ESTIMATED ADDITIONAL OUTLAYS FOR ELEMENTARY AND SECONDARY EDUCATION WITH STATE-FEDERAL EQUALIZATION PLAN

(billions of dollars)

Year	Total Equalization Cost	Federal Share
1975	13.4	3.9
1976	14.2	4.1
1977	14.8	4.3
1978	15.6	4.5
1979	16.5	4.8
1980	17.7	5.2
1981	18.6	5.4

Source: Based on Table 7-10 and assumptions given in text.

ment grants should be given to those students to give them the same level of educational opportunity as their comrades in the public school system.[12]

Higher Education

1974 Budget and Budget Outlook. The administration's commitment to higher education in the 1974 budget again reflects its view that education is the primary responsibility of state and local governments and that the federal role is one which aims at developing and encouraging improvements in the education process, and extending and supporting educational opportunity. In fiscal 1974, federal support to higher education is put at $1.6 billion or about 7 percent of estimated total outlays for higher education (Table 7-12). Of this total, $1.2 billion or 75 percent is directed towards student support, while the remaining $.4 billion or 25 percent of the total is devoted to developing and improving the education process.

The new emphasis on student aid in the 1974 budget represents a shift away from the established practice of channeling aid to institu-

---

[12] If such a program is implemented, the federal-state cost would be higher than that estimated in Table 7-11.

137

Table 7-12

FEDERAL AID TO HIGHER EDUCATION, FISCAL YEARS 1974–81

(millions of dollars)

Program	1974 [a]	1975	1976	1977	1978	1979	1980	1981
Basic opportunity grants	622	987	1,021	1,048	1,072	1,093	1,111	1,156
Work-study	250	260	275	287	300	307	312	320
Guaranteed loans [b]	350	350	350	350	340	325	300	266
Innovation, developing institutions and others	414 [c]	435	437	439	440	442	444	447
Total outlays	1,636	2,032	2,083	2,124	2,152	2,167	2,167	2,189

a *Fiscal 1974 Budget* and *1974 Special Analyses.*
b This amount represents the administrative costs of the loans program.
c This amount is net of HUD reductions in college loans of $20 million.

tions, a step which most people would agree is in the right direction. According to a *Wall Street Journal* editorial, "It makes better sense if the aim of federal aid is to help needy students rather than college employees or the building industry."[13] Assuming that the federal commitment to higher education will grow at about the same rate during the period 1972-74, the budget commitment for higher education in the next seven years is projected to reach almost $2.2 billion by 1981 (Table 7-11).

The major assumptions made in projecting federal outlays for higher education by program category are given below.

Student aid—Basic Opportunity Grants (BOG). Student aid constitutes the largest item in federal aid to higher education in 1973-74 outlays. The 1974 budget estimates outlays on BOGs, the most significant type of student aid, to be about $622 million in fiscal 1974 with 1.5 million students benefiting from it. This implies an average grant per student of $415 in 1974. About 18 percent of all students at institutions of higher learning would receive BOGs. This percent seems low as compared to outside estimates. Hartman estimates that about 26 percent of all college students would have been entitled to receive BOGs in 1970-71; average entitlement was estimated to be $753.[14]

Using Hartman's methodology—distribution of full-time undergraduate students by income class and by type of institution, cost of education, and average family contributions—to project BOG's cost for 1974, it is estimated that 2.3 million students would be eligible, with an average entitlement of $780. This puts the cost of BOG at $1.8 billion if fully funded. If one accepts these figures, the budget estimates would seem to imply funding of BOG at 30 percent of entitlement in 1974.

Assuming that the administration intends to fund BOG at the level shown in the 1974 budget—entitlement equal to 18 percent of college enrollment—we project the number of students entitled to receive BOGs for 1975-81, by applying this percentage rate to projected college enrollment during this period. Average entitlement is estimated on the basis of projection of the cost of education for

---

[13] "Learning a New Way," *Wall Street Journal,* February 29, 1972, p. 10.

[14] Robert W. Hartman, "Higher Education Subsidies: An Analysis of Selected Programs in Current Legislation," in *Economics of Federal Subsidy Programs,* A Compendium of Papers, Part 4, printed for use of the Joint Economic Committee (Washington, D. C.: U.S. Government Printing Office, August 28, 1972). The estimates assume no induced enrollments as a result of basic opportunity grants.

1975-81, and the breakdown of student enrollment between private and public institutions.

Work-study. The projection in this area assumes that work-study grants will reach authorization level by 1981.

Guaranteed loans and students loan funds. Outlays for these programs are projected to decrease during 1975-81. The newly created Student Market Loan Association is assumed to be operative by 1975.

Special institutions, personal development, and innovation. Projections of outlays in this category assume slight increases during this period reflecting the de-emphasis on federal aid to institutions.

The Role of the Federal Government in Higher Education. In order to evaluate critically federal aid to higher education, we must first pose two questions: Is federal aid adequate, and is it efficient? Unfortunately, the question of adequacy cannot be answered in simple yes-or-no terms. It clearly depends on one's value judgment about what the federal role in higher education should be and the extent of resource commitment one is willing to divert from other functions to fulfill it. As to the efficiency issue, this requires an extensive analysis of alternatives to determine the effectiveness of a dollar of expenditures in accomplishing a given educational objective. However, defining the federal role or federal objectives must precede any attempts at evaluating federal aid to education or the analysis of alternatives.

In a "free" society, where no externalities[15] exist and where the market system is assumed to function properly, market choices are assumed to yield an optimum solution. In the field of education, as in any other market area, the price system would determine the amount of resources directed towards education in accordance with the demand for and supply of educational services. However, the market system does not function properly and externalities are associated with the consumption of education. The most common arguments advanced for government intervention in the education market are:[16] (1) The market fails to produce the socially desired level of education due to existence of monopoly or other imperfections which preclude effective competition, and (2) the market fails to "internalize" externalities; that is, private costs and benefits are

---

[15] Externalities are those benefits accruing to—or costs imposed on—society over and above those which accrue to individuals consuming or producing a given activity.

[16] See, for example, Milton Friedman, "The Role of Government in Education," in Robert A. Solo, ed., *Economics and the Public Interest* (New Brunswick, New Jersey: Rutgers University Press, 1955).

considered by decision makers but social costs and benefits are ignored.

The question of market imperfections or monopoly elements seems to be less debatable than the issue concerning social gains from higher education. It is generally agreed that higher education is not significantly monopolistic. On the other hand, views on the social versus private nature of the benefits of higher education differ considerably. Little or no empirical evidence seems to exist to substantiate or refute the existence or magnitude of social benefits or costs in this area. It is probably safe to assume that a large element of total benefits from higher education constitutes "private" benefits. At a minimum, one can argue that private benefits from higher education constitute a larger share of total benefits from education than is the case, for example, with elementary and secondary education. Accordingly, one would expect the government role in this area to be somewhat more limited than in the area of elementary and secondary education.[17] Federal aid to higher education, one might argue, should be looked upon as accomplishing a redistribution of income function—by enabling students from low-income families to have greater access to the educational market, thus raising their income potential and infusing in it some elements of competition.

A number of studies has shown that most federal-state aid to higher education accrues to families with above-average income and the size of the subsidy increases as income rises.[18] This pattern of distribution of federal-state aid to education is clearly inconsistent with a goal aimed at improving the educational opportunity of the poor or the needy and leads to further inequalities in the distribution of wealth or opportunities.

Alternative Federal Programs. Three plans are explored here as alternatives to present federal aid to higher education. In all these plans, the federal role in higher education places emphasis on the educational needs of college students, that is, on providing funds to those who otherwise could not afford the cost of higher education.[19]

---

[17] See, for example, H. Aaron and M. McGuire, "Public Goods and Income Distribution," *Econometrica*, vol. 38, no. 6 (November 1970).

[18] W. Lee Hansen and Burton A. Weisbroad, *Benefits, Costs and Finance of Public Higher Education* (Chicago: Markham Publishing Co., 1969).

[19] Other schemes may also be worth considering, such as a scheme for the full cost financing of higher education. For a detailed discussion of issues in such a program, see W. Hartman, *Equity Implications of State Tuition Policy and Student Loans*, Brookings Reprint 238 (Washington, D. C.: The Brookings Institution, 1972).

The first plan—which may be called a cost-sharing plan (CSP) —is a student grant program similar to the basic student grant in the 1972 amendments to the Higher Education Act. Federal aid, in this case, would be limited to students who qualify for aid under the existing college scholarship test. The minimum grant would be $100. This would be a "shared responsibility" program: the federal government, the state government, and the student would share the cost of education.

A second plan involves only the federal government, since state governments may opt to continue financing higher education by subsidizing the cost of education at public institutions rather than by giving direct aid to college students. The federal government, in this case, would channel direct aid to eligible students under a "liberalized educational opportunity grant to college students" (LEOG). Liberalization of the present basic opportunity grants (BOG) system is essential if the federal role is one which aspires to give needy college students better opportunities for purchasing educational services. The present BOG system, with its $1,400 ceiling on the amount awarded, is tilted towards two-year and four-year *public* institutions; it provides little incentive for eligible students to enroll in private institutions. The proposed liberalized educational grants would eliminate this aspect of the BOG system but would continue to make federal contributions directly related to student needs.

A third federal aid plan, which is less costly than the previous two alternatives, would be to give a tax credit to students enrolled in private colleges. This would be consistent with the administration's proposal to grant tax credits to parents with students enrolled in private elementary and secondary schools. The rationale behind this option is quite simple. Because state governments have elected to subsidize public institutions rather than college students themselves, a student's choice as to the form of institution he will enroll in is clearly distorted. In addition, federal aid under BOG, in effect, adds to the inequality of educational opportunity that already exists due to inequality in the distribution of economic power to buy educational services, rather than providing students with ample funds to freely choose an institution. The tax credit scheme, by lowering the cost of private schools vis-à-vis public colleges, helps correct the existing imbalance in pricing educational services and thus improves market choices.

Cost Sharing Plan (CSP). Under this plan, each student attending or planning to attend an institution of higher education would receive an education cost grant made up of the following shares: (1) A "state of residence" share equal to per pupil expenditures on higher education in his home state, (2) his own contribution equal to the expected family contribution as determined by college scholarship schedules, and (3) a federal share equal to the difference between the total cost of education at his chosen institution less the state share and reduced by the amount of family contribution. Thus, the federal CSP equals total education cost minus per student state expenditure minus expected family contribution.

Under this plan, present forms of federal student aid would be eliminated in favor of direct payment to students. Efforts by state governments in the higher education area and the scholarship test presently used by financial aid offices to determine the family contribution would be continued. The federal programs that would be eliminated are (1) student aid, including BOGs, (2) social security benefits to dependents of survivors attending college under the OASDI program, and (3) the double exemption given for taxpayer dependents who are college students.

Tables 7-13 through 7-16 show the federal share per student, number of beneficiaries, reductions in federal outlays due to the

Table 7-13

CSP PLAN: FAMILY CONTRIBUTION SCHEDULE, AVERAGE PER STUDENT STATE CONTRIBUTION, AND FEDERAL CONTRIBUTION BY INCOME CLASS, 1975

Income Class	Average Family Contribution [a]	State Contribution [b]	Federal Contribution [c]
Less than $5,000	0	$1,400	$1,400
$ 5,000 – $ 7,500	$ 160	1,400	1,240
$ 7,500 – $10,000	720	1,400	670
$10,000 – $15,000	1,327	1,400	73 [d]
$15,000 and over	1,533	1,400	0

[a] Based on 1971 College Entrance Examination Board estimates.

[b] State contribution is equal to per student state expenditure in 1971 excluding federal grants to states for higher education. This aid is assumed to remain constant for 1975-81.

[c] Federal contribution is equal to average cost of education less family contribution and state contribution. Federal contribution will be different for the period 1976-81 because the cost of education is different (family and state contributions are assumed to remain the same).

[d] No aid would be granted for amounts less than $100.

Table 7-14

CSP PLAN: PROJECTED ENROLLMENT, INDUCED ENROLLMENT, AVERAGE COST OF EDUCATION AND FEDERAL CONTRIBUTION, FISCAL YEARS 1975–81

Year	Projected Enrollment (thousands)	Induced Enrollment (thousands)[a]	Number of Beneficiaries (thousands)	Average Cost	Average Federal Contribution
1975	9,147	1,810	3,457	$2,800	$1,018
1976	9,457	1,900	3,583	2,950	1,177
1977	9,710	1,926	3,679	3,120	1,334
1978	9,930	1,983	3,749	3,292	1,518
1979	10,125	1,982	3,837	3,472	1,700
1980	10,284	2,062	3,890	3,665	1,892
1981	10,438	2,096	3,952	3,866	2,093

[a] Based on enrollment rates of eligible population by income class. It is assumed that each income class up to $15,000 and over enrollment rate as a percent of eligible population is raised to the level of the income class above it.

Sources: Based on U.S. Office of Education 1970-71 distribution of students by income class, unpublished data; College Entrance Examination Board, *Estimates of the Distribution of the Federal Student Grant Funds;* College Entrance Examination Board, *Manual for Financial Aid Officers, 1971;* AEI LRBP estimates and assumptions given in footnote 20, this chapter.

elimination of some federal programs, and the net federal cost under this plan.[20] From these tables, it can be seen that budget outlays on higher education would be increased by $1.2 billion over the level

---

[20] The estimated federal cost under the CSP plan for the period 1975-81 was based on the following data and assumptions: (1) The percentage distribution of students in each income class remains the same as the distribution for 1970-71. (The 1970-71 data are based on Office of Education unpublished estimates.) (2) The average cost of education in each type of institution for the period 1975-81 is based on estimates of the College Entrance Examination Board for 1970-71 adjusted for increases in the cost of education. [The education cost index for each type of institution is given by: for public institutions $= .2$ (Δ compensation per man-hour plus .8 rate of growth, private GNP deflator); for private institutions $= .5$ (Δ compensation per man-hour plus .5 rate of growth, private GNP deflator).] (3) Average expected family contribution is assumed to remain the same as that given by the College Scholarship Service for 1971. (4) By income class, enrollment is expected to rise at least to the enrollment level of the next income class, since the proposed grant provides students in each income class with better opportunities than those already available to them under the present system to purchase educational services. (5) Per student state contributions are equal to average state expenditure *net* of federal aid, which would be eliminated under the plan. (6) The distribution of students between private and public institutions is assumed to rise to 40:60 in lieu of the existing 29:71 ratio.

Table 7-15

CSP PLAN: REDUCTION IN ADMINISTRATION OUTLAYS ON HIGHER EDUCATION BY PROGRAMS AND INCREASE IN PERSONAL TAX REVENUES, FISCAL YEARS 1975–81

(millions of dollars)

Item	1975	1976	1977	1978	1979	1980	1981
Basic grants (BOG)	987	1,021	1,048	1,072	1,093	1,111	1,156
Work-study	260	275	287	300	307	312	320
Federal cost of guaranteed loans	358	350	350	340	325	300	266
Social security benefits[a]	638	695	758	826	901	982	1,071
Other[b]	360	360	360	360	360	360	360
Total outlay reduction	2,603	2,701	2,803	2,898	2,986	3,065	3,173
Tax increase due to elimination of double exemptions[c]	749	772	792	811	831	842	854
Total savings	3,352	3,473	3,595	3,709	3,817	3,907	4,027

[a] Social security benefits to students are assumed to grow during 1975-81 by the same rate of growth as that for 1971-75, or by 9 percent. About 94 percent of social security recipients are from families with incomes below $15,000.

[b] Includes special institutions aid, personnel development and innovation.

[c] Based on S. Surrey estimates for revenue gain in 1971 due to elimination of double exemption for college students.

Sources: AEI LRBP model; S. Surrey, "Tax Subsidies as a Device for Implementing Government Policy," *The Economics of Federal Subsidy Programs*, a compendium of papers, U.S. Congress, Joint Economic Committee, Part 1, p. 77.

Table 7-16

CSP PLAN: ESTIMATED FEDERAL COST, FISCAL YEARS 1975–81

(millions of dollars)

Year	Gross Federal Cost	Savings from Reductions in Present Programs	Add-on to Budget Outlays	Increase in Personal Income Tax Revenue Due to Elimination of Double Exemptions	Net Federal Cost
1975	3,520	2,603	917	749	168
1976	4,218	2,701	1,517	772	745
1977	4,909	2,803	2,106	792	1,314
1978	5,692	2,898	2,794	811	1,983
1979	6,523	2,986	3,537	831	2,706
1980	7,360	3,065	4,295	842	3,453
1981	8,270	3,173	5,097	854	4,243

Sources: Tables 7-13, 7-14, and 7-15.

estimated for the administration's 1975 budget (including the relevant portion of social security benefits). This increment would grow to $5.1 billion by 1981. Grants to state and local governments—under existing student aid programs—would be eliminated, while federal aid direct to students in the form of increased federal transfer payments to persons would be increased.

Liberalized Educational Opportunity Grants (LEOG). Under this alternative, the present BOG program would be modified in two respects. First, the $1,400 ceiling would be eliminated. In its place a limit equal to one-half of the cost of education would be used. Second, the value of the grant would decrease by the amount of the expected family contribution, social security benefits, or G.I. Bill benefits.

The plan calls for extending aid to college students in relation to their own or their family's income. For example, students (or their families) with incomes below $5,000 would receive half the cost of education at any institution of higher learning, whereas students from families with income above that level would receive decreasing amounts of aid. To determine eligibility for aid, as well as its amount, a financial statement would be submitted to college aid officers. In Table 7-17, average federal aid to college students, exclusive of family contribution by income class, is shown for fiscal

Table 7-17

LEOG PLAN: AVERAGE FEDERAL AID BY INCOME CLASS, FISCAL YEARS 1975–81

Income Class	1975	1976	1977	1978	1979	1980	1981
Less than $300	$1,400	$1,475	$1,560	$1,646	$1,737	$1,833	$1,933
$ 300 – $ 500	1,400	1,475	1,560	1,646	1,737	1,833	1,933
$ 500 – $ 7,500	1,240	1,315	1,400	1,482	1,577	1,673	1,773
$ 7,500 – $10,000	670	740	830	916	1,007	1,103	1,203
$10,000 – $15,000	73[a]	148	233	319	410	506	606
$15,000 and over	0	0	27[a]	113	204	300	400

[a] No aid would be granted for amounts less than $100.

Source: Based on data in Table 7-12, and projection of cost of education for 1975-81 (see footnote 20, this chapter).

1975-81. Table 7-18 shows the number of eligible students, including veterans, and the federal cost of the program assuming that: (1) enrollment in each income class would be expected to rise due to this new program to the level of the income level above it, (2) eligible veterans are treated as additional enrollment, and (3) other forms of federal aid to college students, including social security and veterans benefits (G.I. Bill), would in effect be eliminated.

As Table 7-18 shows, liberalization of the basic opportunity grants to cover virtually all of the eligible college population by 1978, although costly in terms of additional funds that would be needed, guarantees all college-age students an opportunity to attend the college of their choice. Since the grant benefits both private and public colleges, some of the state funds for higher education, which aim at subsidizing education only at state colleges, would be freed to provide supplementary state scholarships to those who need additional funds to meet the full cost of private institutions.

Perhaps one of the most salutary effects of such a program would be its impact on educational changes at public institutions.

Table 7-18

LEOG PLAN: NUMBER OF BENEFICIARIES, FEDERAL COST, AND NET INCREASE IN FEDERAL OUTLAYS FOR HIGHER EDUCATION, FISCAL YEARS 1975–81

Year	Number of Beneficiaries[a] (thousands)	Total Federal Cost[b] (millions)	Reduction in Existing Programs[c] (millions)	Net Increase in Outlays (millions)
1975	5,118	$ 5,846	− $3,535	$2,311
1976	9,770[d]	6,740	− 3,402	3,338
1977	9,780[d]	7,627	− 3,540	4,087
1978	12,972[e]	8,459	− 3,553	4,906
1979	12,998[e]	9,507	− 3,545	5,962
1980	13,097[e]	10,659	− 3,563	7,096
1981	13,145[e]	11,860	− 3,628	9,232

[a] Eligible veterans under G.I. Bill are included.
[b] Veterans are assumed to have zero family contributions.
[c] Includes veteran payments under the G.I. Bill which is equal to the difference of this column and column (2), Table 7-16.
[d] Includes students from families in income classes of $10,000–$15,000.
[e] Includes students from families with income above $15,000. In effect, beginning in 1978, the income limit does not apply and the number of beneficiaries would be equal to total college enrollment, including induced enrollment plus veterans covered under the G.I. Bill.

Since the proposed federal grant program would cover half the cost of education at any institution, public institutions would be induced to follow a more rational pricing policy for their educational services. Furthermore, since students enrolled in private institutions would have effective access to these funds (LEOG), both types of institutions, but especially public institutions, would have to intensify their efforts to attract college students. Although such competition may lead to higher education costs and, thus to higher federal outlays, one can argue that such a price may be warranted, if it leads to an improvement in the quality of higher education.

Refundable tax credits. In the same spirit that the President expressed in his 1974 budget message to Congress in proposing "legislation to provide an income tax credit for tuition paid to nonpublic elementary and secondary schools," a case can be made for a tax credit for tuition paid to nonpublic colleges and universities. Most private institutions of higher education are faced with a financial crisis in this and the following decade. This financial crisis, in large part, is thrust upon them by the underpricing of educational services at public institutions. Because state aid to higher education is in the form of institutional aid rather than direct aid to college students, public institutions have no incentive to charge tuition that is closely related to educational costs. In 1969-70, public institutions, on the average, charged tuition which was about 44 percent of their total current expenditures, while private institutions were charging tuition of about 62 percent of cost. In addition, federal aid to higher education, if not adding to this imbalance in the price structure, is not sufficient to counteract the state subsidy to public institutions. Clearly, the delivery of educational services would be vastly improved if a more rational price policy were followed by public institutions. A tuition charge equal to 50 percent of the cost of education at both private and public institutions—coupled with state-federal scholarship programs—would provide college students with the opportunity to choose the educational system they prefer. Proposals along these lines are undoubtedly controversial because they depart from the long-established philosophy of subsidizing sellers of education rather than those who consume it. The tax credit scheme may be thought of as a *third* best solution to the problem of higher education financing in that it would provide enough aid for the poorest students to be able to attend college.

The basic ingredients of the tax credit plan can be summarized briefly. A tax credit for tuition paid by students in private colleges would be allowed with (1) a maximum equal to the amount of public subsidy—the difference between tuition charges in public institutions and the cost of education at these institutions, and (2) refundable credit for amounts in excess of $100.

Because students enrolled in public colleges receive a direct subsidy in terms of lower tuition charges than those enrolled in private institutions, a tax credit would in effect remove such vast differences, thus improving the distributional effect of the state subsidy system. Furthermore, since the credit is refundable, all families with students in private schools would benefit from it irrespective of their tax liabilities. This feature would provide buyers of educational services with additional incentives to evaluate more carefully the educational services offered in both types of institutions, since the credit would in effect lower the tuition differential between public and private institutions.

The impact of this proposal on private and public schools is clearly warranted. In addition to easing some of the financial difficulties facing private schools, the tax credit plan increases the competition between public and private institutions because it lowers the supply price of private institutions and thus indirectly improves the functioning of the price system in the educational market. The cost of the tax credit plan will clearly depend on: (1) whether or not an income limit is imposed, (2) the number of induced enrollments in private schools, and (3) tuition charges at both public and private institutions. Assuming that the credit is not limited to specific income classes and that 15 percent of full-time students enrolled in private schools receive tuition grants, the maximum cost of a tax credit plan, at 1971-72 levels of tuition and enrollment, would be about $2 billion.[21]

Occupational, Vocational and Adult Education, Other Educational Aids, and General Science

Occupational, Vocational and Adult Education. Categorical aid by the federal government for these activities is being sharply curtailed for 1974. In 1973, for example, grants totaling $504 million were made to state governments, including $384 million for basic vocational educational programs, $20 million for programs for students with special needs and work study, $26 million for consumer and homemaking, $23 million for cooperative education, and $51 million for

---

[21] Data used in the estimates are from *Projections of Educational Statistics to 1979-80*, 1970 edition, National Center for Educational Statistics, pp. 29, 99 and 110.

adult education. In the 1974 budget, these "categorical" aid programs are eliminated and most, but not all, will be absorbed by the newly proposed special revenue sharing for education. Estimated outlay on these activities under revenue sharing is put at $238 million (with requested authorization for $443 million). Support for other vocational education categories, such as research and career education, will remain at about the same level in 1974 (about $45 million) as in 1973.

The budget outlook for vocational and adult education during the period 1975-81 is given in Table 7-19. The projection reflects the administration move towards a "more flexible" approach to education, that is, eliminating categorical grants in favor of special revenue sharing.

Other Educational Aids. "Other educational aids" covers a wide range of activities including library resources, educational (renewal) development, educational activities overseas, the National Institute for Education, the National Foundation for the Arts and Humanities, the Smithsonian Institution, and the Corporation for Public Broadcasting. Major changes in these activities in the 1974 budget are:

(1) Proposed rescission of appropriations of $12 billion for educational renewal and $3 million for library resources.

(2) Termination of some programs, under educational renewal, including new careers in education, drug abuse education, environmental education, and nutrition and health education.

(3) Discontinuance of support of library programs (except college libraries).

(4) Transfer of special technology demonstration projects to the National Institute of Education.

Projected outlays for other educational aids for the period 1975-81 are shown in Table 7-19. The projection assumes that the administration continues its support for research, innovation, and reform in education. Outlays for cultural activities also increase, especially in 1975 and 1976, to finance the American Revolution Bicentennial activities.

General Science. Outlays by the National Science Foundation are estimated to be about $585 million in 1974, representing a 2 percent increase in outlays over the 1973 level. For the projection period 1975-81, the growth rate assumed is 2.5 percent per year. Table 7-19 shows projected outlays by the National Science Foundation for this period.

Table 7-19

PROJECTED FEDERAL OUTLAYS FOR VOCATIONAL AND ADULT EDUCATION
AND OTHER EDUCATIONAL AID, FISCAL YEARS 1975-81

(millions of dollars)

Program	1975	1976	1977	1978	1979	1980	1981
Occupational, vocational, and adult education							
Special revenue sharing[a]	443	443	443	443	454	465	477
Vocational research, and career education	47	49	51	53	55	57	59
Other educational aid							
Library of Congress	100	106	113	125	138	148	161
Salaries and expenses	86	90	95	100	105	11	117
Library resources	73	0	0	0	0	0	0
Educational development	120	124	134	138	144	149	154
National Institute of Education	160	187	205	226	249	274	300
Corporation for Public Broadcasting	46	47	48	50	51	52	53
National Foundation on Arts and Humanities	140	160	120	128	126	128	130
Smithsonian Institution	114	133	156	175	196	217	239
Other							
National Science Foundation	10	12	14	16	18	20	22
Special foreign currency program	600	615	631	646	663	679	696
	4	4	4	4	4	4	4
Total	1,940	1,970	2,014	2,104	2,203	2,304	2,412

a Figures for years 1975 through 1978 are U.S. Office of Management and Budget estimates.
Note: Totals may not add due to rounding.
Source: Based on assumptions given in text.

8

MANPOWER

Dave M. O'Neill

In a general way federal manpower programs have always been directed at improving access to jobs and job-related services for persons experiencing more than average difficulty in the labor market. Until the late 1950s the program area was straightforward and easy to describe. The individuals served were primarily workers who, although otherwise self-sufficient, had become involuntarily unemployed. The major services offered were job-finding assistance and formal skill training. However, since the early 1960s the situation has become much more complicated as a greater variety of groups have come to be served and a number of quite different program services developed. This chapter examines the budget outlook for this area and the rationale for and objectives of the various manpower programs and possible ways to improve their efficiency.

The Budget Outlook

In 1974, outlays for manpower programs will amount to $3.3 billion, $.6 billion less than estimated 1973 outlays. This 15 percent decline is mainly due to the administration's phase-out of the Emergency Employment Act programs. The administration's 1974 budget lays primary emphasis on assisting state and local governments—through revenue sharing—to meet their own specific local labor market needs. Thus about 40 percent of total federal outlays for manpower will be in the form of revenue sharing. The remaining 60 percent is to be directed towards specific "high priority national objectives," including employment of welfare recipients, research and experimental matching of workers and jobs, and insuring equal access to the job market. The budget outlook for manpower during fiscal 1975-81 is presented in Table 8-1.[1]

The Array of Manpower Programs

The groups served by the present array of manpower programs range from very disadvantaged youth (Job Corps, Neighborhood Youth Corps) through AFDC mothers and the physically disabled (Work Incentive Program and vocational rehabilitation) all the way to groups of fairly well educated adult workers who, although temporarily unemployed at the time of entry into the program, are not disadvantaged in any permanent sense. The types of programs now include, in addition to formal skill training in classrooms, skill training on the job, direct provision of jobs (job creation programs), fairly elaborate and computerized employment exchange services and, finally, provision of a variety of so-called supportive services like child care, counseling for health and emotional problems, et cetera. Some program categories specialize exclusively in one type of distressed group (for example, Job Corps, vocational rehabilitation, WIN) while others serve individuals from a number of sociodemographic groups (for example, MDTA-Institutional and the Public Employment Program). Table 8-2 shows estimated outlays for both fiscal 1973 and 1974 for the various program categories. (The programs included in this tabulation include some which are put into different functional

Table 8-1

MANPOWER OUTLAYS, FISCAL YEARS 1975–81
(unified budget, millions of dollars)

Spending Category	1975	1976	1977	1978	1979	1980	1981
Manpower training	1.5	1.6	1.7	2.9	2.1	2.2	2.4
Employment services	.9	1.0	1.1	.1	1.1	1.2	1.3
Other training services and manpower aids	.5	.5	.5	.6	.6	.6	.7
Total	2.9	3.1	3.3	3.6	3.8	4.0	4.4

Source: LRBP estimates.

[1] The projection assumes a national unemployment rate of 4 percent. Divergences in unemployment rates between certain segments of the labor force are, however, assumed to exist.

Table 8-2

ESTIMATED OUTLAYS ON FEDERAL MANPOWER PROGRAMS BY TYPE OF PROGRAM, FISCAL YEARS 1973–74

(millions of dollars)

Program Category	1973	1974
Special Manpower Revenue Sharing (SMRS)		943
Training programs		
MDTA–Institutional[a]	393	SMRS[d]
JOBS program	92	96
Other OJT programs[b]	171	SMRS[d]
Job Corps	177	111
Veterans OJT programs and other	260	287
Job creation programs		
Public Employment Program	1,088	574
Neighborhood Youth Corps (all programs)	407	SMRS[d]
Operation Mainstream	82	SMRS[d]
Other specified job creation[c]	61	SMRS[d]
Other not specified	119	128
Work Incentive Program		
Training	320	381
Job creation	70	102
Child care (employment related only)	517	582
Vocational rehabilitation	756	824
Labor market and employment services	578	588
Program direction, research and support	205	192
Total	5,296	4,808

[a] Includes institutional training under the Concentrated Employment Program (CEP).

[b] JOBS Optional, Public Service Careers, CEP.

[c] CEP and Public Service Careers.

[d] Transferred to Special Manpower Revenue Sharing.

Source: *1974 Special Analyses,* Part 2-I, Federal Manpower Programs, pp. 119-135.

categories in the budget projection model. Hence the outlay levels differ from those mentioned above in connection with Table 8-1.)

Table 8-3 shows data on flows of new enrollees served during fiscal 1972. None of the individual federal programs (except perhaps for the Work Incentive Program) appears very large relative to the total number of individuals who fall into the various target group

Table 8-3
NEW ENROLLEES IN SELECTED MANPOWER
PROGRAMS, FISCAL YEAR 1972

Program Category	Number of New Enrollees[a] (thousands)
Training programs	
MDTA–Institutional	150,600
JOBS Program	82,800
JOBS Optional	82,100
Job Corps	49,000
Job creation programs	
Public Employment Program	226,100
Neighborhood Youth Corps (all programs)	1,010,900
Operation Mainstream	31,400
Work Incentive Program	120,600
Total new enrollees	1,753,500

[a] The average time spent in the various programs by the new enrollees is about four months. Thus, to convert the flow figures in this table to estimates of man-years of training and job slots, divide by a factor of three.
Source: *Manpower Report of the President*, March 1973.

categories. For example, each year the number of individuals who experience unemployment at some time during the year runs to about 14 or 15 million, while the number of teenagers (14-19 years) in poverty families is over 3 million.

Although none of the individual programs has grown very large, the expenditure level for the sector as a whole is significant as federal programs go. Moreover, until the recent budget stringency this program area had been characterized by immunity to both budget cuts and serious evaluative assessment. The importance of the problems being tackled by the programs (helping disadvantaged youth, welfare mothers, the disabled, the unemployed) was always taken as proof of objectives actually being achieved. But the tenor of the times is changing. The mere existence of a social program is no longer taken as evidence that worthwhile services are actually being delivered. More hardheaded scrutiny of program performance has become the order of the day.

The following sections address these questions:

- What precisely are the rationales and objectives of the various federal manpower programs?

- What is the evidence on the cost/effectiveness of the existing programs in actually achieving their objectives?
- Have the recent cuts in manpower spending by the Nixon administration been in line with the evidence on relative program performance?
- What long-range changes in the role of manpower programs is suggested by the evidence?

Rationale and Objectives of the Various Programs

The major objective of manpower training programs is to raise the long-run earning capacity of participants.[2] The underlying rationale for having the government provide this service is that the groups being served do not have access to the knowledge or financing required to do it themselves—that is, there are significant imperfections in the human capital market. In thinking about the validity of this rationale, it is important to distinguish sharply between the various groups being served by the training programs. For mature adult males, especially those with formal education through or beyond high school, the imperfections argument does not have nearly the plausibility that it does for disadvantaged youth. The job skills that might be useful to adult workers are at present widely available in the private sector of the economy. And the notion that these men would lack the information or motivation to undertake these investments (in the absence of direct governmental provision) is belied by the vigorous growth in the private vocational-technical school industry over the last few years.

Among the set of job creation programs it is important to distinguish the Neighborhood Youth Corps (NYC) program from the others. NYC is aimed exclusively at disadvantaged school-age youth and its objectives are primarily dropout prevention and prevention of juvenile crime and other antisocial behavior. The NYC summer program provides about 500,000 summer jobs mainly for inner-city disadvantaged teenagers. Its primary objective is that of reaching youngsters who would otherwise be likely to get into trouble in the summer months. The other part of the NYC program is primarily aimed at dropout prevention. Its role is to provide youth with jobs that easily dovetail with school attendance so that they do not have to drop out of school in order to help with family support.

---

[2] For the Job Corps program, which deals with very disadvantaged youth, other objectives are also important—improved health habits, reduced propensity for crime, et cetera.

The other job creation programs are aimed at adults with the objective of reducing unemployment, primarily among the long-term unemployed poor. The new Public Employment Program (PEP) has the additional objective of providing for local public services that would have gone underfunded at the local level. The small Operation Mainstream program is targeted specifically toward creating rather modest public jobs for older long-term unemployed workers. The rationale for these programs appears to be based on two assumptions. One is that long-term involuntary unemployment is a significant cause of poverty. The other is that these types of hard-to-employ workers can be helped more efficiently with this approach than they can with alternative policy approaches to reducing unemployment—monetary and fiscal policy, migration assistance, et cetera.

The Work Incentive Program (WIN) grew out of 1967 amendments to Title IV of the Social Security Act. In addition to the "income disregard" provision—providing a direct work incentive by exempting the first $30 a month and one-third of any additional earnings from welfare payments reduction—the 1967 amendments established the WIN training program. Subsequently, large amounts of work-related child care services also came to be provided under the WIN program. The main objective of WIN appears to be to enable welfare mothers to become self-supporting, or at least to reduce the overall costs of the AFDC program by having their earnings substitute for some welfare payments.

The other major type of program in the manpower sector is the free employment exchange services provided by the network of federal-state Employment Service systems (ES).[3] In a sense ES is the oldest of the manpower programs. It was created in connection with the introduction of the federal-state system of unemployment insurance in the 1930s. It experienced a tremendous surge of growth beginning in the late 1950s as it became the focal point for administering the myriad of manpower programs that began to develop at that time. Its latest surge of growth began in 1969 when President Nixon became convinced that computerized job-matching was a solution to unemployment problems.

Why should the government provide free employment agency services? The belief that the private market will not provide the socially optimal amount of job information is deeply embedded in the

---

[3] A discussion of the vocational rehabilitation program is omitted. The major issue here appears to be one of estimating whether all the disabled who could benefit are being covered by the current level of program funding. This is touched on briefly below.

public's mind and is probably related to bad experiences of early immigrants and migrants with private employment agencies. However, it is not at all clear that this picture is valid today. The vast majority of modern workers are much more mobile and well informed than the early immigrant workers were. Moreover, modern labor market research has revealed that informal channels of information (friends and relatives, business associates) are a much more important part of the job search picture than formal channels. However, recent surveys have also revealed that disadvantaged and minority groups have much less access to these informal channels of job vacancy information than advantaged and majority workers do. Thus there is probably some role for government assistance in this area, but whether or not it should be in the form provided by the present ES system is not clear.

As a final point, it should be noted that the objectives of manpower programs are sometimes loosely stated in terms of global macropolicy variables (for example, "reducing the unemployment rate," "shifting the Phillips Curve," "reducing poverty," et cetera). For a number of reasons this way of specifying objectives can be very misleading.

For example, the aggregate unemployment rate is influenced by a host of other variables that would swamp any effects of existing programs even if they were highly successful in reducing the amount of unemployment experienced by participants. Moreover, for some of the programs (for example, training programs) success need not result in lowered unemployment experience—the primary effect may be on wage rates. For others (WIN, ES) success might actually be associated with an *increase* in measured unemployment—more efficient job-search methods might induce workers to quit to look for better jobs; greater work effort by AFDC mothers means higher labor force participation and, perhaps, higher measured unemployment also. And, finally, while it is true that existing manpower programs could be put in a position to exert a significant influence on the overall poverty problem, to do so they would have to be greatly increased in size. Clearly, this would be highly inadvisable unless there is some hard evidence that they have been achieving their objectives.

Program Objectives and Program Performance

Manpower programs have worthy objectives. But have they worked in practice to achieve these objectives? For some of the programs and groups (training programs for the nondisadvantaged and the PEP) the existing evidence is distinctly unfavorable. This evidence, combined with the existence of promising alternative approaches to the same problems addressed by these programs, strongly suggests that they should be phased out completely. For other programs and groups (ES, WIN), the picture is a mixed one—unfavorable evidence on performance combined with no firmly established alternative approaches to the problems addressed. These programs should be frozen at fiscal 1973 levels of effort, and a serious effort at experimentation with alternative approaches undertaken. Finally, for one distressed group (disadvantaged youth) some evidence of favorable program performance is discernible.

Training Programs. There is a voluminous and, except for the Job Corps program, mostly discouraging evaluative literature on most of the training programs, especially for the venerable MDTA-Institutional program.[4] Put charitably, it is hard to find any solid evidence that the institutional training carried out under the MDTA has had any significant effect on the post-program earning capacity of its participants. This discouraging finding has been slow to permeate the consciousness of policy makers for two reasons. First, there have been a large number of what can be called "public relations" evaluation studies that always report finding significant program impact. However, on closer scrutiny one invariably finds that no control groups have been used and that only persons who complete the program (or some other select group like those found to be employed ninety days after termination) have been utilized in the "before and after" calculation.

A second reason for the favorable reception given MDTA-Institutional training is the fact that large numbers of eager enrollees have always been available to sign up for MDTA-Institutional classes. A reasonable person might ask, "If the program really has no post-program impact on earnings capacity, then why would sensible people keep on enrolling in the program?" The answer is simple. The individual enrollee receives a relatively generous training allowance as long as he is enrolled in the program. The MDTA legislation structured the computation of training allowances so that an unemployed person who is eligible for unemployment insurance benefits

---

[4] For detailed surveys of existing studies see: Dave M. O'Neill, *The Federal Government and Manpower: A Critical Look at the MDTA-Institutional and Job Corps Programs* (Washington, D. C.: American Enterprise Institute, 1973), and Ernst Stromsdorfer, *Review and Synthesis of Cost/Effectiveness Studies of Vocational and Technical Education*, Eric Clearinghouse on Vocational Education and Technical Education, The Center for Vocational and Technical Education (Columbus, Ohio: Ohio State University, 1972).

can both significantly extend the duration of his benefits as well as increase the weekly amount received.

The only glimmer of what looks like favorable evidence for training program results is in connection with the Job Corps. The sparse empirical evidence available [5] indicates that the Job Corps has a beneficial effect on the earning capacity of disadvantaged youths who have gone through the program. Although the magnitude of this effect may be difficult to assess with existing data, it does appear to be greater than that provided by any of the other manpower programs serving disadvantaged youth.

Job Creation Programs. The most extensively evaluated program in this group has been the NYC.[6] Most of the careful studies are discouraging with regard to the objective of dropout prevention. Usually NYC enrollees end up with the same dropout rates as a similar comparison group of nonenrollees. However, the NYC program does get high marks in terms of the objective of actually placing its target group in jobs.

It may appear at first blush to be a simple matter for a public job creation program to result in placement of a specified target group in the jobs actually created. Although this has turned out to be the case for NYC (and also for the very small Operation Mainstream program), it appears not to have been the case for the PEP.

What appears to have happened in practice is that local governments utilized part of the PEP funds to ease their own tax burdens. In other words, some unknown (but possibly very large) percentage of the program's 150,000 slots went to fill posts that would have been funded out of local borrowing or taxes in the absence of federal funds. Also, not surprisingly, the characteristics of persons actually hired is anything but a profile of the disadvantaged working poor population. For example, fully 78 percent were high school graduates or higher, including many old, retired military officers who slipped in under a veterans preference clause that was supposed to apply only to Vietnam veterans.[7]

In short, the PEP in all likelihood has been a failure in attaining either the objective of reducing unemployment of the poor or in creating a net add-on to local public services.

---

[5] O'Neill, *MDTA and Job Corps Programs.*

[6] Stromsdorfer, *Review and Synthesis of Cost/Effectiveness Studies.*

[7] See Sar A. Levitan and Robert Taggart, "The Emergency Employment Act: An Interim Assessment," *Monthly Labor Review,* June 1972; and *The Public Employment Program: An Evaluation by the National Urban Coalition* (Washington, D. C.: The National Urban Coalition, September 1972).

To be fair, it should be noted that the Emergency Employment Act of 1971 created a public employment program that is a far cry from what was wanted by the more vigorous proponents of the public job-creation approach to poverty. The Nixon administration opposed the concept of public employment to combat poverty from the outset.

However, it still appears that the failure of PEP has significance for conjecturing about the performance of more ambitious programs. After all, the only important difference between the existing EEA and the proposals of such legislators as Senators Walter F. Mondale and Alan Cranston is in the size of appropriations involved.

The WIN Program. It is important to distinguish between the "income disregard" and training program aspects of WIN. There have been a large number of studies [8] of WIN training program terminees. These studies usually conclude that the training received had little effect. "Placement rates" (the percent of all program terminees that were in jobs 90 or 180 days after termination) are so low (10-15 percent) that it does not appear likely that the training programs of WIN have had much effect on anything except the overall costs of the AFDC program.

There have not been many studies of the effects of the income disregard provisions of WIN. This is most unfortunate because this factor clearly has a large potential for inducing work effort among AFDC mothers. Moreover, and this is a factor frequently overlooked by students of welfare policy, the income disregard provision also has the potential for *increasing* the AFDC caseload. This is because there are women with dependent children who, prior to the 1967 amendments, chose to work at jobs paying a little more than the AFDC need standard. These women are now in a position where, for the same work effort, they can increase their total disposable income if they can manage (and they desire) to qualify for the AFDC program. Thus, although the income disregard provision of WIN is probably a powerful tool for increasing work effort among AFDC women, on balance it could turn out to be very costly.

Indeed, one careful empirical study [9] concluded that in addition to increasing the average amount of work effort among AFDC women the amendments had increased both overall AFDC costs and case-

---

[8] See the articles in the supplement to the *Journal of Human Resources*, volume 8 (1973).

[9] See Gary Appel, *Effects of a Finance Incentive on AFDC Employment: Michigan Experience between July 1969-70* (Minneapolis, Minn.: Institute for Interdisciplinary Studies, 1972).

loads. Thus for the program to be considered cost-effective it must be assumed that the nonmonetary benefits of having AFDC mothers increase their work effort (improved self-image, improved child development) outweigh these additional pecuniary costs.

It would appear that the general public as well as many in Congress do not perceive the WIN program as presenting this kind of difficult cost-benefit comparison. Most people surely think that WIN operates to get people off welfare and therefore to reduce total welfare costs and caseloads.

Employment Service. Although there exist numerous critical studies of the ES, none of them questions the rationale or need for having a publicly financed *and operated* employment exchange. Very radical alternatives to the current delivery system have not received much attention. And this is unfortunate for, although one can make a convincing argument for the need for government to help *finance* job search costs (especially for very low skill and poor workers), it does not follow that the most efficient way to deliver these services is via publicly operated employment offices. For example, it may be more cost-effective to allow the individual to utilize private employment agency services and then reimburse him for the fee he has to pay. Clearly what is needed here are more wide-ranging evaluative studies than have been done in the past.[10]

The recent ES computerization of man-job matching has been subjected to evaluative study. The first major phase of computerization is now almost complete. Over 100 local "job banks" are in operation, covering almost all of the important ES systems in the country. These local job banks contain inventories of all the job openings in the local ES system and make daily listings of them available, via "job bank books," to all the system's local offices. Thus, information on all available job openings in a given ES system are available to any applicant walking into any local office. The next phase will involve computerization of the applicant's search

---

[10] In this connection it will be important for the Labor Department to monitor closely the results of an experimental project in California in which the costs and benefits of having private employment agencies place disadvantaged job-seekers were compared with those of the public employment service. This little-publicized project was funded by the Office of Economic Opportunity (Grant Number CG 9831 A/1) in August of 1971, and it closely resembles the "performance contracting" experiments that OEO funded in the education area. More information can be obtained by writing the Assistant Director for Program Development, Office of Economic Opportunity, 1200 19th Street, Washington, D. C. 20036.

through job bank inventories. This is called on-line "man-job matching."

At present there has been only one evaluative study of the effects of job banks on ES performance.[11] This study concluded that local job banks alone (without on-line matching) have had no effect on any of the easily measurable indicators of ES performance: time to fill job orders, quantity and quality of placements, et cetera. Although the quality of the evaluative evidence can be questioned, it is such as to clearly place the burden of proof on those who assert that adding on computerized matching will make a difference. This is quite a change from the situation in 1967, when the idea that computerization was a useful answer to the job search problem stood almost unquestioned.

Proposed Cuts in Manpower Programs

Table 8-2 above shows estimated outlays on federal manpower programs in fiscal 1973 and 1974.[12] The figures for 1974 are those proposed in the President's budget message (in the table, program categories that have been targeted by the President for special manpower revenue sharing are indicated).

On balance, for the entire manpower sector, the President's proposed budget implies a cut from 1973 levels of about 9.3 percent. For the group of programs included in revenue sharing, the cut amounts to 15.3 percent—from the $1,114 million that was spent on each categorically in 1973, to the $943 million earmarked for special manpower revenue sharing in 1974. For the programs that retain categorical funding, the distribution of the cuts is exceedingly varied. The Public Employment Program (PEP) and the Job Corps are cut by 47 percent and 37 percent, respectively, while the Work Incentive Program (WIN) and the vocational rehabilitation program are slated for increases in outlays of 17 percent and 9 percent, respectively.

Is the distribution of these proposed cuts in line with the evidence on individual program cost/effectiveness just reviewed? The President's proposals appear to go in the right direction with regard to PEP and MDTA, but in the wrong direction with regard to Job Corps and WIN. At the least it would appear reasonable not to

---

[11] See *Job Banks and Job Matching: Evaluation Results and Plans,* INS Memorandum, 1962-72 (Arlington, Va.: Center For Naval Analysis, 1972).

[12] The reader is reminded that the programs shown in Table 8-2 include some which are not classified as manpower programs in the budget.

increase the WIN program, given the ambiguity of the evaluation findings discussed above.

Is there enough money going to manpower overall? There appear to be three issues involved here. First, can the Job Corps, NYC, and Operation Mainstream be boosted up to their universe-of-need levels by trimming down the proposed spending levels for the MDTA, PEP, and WIN programs? Second, with a practically nonexistent PEP and an overall unemployment ratio of 5 percent, what is to be done about unemployment? Third, given that outlays for vocational rehabilitation are programmed to *increase* by 9 percent, what is the recent angry reaction concerning this program all about?

The answer to the first question is a definite yes. It is estimated that an expansion of about 20 percent in the size of the Job Corps over its fiscal 1973 level would suffice to extend its services to all very disadvantaged female as well as male youth.[13] In terms of the figures in Table 8-2, this translates into an "add-on" of $139 million to the proposed fiscal 1974 funding for the Job Corps. This amount could be obtained by holding the outlays on WIN in fiscal 1974 to their fiscal 1973 level. Similarly the NYC programs could be returned to their peak year funding levels (fiscal 1972) by cutting into MDTA and PEP funds by about 10 or 15 percent.

The answer to the second question is that there are many more efficient approaches to lowering unemployment than the public service employment approach. The able-bodied, nondisadvantaged individuals who end up in the PEP slots would be better served by a combination of policies involving extended unemployment-insurance benefits and improved labor-market information services. Their long-run career prospects would probably be enhanced considerably over the career patterns induced by PEP employment. As far as the very hard-core structurally unemployed individuals are concerned, what is required is a much more targeted approach to job creation than that implicit in the PEP-type approach. In this regard, the success of the small Operation Mainstream program in placing very aged unemployed individuals should be studied.

To answer the third question, one must know how many disabled people there are who could benefit from the program. Without this knowledge it is not possible to judge the validity of the current concern over funding shortfalls for vocational rehabilitation. It is true that the annual rate of increase of outlays for vocational rehabilitation in recent years has slowed considerably from what it was in the late 1960s—from about 25 percent to 9 percent. Similarly, in

---

13 O'Neill, *MDTA and Job Corps Programs.*

terms of numbers of individuals served per year, the annual rate of increase has slowed from 14 percent to 3 percent. In 1973 the program served 1.2 million deaf, blind, and other types of physically and mentally disabled individuals. Is the fiscal 1974 level of funding (covering about 1.22 million disabled) sufficient to reach all who could benefit by this program? A good answer to this difficult question would require detailed analyses of data on numbers of disabled, numbers of disabled being served sufficiently by other programs (for example, Medicare, et cetera). If needed, the administration could reprogram some PEP and MDTA funds to vocational rehabilitation for fiscal 1974.

A Revised Role for Manpower Programs

It is relatively easy to criticize existing manpower programs. It is much harder to be positive and suggest better approaches to the social problems that manpower programs have wrestled with. However, in this section an attempt is made to suggest a redirection of efforts in three areas of concern. New manpower program approaches are discussed for (1) disadvantaged male youth, (2) disadvantaged female youth, and (3) the elderly poor.

Training and Other Programs for Disadvantaged Youth. First and foremost, for the *non*disadvantaged clientele served by some of the training programs (for the MDTA-Institutional program this has run about 40-50 percent in the last few years) the government should get out of the business of trying to produce and supply directly a very difficult product that is widely produced and available in the private sector. At most, this effort should be turned into a vocational-technical subsidized loan and voucher type of program and be administered by HEW along with its student loan guarantee program.

The private sector is efficient in getting much human as well as physical capital financed and produced. Manpower policy makers should recognize this fact and keep manpower programs away from problem areas that are much better handled by the private market.

However, there is one situation where the private market mechanism would be expected to fail—the case of the disadvantaged youth who, because of lack of information, funds, and motivation, fails to make the proper investments in human capital at the crucial early stage in life. This type of case should be the major focus of manpower policy in the 1970s. Manpower policy should be integrated with existing policies relating to disadvantaged youth—rehabilitation of juvenile offenders, dropout prevention, career counseling, et cetera. In fact, it would probably be a wise strategy to drop the term "manpower" altogether. A better name for the overall program area dealing with youth would be "career development assistance." Its starting point should be the early years of high school (and the juvenile courts) and it should make available to disadvantaged youngsters a veritable avalanche of options and treatments—Job Corps, on-the-job training, two-year college, four-year college, migration assistance, marriage counseling, psychotherapy, et cetera.

Disadvantaged Girls. A particular problem with disadvantaged girls is to prevent them from getting on the AFDC rolls. The current manpower policy approach to welfare mothers (the Work Incentive Program), although it has increased the total amount of work effort among AFDC mothers, has not dented either overall welfare costs or caseloads. It would appear that the only permanent solution to the dependent children problem is through prevention rather than cure. Somehow, programs must be devised to make a young girl growing up in the ghetto feel that she will be better off if she foregoes the welfare "life style" and opts instead for an independent life with broader horizons. The precise nature of a program that will produce this result is one of the major challenges for social research in the 1970s. Among the existing manpower programs, the Job Corps offers some promise as being one possible device for steering disadvantaged girls away from AFDC rolls.

Detailed follow-up studies of female Job Corps terminees should be launched to see how well the Job Corps approach works in helping disadvantaged young girls avoid the welfare rolls. These studies would be expensive but clearly worth the cost, given the enormous importance of the problem.

A Realistic Role for Public Job Creation Programs. Most of the proponents of large-scale public employment programs argue that unemployment is an important cause of poverty. Although this may have been the case in 1933, it is definitely not the case in 1973.[14] Stereotyped thinking notwithstanding, unemployment is no longer a significant cause of poverty. The vast majority of people who experience unemployment during any year are not part of the poverty population and, conversely, the vast majority of the poverty popula-

---

[14] For a more detailed discussion see Dave O'Neill, "Against a Federal Guaranteed Employment Program," *Current History*, vol. 65, no. 384 (August 1973), pp. 76-79, 88.

tion does not experience involuntary unemployment. If modern poverty is related in any way to the labor market, it is via the low wages that the working poor earn. Government policy may have a role here but it is probably not in the form of large-scale job creation programs.

Table 8-4 gives the distribution of poor family heads and poor unrelated individuals by work experience in 1971. Note that fully half of all poor heads and unrelated individuals are in poverty for reasons that are not only totally unrelated to unemployment but are also only remotely connected to the labor market in any way—old age, disability, disease, and family disorganization. For the other half, those who worked either full-year/full-time or part-year, the inability to obtain anything but low-paying jobs, rather than unemployment, is the major cause of their poverty. Although the annual incidence of unemployment among the working poor is about twice that among the working nonpoor, the fact that work is only possible for about half the poor means that unemployment is only a very minor cause of poverty in the present U.S. economy.

Thus, the size of the job creation program that would be implied

Table 8-4

WORK EXPERIENCE OF FAMILY HEADS AND UNRELATED INDIVIDUALS BELOW THE LOW-INCOME LEVEL, 1971

(in thousands)

Work Experience	Family Heads		Unrelated Individuals	
	Number	Percent	Number	Percent
TOTAL	5,231	100.0	5,151	100.0
Worked	2,809	54.0	1,622	31.5
Full time, full year	1,084	20.7	292	5.6
Part year (u)[a]	655	12.5	1,330[b]	25.4
Part year (other)	1,070	20.4		
Did not work	2,422	46.0	3,530	68.5
Unemployment	118	2.2	83	2.3
Other reasons	2,304	43.8	3,447	66.2

[a] Those who gave unemployment as the reason for not working a full year.

[b] No data are published showing reason for the part-year experience of unrelated part-year workers.

Source: U.S. Bureau of the Census, *Current Population Reports,* P-60, no. 86, "Characteristics of the Low-Income Population, 1971" (Washington, D. C.: U.S. Government Printing Office, 1972), Table 26, p. 97.

by the relation between unemployment and poverty would be a very modest one, perhaps about 100,000 job slots at the very maximum.[15] However, in order to ensure that this small-scale program actually reaches the long-term unemployed poor, major changes in the administrative methods used to implement public job creation programs will be required.

Perhaps the most important administrative innovation would be to stop using simple measures of unemployment incidence as a basis for geographical allocation of funds and individual eligibility. Under the EEA's allocation rule, the amount a state receives is a direct function of the number of unemployed individuals in the state regardless of their distribution, either by reason for becoming unemployed or by duration of unemployment. Although this simple-minded allocation might have been sufficient in the 1930s, when unemployment and poverty were largely overlapping, it can lead to inequitable allocations by area in the current period. Many relatively prosperous, high growth areas of the country (for example, California) have had above-average unemployment rates for the past fifteen years. The reason for this phenomenon has absolutely nothing to do with poverty. Indeed, it has to do with something opposite to poverty—the migration of large numbers of nonpoor people seeking to better their economic opportunities. In-migrants always experience above-average unemployment after they arrive in a new area. Thus in order to ensure that funds will actually get targeted on the structurally unemployed poor, the legislative rules for area allocation and eligibility must utilize information on duration of unemployment, age, wage in last job, reason for becoming unemployed, et cetera.

Another key aspect of a well-targeted job creation program is that the types of job slots created be realistically in line with the abilities of very low productivity, older workers. If the legislation mandates the creation of fairly high quality jobs (along with moderately high salaries), this will greatly reduce the probability of the poor actually being hired into them. Also, it might create serious inequities between the working poor in the private sector and those structurally unemployed poor who end up in public jobs.

---

[15] This figure is arrived at by dividing the total number of poor people who experienced any unemployment in 1971 (about 1,000,000; see Table 8-5) by 5 and dividing the result in half. Dividing by 5 assumes that the average duration of unemployment is about 12 weeks. Dividing the result in half is to allow for the usual amount of short duration unemployment experienced by all groups in the labor force.

Expenditure Effects of the Proposed Redirections

It is difficult to draw any precise implications about changes in manpower sector expenditure levels from the foregoing analysis. Table 8-5 shows one possible redistribution of the fiscal 1974 expenditure total of $4.8 billion (see Table 8-2).

A somewhat revised set of program categories is suggested by the above discussion of program redirection. The expenditure figure for the older worker job-creation program assumes that the program would consist of 100,000 job slots at an average salary of $6,000 per slot. The figure for the NYC summer program would suffice to put that program about 100 percent above its previous peak year (fiscal 1972) level. The expenditure levels for ES and vocational rehabilitation would just about keep them at their current (fiscal 1974) levels. However, the expenditure level for ES should be significantly increased during the 1970s if the computerized matching of people and jobs proves successful. Finally, the $2 billion figure allocated to the career development programs is based on only very rough conjecture. It more or less represents all the fiscal 1974 training program category funds plus all the WIN program funds. To determine whether this will be enough to handle the problem of getting (and keeping) disadvantaged youth on the right track during the 1970s, two important questions will have to be researched: What is the level and quality of local, state, and private charity efforts in this area? And, what is the precise size of the disadvantaged youth population that will have to be served?

Table 8-5

A REDISTRIBUTION OF FISCAL 1974 EXPENDITURES BY A REVISED SET OF MANPOWER PROGRAM CATEGORIES
(millions of dollars)

Program Category	Expenditure Level
Career development programs[a]	2,000
Job creation programs	1,200
Older worker program	600
NYC (summer program)	600
Vocational rehabilitation	1,000
Employment Service	600
Total	4,800

[a] Can include Job Corps-type programs, counseling programs, disadvantaged girls' programs, and others.
Source: See text discussion.

9
HEALTH

Rudolph G. Penner

The Budget Outlook

Federal outlays on health have grown at an enormous rate over the last decade. In fiscal 1964, the total amount spent was only $1.7 billion. For fiscal 1974, the budget estimates the spending of $21.7 billion, a twelve-fold increase or, put another way, an annual growth rate of almost 30 percent per year. Of course, the main reason for this huge increase was passage of Medicaid and Medicare legislation in 1965. Spending on these two government programs will continue to grow rapidly, fueling a large expansion in health outlays despite some important health budget cutbacks discussed later in this chapter. The projections shown in Table 9-1 imply an average annual rate of growth in total health outlays of 12 percent per year between fiscal 1974 and fiscal 1981. The annual rate of increase for Medicaid, Medicare, and the Nixon administration's proposed new health plan is assumed to exceed 13½ percent over the same period. In large part, this increase is due to a growing eligible population, increases in utilization, and inflation in medical costs, but recent legislative changes have also added significantly to the growth rate. The most expensive new items are the provision of kidney dialysis to those in the social security system, the extension of Medicare to the disabled, and the expected discovery of new eligibles for Medicaid as the result of federalizing welfare for the aged and disabled (all passed in October 1972).

The Medicare projections were based on data provided in the 1972 annual reports of the board of trustees of the Federal Hospital Insurance Trust Fund and the Supplementary Medical Insurance Trust Fund. The resulting outlay projections were then adjusted upward for legislation passed since the trustees' reports were written. The

Table 9-1

PROJECTION OF OUTLAYS FOR HEALTH, FISCAL YEARS 1975–81, ASSUMING 2½ PERCENT ANNUAL INFLATION RATE
(billions of dollars)

Item	1975	1976	1977	1978	1979	1980	1981
Development of health resources	2.8	2.7	2.7	2.7	2.7	2.9	3.0
Providing or financing health services							
Health insurance [a]	21.0	24.6	27.5	30.7	34.3	38.3	42.8
Other	1.1	1.1	1.2	1.2	1.3	1.4	1.5
Prevention and control of health problems	.7	.7	.7	.7	.7	.7	.8
Total	25.5	29.1	32.1	35.4	39.1	43.3	48.0

[a] Includes Medicaid, Medicare, and the amounts allocated to the administration's new health plan.

Source: See discussion in text.

Medicaid projections were estimated using a base somewhat higher than that found in the 1974 budget. The budget estimate was adjusted upward because H.R. 1 gave states and localities considerable flexibility to cut back their Medicaid programs, and the budget projects savings amounting to $700 million in fiscal 1974 [1] because of this change. The author believes this to be overoptimistic and projects savings of only $400 million.

For programs which were expanded in the budget, for example, cancer, heart, and lung research, outlays were raised to budget authority levels as soon as seemed practicable. Then program outlays were increased at the assumed rate of growth of wages. Where cutbacks occurred, as in health manpower and mental health centers, an attempt was made to discover the rate at which past commitments would be satisfied. Then these programs were held constant at their new budget authority levels. For programs in which no change of policy was indicated by the budget, outlays were assumed to expand at the rate of growth of wages.

---

[1] *Fiscal 1974 Budget, Appendix,* p. 442.

Policy Issues

Health Insurance. In recent years there has been a large number of health insurance proposals. Thirteen major bills were introduced in the 92nd Congress, some of which would expand the size of the federal sector more than 20 percent. Many of these proposals have been reintroduced in the 93rd Congress, and the administration's 1974 budget also promises to resubmit an overhauled version of its 1971 proposal. It is obviously necessary to ask what has stimulated this intense activity.

There are a number of areas of possible concern. Let us first list them, and then proceed with a brief analysis of each, asking whether they justify a fundamental change in our health insurance systems.

(1) There is concern over the general health of the nation, and a feeling that the situation would be improved if all groups—rich and poor alike—consumed more health care.

(2) Another area of concern is centered not on the average consumption of health care, but on its distribution. In particular, it is believed that the poor receive insufficient care, and there is also concern over the doctor "shortage" in rural and urban slum areas.

(3) The continuing increase in the cost of health care is the final major concern. The high cost can, in turn, imply that a serious illness becomes a financial catastrophe even for relatively affluent families.

General level of health care consumption. The view that we do not generally consume "enough" health care may be based on the purely paternalistic notion that people do not know what is good for them and they should therefore be induced to buy more through various subsidy plans. On the other hand, there may be a more selfish motive behind the desire to stimulate more consumption. A person who does not spend much on preventive and therapeutic care may spread communicable diseases to the rest of us. Even if his disease is not communicable, it may become more serious as the result of neglect, eventually forcing the person to become a ward of the state. Such persons can create a drain on the Medicaid or Medicare programs, thus increasing the tax burden on the rest of the populace. However, it should be noted that expenditures on preventable or curable communicable diseases represent a tiny proportion of total health care costs.

To evaluate the view that we are not consuming enough health care, it is necessary to have some information on whether increases in health inputs would have a productive impact on the health of the nation. Unfortunately, the statistics are confusing and experts differ widely on how they should be interpreted. On the one hand, the usual indices of health status paint a bleak picture for the United States. In 1968, we ranked eighteenth in the world in male life expectancy and fourteenth in infant mortality.[2] On the other hand, the United States spends more on health care both per capita and as a share of GNP than do many of the countries that have superior health statistics. Moreover, we have experienced vast increases in expenditures on medical care since 1960 without a significant impact on the trend in life expectancy.

This paradox can be interpreted in very different ways. To those who advocate fundamental reforms in our health insurance systems, the evidence implies that our health care delivery systems are horribly inefficient and that changes in the quantity, composition, and distribution of health care would be highly productive.[3] To those who are more cautious about radically changing our approach to health care, the evidence indicates that there is only a weak functional relationship between the consumption of health care and health status. These observers feel that life style, diet, and cultural heritage are also important factors. Evidence is cited which indicates that male life expectancy actually varies inversely with income levels.[4]

Obviously, we cannot resolve this complex issue in this brief analysis. We can only note the major uncertainties and advocate some caution before undertaking any enormously expensive reforms in our health care delivery systems.

Distribution of health care. This concern takes two forms. First, there is a belief that the distribution of health care across income groups is inequitable, with the poor suffering from inadequate services. Second, there is also concern over the geographical distribution of

---

[2] Data cited by Arnold Packer, "The Health-Care Financing and Payment Systems," unpublished manuscript, Committee for Economic Development, Washington, D. C., 1972, p. 2.

[3] For example, see Victor Fuchs, "Impact of National Health Insurance Plans on Costs: A Framework for Determination," published in *National Health Insurance: Conference Proceedings*, ed. R. D. Eilers and S. S. Mogerman (Homewood, Illinois: Richard D. Irwin, Inc., 1971), pp. 184-200.

[4] Charles T. Stewart and Corazon M. Siddayao, *Increasing the Supply of Medical Personnel* (Washington, D. C.: American Enterprise Institute, 1973), Chapters 2 and 5. For detailed discussion of the uncertainties involved in interpreting the data, see Rita R. Campbell, *Economics of Health and Public Policy* (Washington, D. C.: American Enterprise Institute, 1971), pp. 41-52.

health care with an alleged doctor shortage in rural areas and in the slums of our largest cities.

The problems posed by the lack of health care consumption among the poor have been mitigated somewhat by the institution of Medicaid in the middle 1960s. Between 1962 and 1968, the rates of hospitalization for the low income population rose from 94.7 per thousand to 114.5 per thousand. Between 1964 and 1969, physician visits per capita for the same group rose from 4.3 to 4.6. By these measures, low income groups are actually now consuming more health care per capita than middle and high income groups whose consumption has fallen in the Medicaid era,[5] although perhaps not more relative to their needs.

Moreover, these data do not imply that the treatment of the poor is equitable. Medicaid plans are designed at the state and local levels with the federal government providing financial support totaling roughly 55 percent of costs. Plans vary greatly from state to state and two states have no plan at all. Some states serve only those on welfare, while others also serve the "medically indigent"—basically the working poor. Some states provide dental care, others do not.[6] Consequently, the federal government's contribution varies greatly from state to state. For reasons of equity, to some it seems preferable for the federal government to guarantee at least a minimal level of benefits which state and local governments could supplement solely out of their own funds if they wished. In this regard, the administration proposed a Family Health Insurance Plan in 1971 to replace Medicaid for families with children and has promised that a new version will soon be presented. The administration approach will be analyzed in detail later. Here, it must only be emphasized that arguments for treating the poor more equitably only pertain to plans which focus on the poverty population, however defined. They do not provide any support for making huge resource expenditures on comprehensive plans which would serve the entire populace.

Another alleged medical problem is the maldistribution of medical services around the country, particularly the "shortage" of doctors in rural and slum areas. In part, the rural problem may be one of severe discontinuities in the production of medical care in sparsely settled areas. For example, in certain places there may only be enough

---

[5] Charles L. Schultze et al., *Setting National Priorities: The 1973 Budget*, pp. 224-225. Low income is defined as under $4,000 in 1962 and 1964 and below $5,000 in 1968 and 1969.

[6] The 1974 budget suggests ending federal support for the provision of dental care.

demand to provide an adequate income for one-half of a doctor, but in many places part-time service may not be feasible and doctors may be available only in units of one. In other places, one doctor may have too much to do and medical ethics may prevent him from charging a high enough fee to reduce demand. Yet, at existing fee levels there may not be sufficient demand to warrant doubling inputs to two doctors. In slum areas, the problem is two-fold. On the one hand, doctors demand higher incomes to work under unpleasant conditions and, on the other, low patient incomes make it difficult to generate the demand necessary to provide remuneration sufficiently high to attract more doctors.

While such problems are often used to provide evidence of a health care "crisis" in this country and the health care crisis is in turn used as a justification for a comprehensive health insurance plan, it must be noted that a health insurance plan applying to all areas and all income groups may in fact intensify the problems noted above. A comprehensive plan will increase the demands of the affluent as well as those of the poor. Since the affluent, educated members of our society usually prove to be more adept at taking advantage of government programs than do the rural and urban poor, the result may be that the doctor shortage will actually be intensified in rural and slum areas. Even if this hypothesis is incorrect and a national health insurance plan does increase the demands of the slum and rural population relative to the urban and affluent population, it is a terribly crude weapon for a very special, narrow problem. Many who have studied the slum problem feel it might be better attacked by a plan focusing on the poor, while the rural problem is probably handled better by collective action at the local level to subsidize rural doctors. In either case, the problem should become somewhat less serious in the future if no further legislation is passed, because most projections imply a substantial increase in the supply of doctors.

The discussion thus far has not uncovered an important need for a universal health insurance plan. It is necessary to consider the possibility that the impetus for a comprehensive plan may have gained momentum not because of a vital need for such a plan, but rather because its provision is very much easier now than it would be if the need were greater. Governments often find it most feasible to take over services that are already being consumed by the vast majority of the population. Then, the amount of resource reallocation and the concomitant disruption to society is less severe than it would be if none of the service were currently being consumed. For example, E. G. West argues that vast amounts of education were consumed privately before public education was contemplated in Britain in the nineteenth century and that this greatly eased the transition to public education.[7] In the same manner, the fact that 80 percent of the portion of the population under age 65 already have some sort of private health insurance, another 20.6 million receive Medicaid, and 95 percent of the over-65 population have Medicare[8] would greatly reduce the net resource costs of a comprehensive public plan, because it would simply take over the financing of services already publicly or privately financed. This should not be interpreted to mean that a comprehensive medical plan would be cheap. Cost estimates will be discussed later in our analysis of the Kennedy-Griffith legislation. However, the net cost will be very much less than it would be if we were not already consuming so much private and public health insurance. On the other hand, it seems foolish to implement a completely universal health insurance plan in order to serve that 10 percent currently not covered by either private or public insurance (this group consists largely of the self-employed of low income, people working for small employers, and female-headed households whose income is greater than the Medicaid limits) and to add somewhat to the generosity of the plans now serving the other 90 percent of the population. A plan which focuses directly on the problem areas would seem more sensible.

The cost of catastrophic illness. The possible financial burden imposed by a serious illness has risen rapidly in recent years for two reasons. First, highly sophisticated and expensive life preserving technologies have become available that did not exist previously. Second, the relative price of all forms of medical care has risen rapidly in the last decade. Between 1960 and 1971, the medical care component of the consumer price index rose 62 percent, physicians' fees rose 69 percent, and hospital daily charges rose 186 percent. This compares to an overall rise in the consumer price index of 37 percent.

There are a number of possible reasons for this significant increase in the relative price of medical care. First, the price indices are imperfect and do not completely reflect the fact that there have

---

[7] See "Resource Allocation and Growth in Early Nineteenth-Century British Education," *The Economic History Review*, vol. 23, no. 1 (April 1970), pp. 68-95; and E. G. West, *Education and the State* (Levittown, N.Y.: Transatlantic Arts, Inc., 1965).

[8] Department of Health, Education, and Welfare, *Towards a Systematic Analysis of Health Care in the United States, A Report to the Congress* (Washington, D.C.: U.S. Government Printing Office, October 1972), p. 18.

been rapid technological changes in medicine and that we are now buying higher quality services with each physician's visit or stay in the hospital. In other words, part of the increase in price is not true inflation but simply reflects the fact that we are buying a slightly different, and presumably better, product than we did in' 1960. On the other hand, some of the price increase certainly does reflect the fact that we are also paying more per quality unit than we did in 1960. A large part of this change is the result of a rapid increase in relative demand stimulated by the spread of private insurance and the implementation of Medicaid and Medicare in the middle 1960s. When a person is insured, he is much more likely to consume the so-called discretionary medical services than he is if he must pay the whole cost himself. (Discretionary services are those whose value is highly uncertain, but which may possibly have some expected net benefit.) Because of this phenomenon, the demand for total medical services is quite sensitive to the portion of cost borne by the patient. For example, a study by Rosett and Huang estimates that expenditures for physicians and hospital services will be almost doubled if the patient's share of costs is lowered from 35 percent to 10 percent for zero deductible insurance policies. Where the patient pays 10 percent of the cost, an increase in the deductible from zero to 20 percent of income reduces expenditures by more than 50 percent.[9] As additional evidence, Stewart and Siddayao note that "after the institution of Blue Shield there were four times more tonsillectomies performed, and twice as many appendectomies, mastectomies, and hysterectomies as before."[10]

The discretionary demands induced by the spread of insurance have, of course, raised the prices of both discretionary and more essential services. This and, more important, the availability of very sophisticated and expensive life-prolonging technologies means that a very serious, long-lasting illness can become enormously expensive. Even relatively affluent families must face the possibility that a serious illness can make them destitute.

It may be this possibility and not a general lack of medical care for ordinary illnesses which represents a most serious contemporary medical problem. An immediate question is why has the private

---

[9] See "The Effects of Health Insurance on the Demand for Medical Care," part 1, *Journal of Political Economy*, vol. 81, no. 2 (March/April 1973), pp. 281-305. Of course, such estimates are subject to numerous qualifications and various studies have produced quite different results, but, in general, numerous studies document significant sensitivity of demand to the presence of insurance. For a brief review, see HEW, *Towards a Systematic Analysis of Health Care*, p. 19.

[10] *Increasing the Supply of Medical Personnel*, Chapter 4.

insurance market not provided adequate protection against cata-strophic illnesses. To a large extent it has, and the sales of insurance which provide such protection are growing rapidly. However, such insurance currently covers only about a third of the population and a large part of the remaining population is covered by insurance which pays only for ordinary expenditures and which has an upper limit on benefits that is insufficient to cover true catastrophies. This is known as "shallow coverage" insurance.

The next question is whether the government should intervene and provide catastrophic coverage or whether it should wait for the growing private market to take care of the problem. There are certain market distortions which encourage "shallow coverage" insurance and retard the spread of catastrophe insurance. Of course, govern-ment does not intervene in every case where distortions exist.

One of the artificial inducements to purchase shallow coverage insurance is of the government's own making and originates in the tax system. Under income tax law one cannot deduct direct medical expenditures which total less than 3 percent of adjusted gross income, but an individual or an employer can deduct all or part of a premium for health insurance covering such expenditures, whether it is paid on one's own or on an employee's behalf. The value of this tax deduction is substantial, and Feldstein and Allison have shown that it lowers the after-tax cost of health insurance for the average person to 3 percent less than the actuarial value of the benefit provided.[11] Once the net cost of an insurance premium is lower than the expected value of the benefits, one's behavior toward insurance is altered radically. In the normal case where tax subsidies do not apply—or apply equally to insurance premiums and uninsured outlays—one buys insurance only against large expenditures which cannot be anticipated with any degree of certainty, and one must pay for such protection by paying a premium higher than the actuarial value of benefits because the insurance company must cover not only its claims but also its operating expenses while providing some profits for its owners. Because insurance is expensive in this sense, one does not normally buy it for protection against regular expenditures, which can be anticipated with some degree of accuracy. For example, if one knew with virtual certainty that one would do $50 damage to one's auto per year, one would ordinarily plan ahead for this outlay and would not buy insurance against this sort of damage because the

---

[11] Martin S. Feldstein and Elizabeth Allison, "Tax Subsidies of Private Health Insurance: Distribution, Revenue Loss and Effects," unpublished manuscript, Harvard Institute of Economic Research, Discussion Paper No. 237, April 1972.

cost of the latter would significantly exceed $50. However, if the premium for this type of insurance was tax deductible whereas the damage was not, and if the value of the tax deduction brought the net cost of the premium down to, say, $49, one would be foolish not to buy it because one could be virtually certain of getting $50 worth of benefits at a cost of $49. This is exactly the situation which prevails for shallow coverage health insurance. Consequently, people are induced to buy insurance against fairly small, readily predictable, health expenditures, even though they would never contemplate buying such insurance without the tax subsidy. Once insured, they, of course, consume more health services, and as noted previously, this has undoubtedly been one of the main factors driving up health costs since World War II.

The tax system does not provide the same incentive to buy catastrophe insurance because medical expenditures in excess of 3 percent of income are deductible from taxable income. In other words, both the insurance premiums and uninsured expenditures are subsidized equally by the tax system. Put still another way, the tax system already provides partial insurance against catastrophes. The deductible is equal to 3 percent of income while the taxpayer's share of medical expenditures above this amount is lower, the higher his marginal tax bracket. It should be noted, however, that this tax-subsidized catastrophe insurance system is only relevant to people who itemize on their tax return; in other words, it is primarily for the middle and upper income classes.

There are other institutional arrangements which probably retard the sale of private catastrophe insurance. People realize that they would seldom be required to bear the entire cost of a very serious illness. Once the financial burden reached a certain level, the depletion of their financial resources would qualify them for some sort of state aid, and even before this point is reached, the medical establishment might show some leniency in collecting bills that are very large relative to a person's financial resources. In other words, public and private charity provides a floor of protection against severe catastrophes. (In the extreme, bankruptcy laws place an upper bound on one's maximum liability.) On the other hand, if the person was insured, the insurance company would be expected to pay the whole bill and the premiums reflect this fact. Consequently, catastrophe insurance might seem expensive to someone who was not wholly adverse to becoming a ward of the state or a recipient of private charity. This point may be especially relevant to lower income groups for whom the purchase of catastrophe insurance would involve a more substantial financial sacrifice.

Because private and public charity is quite haphazard and uncertain, many make an argument for an explicit government plan which provides more systematic and more equitable protection against medical catastrophes. In fact, recent changes in social security legislation already provide protection against certain catastrophes, albeit in a highly peculiar manner. In October 1972, anyone insured by social security became eligible for free kidney dialysis—one of the most financially devastating forms of treatment. While such protection can be justified on the basis of the arguments outlined above, we have now created a world in which it is better to have one sort of catastrophic illness than another. Thus, the person suffering from kidney disease is protected, while someone can still be bankrupted by heart intensive care. Very obviously, it would be more equitable to have protection against all catastrophic eventualities at once, rather than to provide protection gradually disease by disease.

One other sort of catastrophe is taken care of by the October 1972 amendments. For the first time, the disabled have been made eligible for Medicare. This provides protection against long-lasting debilitating illnesses, but a substantial financial burden can be suffered in the months before one is officially declared to be disabled.

Summarizing the argument thus far, there are certain biases against the spread of insurance against catastrophes. One may or may not believe that these biases are sufficiently important to warrant government interference, but the fact of the matter is that government has already begun to move toward catastrophe insurance in a piecemeal fashion which will create some very serious inequities. A more systematic approach to the problem might be preferable.

Since even relatively small medical expenditures can represent a financial catastrophe to a poor family, a systematic approach to catastrophe insurance would involve the provision of fairly shallow insurance for the lower income groups. Such insurance could be used to replace Medicaid and thus make the treatment of the poor more uniform from state to state.

The key question is, of course, how much would it cost, and here we enter an area of great uncertainty. First and foremost, cost will depend on the choice of a definition for a medical catastrophe, and opinions are likely to differ greatly on this point. As noted previously, the burden imposed by a given medical expense certainly varies inversely with income. For a given income, the implied burden varies directly with family size. The quantity and liquidity of family assets, the variability of income, and many other factors also affect a family's ability to pay for medical services. Ideally, the design of a catastrophe insurance plan should take account of all of these factors. Practically, it would be impossible to do this with any precision, but a good approximation could be achieved by taking account of the most important variables—income and family size.

For a given family size, one approach to designing a catastrophe plan would be to define arbitrarily a medical catastrophe as anything which imposes medical bills in excess of some proportion of income. Let us be extremely generous and say that this proportion is 10 percent. A family would bear all costs up to this amount, although they could, of course, buy private insurance against their own cost share if they wished. In any case, the government would bear all costs exceeding 10 percent of income. The problem with this approach is that once expenditures exceeded 10 percent of income there would be no incentive for either the patient or the provider of services to economize. With the government paying 100 percent of the remaining cost, very expensive forms of treatment might be prescribed even if they were of dubious value.

An alternative is to structure the plan so that the patient's cost-sharing ratio is reduced in gradual steps. It could be designed so that the maximum outlay possible for the patient is still 10 percent of his income, but he would pay some share of much larger expenditures than would be the case if there was just a deductible of 10 percent of his income and no cost sharing thereafter. For example, consider a family earning $8,000. With a straight deductible equal to 10 percent of income, they would pay 100 percent of expenditures up to $800 and nothing thereafter. Alternatively, the plan could have them pay 100 percent of costs up to a deductible of $250, 25 percent of expenditures between $250 and $2,450, and nothing thereafter. The maximum total burden would still be $800, but there would be an increased incentive for efficiency for expenditures between $800 and $2,450. On the other hand, there would be less incentive for efficiency between $250 and $800.

Given our uncertainty about people's responses to different insurance structures, it is not clear which structure would be more efficient on balance. However, there may be some reason for favoring the approach which reduces the patient's cost sharing in gradual steps. This conclusion is based on the feeling that the doctor would be reluctant to prescribe dubious treatment procedures as long as there is any cost sharing on the part of the patient. On the other hand, with government paying part of the cost down to $250 there would be less disincentive to buy useful treatment over a wider range of expenditures. However, this is all speculation and cannot be substantiated scientifically. It should be noted that the above discussion compares two structures which impose the same maximum cost on the family earning $8,000 per year. This does not mean that they would consume the same amount of medical care under the two approaches, and that therefore the costs to the government would be the same. Comparative costs depend on how the family would respond to the different cost-sharing formulae over different ranges of medical expenditures and, here again, we do not have sufficient information to provide a definitive answer.

Another important problem involves defining the coverage of a plan. The most serious difficulties arise with psychiatric, dental, and nursing home care. In all of these areas, heavy subsidies can induce a vast increase in demand and this can add significantly to the plan's budget cost. Therefore, even the most generous plans typically impose limits on the utilization of these types of services.

A variety of different cost-sharing structures has recently been described and analyzed by the Department of Health, Education, and Welfare. One example which implies an extremely generous definition of catastrophe is set forth in Table 9-2.[12]

Table 9-2

DEDUCTIBLES AND COINSURANCE RATES BY INCOME CLASS

Gross Income Class	Deductible	Coinsurance Rates
Under $3,000	0	20%
$ 3,000 – $ 4,000	$ 50	21
$ 4,000 – $ 5,000	100	22
$ 5,000 – $ 6,000	150	23
$ 6,000 – $ 7,000	200	24
$ 7,000 – $ 8,000	250	25
$ 8,000 – $10,000	300	26
$10,000 and up	350	27

[12] This is a slight variation of a plan described by the U.S. Department of Health, Education, and Welfare in *Towards a Systematic Analysis of Health Care in the United States.* Somewhat different plans following a similar philosophy have been proposed by Mark V. Pauly, *National Health Insurance: An Analysis* (Washington, D. C.: American Enterprise Institute, 1971), and Martin Feldstein, "A New Approach to National Health Insurance," *The Public Interest*, Spring 1971, pp. 93-105.

Some limits are placed on psychiatric, dental, and nursing home care. All cost sharing could be waived once a family's cost share exceeded 10 percent of income. For example, a family earning $9,000 would pay 100 percent of the first $300 of medical outlays, 26 percent of the cost of outlays between $300 and $2,608, and nothing on expenditures exceeding this amount. Cost sharing is not varied with family size. On the one hand, a given amount of cost sharing is more burdensome for a larger family in any income class, all other things equal, but on the other hand, larger families derive higher expected benefits from any given structure. Accordingly, whether or not an adjustment is made for family size is purely a value judgment.

HEW did not provide cost estimates for various cost-sharing structures and it is not possible for this author to provide anything more than a very crude guess. However, using the sort of demand elasticities for medical care estimated by Rosett and Huang,[13] it seems probable that the structure described above could be financed for the under-65 population for a gross cost less than $30 billion in fiscal 1975. The net cost would be about one-half of this amount, since the plan would replace Medicaid, saving about $7 billion in federal outlays; kidney dialysis and Medicare for the disabled under 65, saving in excess of $2 billion; and the administration's new health plan for which they allocate $200 million in fiscal 1975 ($800 million in fiscal 1976). In addition, it could be argued that the plan would eliminate the need for deductions for medical expenses in excess of 3 percent of adjusted gross income and the reform would present a golden opportunity to eliminate the tax subsidy to shallow coverage insurance. This would increase tax revenues by more than $5 billion in fiscal 1975. In total, this provides more than $14 billion in federal budget savings.

The excess cost could be financed by a tax increase or an insurance premium. The structure of the tax or premium is only important to income distribution and can be made as progressive or regressive as is desirable politically.

Of course, the gross cost of the plan and the resulting tax increase could be significantly lowered by slightly raising cost sharing by the family, and conversely, any reduction in cost sharing would significantly increase the cost of the plan. The budget cost is sensitive to cost sharing both because with higher cost sharing the government bears a lower share of the burden at each utilization level and because increased cost sharing reduces utilization. Thus, by manipulating

---

[13] "The Effects of Health Insurance on the Demand for Medical Care."

the schedule given in Table 9-2, the net cost of the plan can be made to approximate anything that the government thinks it can afford.

The most important point is that any cost sharing on the part of the patient greatly reduces the cost of health insurance and generally provides an incentive for health care to be delivered more efficiently. While a plan similar to that described above could have a gross budget cost less than $30 billion and a net cost of less than $15 billion, and while this may seem extravagant, it is modest compared to the cost of a plan such as the Kennedy-Griffith proposal.

In the Kennedy-Griffith plan, there is no cost sharing on the part of the patient. In other words, everything is free and the only restrictions on the consumption of medical services are applied to psychiatric, nursing home, and dental care and to purchases of some prescription drugs. Even these limitations are fairly lenient, with the limit on dental care being relaxed through time.[14] The plan is enormously expensive both because it takes over virtually all private expenditures on the current consumption of medical care and because it would stimulate significant increases in the quantity demanded. In an earlier publication, we estimated that the net budget cost would be about $57 billion in fiscal 1975, with about $50 billion reflecting the takeover of private expenditures that would have been made in the absence of the plan and $7 billion representing the cost of new demand.[15] It is the latter figure which represents the true direct burden on the economy, although the taxes necessary to finance the gross cost of the plan would distort incentives and impose extra inefficiencies on the economy. In any case, these estimates are highly conservative and costs could easily exceed these amounts by a wide margin unless medical care is severely rationed. The proposed Kennedy-Griffith legislation contains the mechanism for such rationing by establishing a national health budget which is allocated among different regions of the country on a per capita basis and each region would be expected to live within its budget. It is not clear how the scarce medical resources within each area would be allocated among patients, but it would clearly involve a massive bureaucratic effort. Put another way, the choice between Kennedy-Griffith and a catastrophe insurance plan is not really a choice between completely free care

[14] U.S. Department of Health, Education, and Welfare, *Analysis of Health Insurance Proposals Introduced in the 92nd Congress*, August 1971. A somewhat different version of the proposal has been introduced in the 93rd Congress.

[15] See David J. Ott et al., *Nixon, McGovern and the Federal Budget* (Washington, D. C.: American Enterprise Institute, 1972), p. 55. New legislation, passed since these estimates were published, would change the estimates slightly, but by only a small amount relative to the margin of error in such computations.

and care whose cost is partially shared by the patient. Rather, the choice is between two forms of rationing—one bureaucratic and the other depending partly on the price mechanism. Of course, the cost estimates attached to Kennedy-Griffith imply that a greater quantity of care will be consumed than under the catastrophe plan described above.

It is useful to compare the two plans described above to the original administration health insurance proposal, even though the administration may propose quite a different plan in the near future. The old plan consisted of two parts. The first was the Family Health Insurance Plan. It was a plan which replaced Medicaid for poor families with children, thus eliminating wide differences in coverage from state to state. It bore some similarity to the catastrophe plan described earlier in that there was some cost sharing, the extent of which varied directly with income and inversely with family size. The plan was partly financed by premiums which also varied directly with income and inversely with family size. However, there was no limit on cost sharing and some limit on hospital and outpatient benefits, and therefore the family was not protected against severe catastrophes. Moreover the plan provided no protection to childless couples and unmarried individuals.

The second part of the administration's plan was called the National Health Insurance Standards Act (NHISA). It required all employers to offer their employees a private insurance plan providing a specified set of benefits. The employer was eventually to pay 75 percent of the premium cost while the employee paid 25 percent. The employee could opt out of the plan if he wished.

The plan called for significant cost sharing on the part of the patient and thus would be more economical and efficient than Kennedy-Griffith. Hospital care was subject to a two-day deductible, and a $100 deductible applied to most other benefits. Beyond the deductible, patients were to pay 25 percent of the costs until $5,000 worth of services were received in a year. Once the limit was reached, all cost sharing was waived for that and the next two years. There was a lifetime limit of $50,000 on total benefits, with a $2,000 annual restoration.

Note that the deductibles, coinsurance rates, and maximum family contributions did not depend upon income. A family might be responsible for over $1,500 of cost sharing per year, and while this could be easily borne by an upper income family, it could be a financial catastrophe for many low income workers. Since premiums were also unrelated to income, the compulsory nature of the plan had the effect of imposing a payroll tax at a percentage rate that declined with income. Because the "employer's share" might be shifted to the worker in the long run, the financing of the plan might be highly regressive. For very low income workers, the plan had the effect of increasing the minimum wage, since the employer must not only pay the minimum but the insurance premium as well, unless employees opted out of the plan. The percentage increase could be quite substantial, especially for people working less than a full work week, because the plan covered anyone who works more than twenty-five hours per week for a ten-week period or more than 350 hours within thirteen weeks. Moreover, coverage had to be continued for 90 days after employment is terminated. Consequently, where the minimum wage prevented backward shifting, the cost could have quite an impact on the employment of low income persons, especially teenagers working only part of the year.[16]

There is also a problem in the relationship between NHISA and FHIP. The unemployed under FHIP would receive better shallow coverage at a lower cost because of the lower deductibles and coinsurance, while the employed under NHISA would receive better catastrophic protection. The net actuarial value of FHIP probably exceeds that of NHISA for most low income people, and therefore, a person might face a significant work disincentive as he moved from one plan to another.

From the point of view of the administration, the compulsory insurance plan has the important advantage that it imposes virtually no budget cost except in that compulsory premiums would be tax deductible. However, from the point of view of true economic cost, the lack of a budget cost is irrelevant. If employers were forced to provide the plan, it makes no difference whether they were forced to finance it with an explicit tax paid to the government or whether they were forced to finance it by paying premiums to private insurance companies. The costs imposed on the private sector would be the same in either case, as would be the resource costs imposed on the economy.

In the author's view, the catastrophe plan described earlier is far superior to the administration package. It seems more equitable in that cost sharing depends on income and there are no serious discontinuities as there are in the administration plan as a person shifts from FHIP to NHISA when he becomes employed.

---

[16] It should be noted that the plan was designed so that typical summer employment remained uncovered.

Before leaving our discussion of health insurance plans, it is necessary to comment on one of the most controversial proposals in the 1974 budget, that is, to increase cost sharing of the aged covered by Medicare. Currently, in the hospitalization part of Medicare, the aged pay a deductible equal to the national average cost of one day in the hospital, regardless of what their hospital actually charges. After that they get 50 days of hospitalization free of charge, paying 25 percent of the cost of the next thirty days and 50 percent of the cost of the sixty days following that. The administration's new proposal would have them pay the actual charges for the first day of care and 10 percent of all charges after the first day. Consequently, some of the burden would be lifted from the aged who have to endure very long hospital stays, but the burden would be raised on those experiencing shorter stays. On average, the costs of hospitalization would rise from $84 to $182 for the typical stay of twelve days.[17]

The philosophy behind the administration's proposal is obvious. Currently, there is no incentive for doctors and patients to economize on hospital stays lasting less than sixty days. Cost sharing would presumably reduce utilization and this, plus the larger contribution by patients, is expected to reduce Medicare outlays by over $1 billion per year currently, with greater savings in the future. For similar reasons, the administration is also recommending an increase in cost sharing for physicians' services covered by Part B of Medicare.

While the administration's move makes good sense from the point of view of economic efficiency, its opponents object vehemently to the implied distributional impact. The whole plan might be much more palatable politically if the extent of cost sharing were made dependent on income. Clearly, the Medicare population contains many fairly wealthy individuals who could easily afford to share a higher ratio of costs than is being proposed by the administration, while all cost sharing could be waived for the aged poor. This would, of course, be more difficult to administer and some would object to the "means test" aspect of the proposal.

Regulation and Efficiency. It was argued above that the soaring cost of medical care has been one of the major causes of the concern that has led to the proliferation of health insurance proposals. At the same time, it has stimulated a call for improving the efficiency of health service delivery mechanisms and for controlling both prices and medical practices.

---

[17] Caspar Weinberger quoted in *The Wall Street Journal*, March 23, 1973, p. 26.

The problem of efficiency has been attacked in two different ways. First, the government has sought to remove all legal barriers to Health Maintenance Organizations (HMO) and to encourage them through subsidization and by favoring them in the structure of their health insurance proposals. An HMO provides all necessary health care to an individual in return for a fixed fee. In theory, such a group has a strong incentive to provide the most efficient mix of preventive and therapeutic cure and to select the optimum combination of health care inputs in the treatment of particular diseases, because by keeping their clientele healthy at the lowest possible cost, they increase their own rate of return. In contrast, a doctor treating an insured patient has no such incentive and expensive forms of treatment can be prescribed at no cost to doctor or patient even though their effectiveness is dubious. In isolation, an HMO can also increase its profits by lowering quality, but again in theory this is prevented by competition among HMOs, and between HMOs as a group and other forms of health care delivery.

Although there is some evidence that HMOs reduce the amount of hospitalization required by patients, this evidence has been disputed,[18] and in general, remarkably little is known about their operation. The main concern about their spread is that competition may not be sufficiently vigorous to ensure that the quality of care will be maintained at a high level. The ethics of the medical profession forbid vigorous competition and it is difficult for the consumer to obtain information on the quality of care that he is receiving.

The other approach to improving efficiency has been the establishment of Professional Standard Review Organizations (PSRO) which examine the quality and appropriateness of medical care under Medicare and, presumably, under any new health insurance proposals made by the administration. The intent is to control overutilization of medical services wherever government pays a large share of the costs. There are two major worries regarding the potential effectiveness of such groups.

First, in an effort to prevent overutilization, they outline a range of standards for the treatment of particular diseases. The danger is that these standards will bias demand. In fact, once standards are explicitly established, patients may demand the maximum standard of care with the threat of malpractice suits lying in the background.

---

[18] For a discussion, see Pauly, *National Health Insurance*, p. 23, and H. E. Klarman, "The Effect of Prepaid Group Practice on Hospital Use," *Public Health Reports*, November 1963.

In other words, a practice aimed at saving money may, in fact, add to medical costs.

Second, the PSROs will be physician-sponsored. Without impugning their honesty, it is necessary to point out that they will come to the problem of setting standards with a certain set of biases and that these are likely to be quite different from the biases of the taxpayers who will be paying the bills. In general, regulatory efforts in areas like transportation, banking, et cetera, have to some degree been hampered by the fact that those who are supposed to be regulated soon gain control of the regulatory mechanism. In the case of PSROs, this arrangement is made explicit from the beginning by the fact that they are physician-sponsored.

In quite another approach to limiting the inflation of medical costs, the administration has paid special attention to the providers of medical services in its various price control efforts. It is far too soon to judge the success or lack of success of these efforts. Obviously, success, if it comes, will depend on the goodwill and altruism of the medical profession, because controls can be readily circumvented using a variety of techniques. The quality of service can be easily reduced since it is so hard to measure; new fees can be levied for services which were formerly provided as part of a broader package; and physicians can prescribe extra, profitable services to compensate for restrictions on profits on services which would normally be provided.

Development of Health Resources

Biomedical Research. The budget estimates that outlays on medical research will total $1.7 billion in fiscal 1974, up from $1.6 billion in 1973. The most important efforts are directed at cancer and heart and lung research. In these two areas, outlays are projected to increase to almost $700 million in 1974 from a 1972 total of about $450 million, or in other words by more than 50 percent. Put another way, about 40 percent of our medical research efforts will be focused on these two areas, while other research programs are to be cut back.

Theoretically, the distribution of funds in medical research should be influenced by two factors. It is necessary to assess first the importance of various diseases to the population and second, the probability that expenditures on research will result in the discovery of methods of mitigating a disease's harmful effects. In general, there has not been much research on either of these factors and therefore it is impossible to evaluate the particular distribution of research funds in the administration's budget. Until recently, the matter was not of great importance, but with the rapid growth of federal expeditures on particular diseases, the matter clearly deserves more attention.

Health Manpower. The 1974 budget makes significant cuts in subsidies to health manpower education. The requested budget authority falls from $673 million in fiscal 1972 to $382 million in fiscal 1974. However, outlays will not fall to the new level for several years because most past commitments will be honored.

There are a number of reasons for making this change. First and foremost, the supply of medical personnel is soaring and the high rate of growth is expected to continue through the 1970s. For example, the budget projects an increase of 27 percent in the number of practicing physicians between 1971 and 1980. Second, doctors and medical researchers are generally among the most affluent members of our society and it is not clear that they should be subsidized in their pursuit of this level of affluence. Third, the high reward to medical training implies that supply is restricted not by lack of incentives but rather by supply limitations, largely imposed by the medical profession. This is done in the name of keeping quality high, but there is considerable evidence that this has been overdone.[19]

An argument against the change is that any new health insurance plan is likely to increase the demand for personnel sufficiently to absorb the projected increase in supply at existing prices. The transition to higher levels of demand might be eased somewhat by continuing the subsidization to medical education. Of course, this point is difficult to evaluate until better information is available on the type of insurance scheme that is likely to be implemented.

It should be emphasized that significant support for medical education will continue if the budget proposals are adopted. Special scholarships will be made available to personnel entering federal service and there will be an attempt to alter the geographical distribution of physicians to mitigate the problem discussed earlier—that of doctor "shortage" in rural and poverty areas. Otherwise, graduate education in the medical professions will receive the same support as graduate education in other fields. Assistance will take the form of guaranteed loans and grants to needy students.

---

[19] Stewart and Siddayao, *Increasing the Supply of Medical Personnel*, Chapter 3.

Prevention and Control of Health Problems

The most controversial budget cut in this area involves the elimination of support for community mental health centers ($63 million in fiscal 1974 and $74 million in 1975). The basic problem is that categorical grants paid a very large share of the construction and operating costs of particular facilities. Because federal support was high, there was not a powerful local incentive to economize and where facilities existed, they tended to be quite generous, implying a large subsidy to the population served. Unfortunately, only about 15 percent of the population which needed help received it. In other words, the situation was very much like that in housing. A few people receive large benefits and are supported by the taxes paid by the rest of the population, some of whom need help at least as much as those actually served. A more equitable method of providing help is to serve all those with equal need equally through whatever national health insurance scheme is eventually proposed.[20]

---

[20] The administration has promised this approach. See *Fiscal 1974 Budget,* p. 139.

10

INCOME SECURITY

Rudolph G. Penner, David J. Ott and Attiat F. Ott

Retirement and Social Insurance

The Budget Outlook. Outlays for social security and the unemployment compensation programs have grown rapidly in the recent past and are expected to maintain a high growth rate throughout the rest of the 1970s. In fiscal 1974, these outlays are expected to be 29 percent higher than they were in fiscal 1972, and between fiscal 1974 and fiscal 1981 the projection here (shown in Table 10-1) anticipates an annual growth rate of about 7.5 percent per annum under the

Table 10-1

BUDGET PROJECTION FOR RETIREMENT AND SOCIAL INSURANCE, FISCAL YEARS 1975–81

(millions of dollars)

Program	1975	1976	1977	1978	1979	1980	1981
Transfers							
OASDI	57.1	62.2	66.9	72.0	77.4	84.1	89.3
Railroad retirement	2.7	2.7	2.7	2.7	2.8	2.9	3.0
Civil service retirement and disability	5.2	5.8	6.4	7.1	7.9	8.8	9.8
Disabled coal miners	1.0	1.0	.9	.9	.9	.8	.8
Unemployment compensation	4.8	5.0	5.3	5.6	5.9	6.2	6.6
Administrative costs and vocational rehabilitation	1.0	1.0	1.1	1.2	1.3	1.4	1.5
Total outlays	71.8	77.7	83.3	89.5	96.2	104.2	111.0

Source: LRBP estimates.

assumption that the rate of growth of the GNP deflator will equal 2.5 percent per annum.

The projections for OASDI utilized projections of the number of beneficiaries provided in the 1972 annual report of the board of trustees of the Federal Old Age and Survivors Insurance and the Disability Insurance Trust Funds, Appendix Table A. Data from that report were integrated with data for shorter-term budget projections made by the Social Security Administration in order to estimate the average rate of growth of the real value of benefits per beneficiary. The rate used was about 2.5 percent per year with a somewhat lower rate early in the period and a slightly higher rate after 1976. Real benefits were then adjusted for inflation. Under the assumption of a long-run rate of increase in the GNP deflator of 2.5 percent, it was assumed that the first automatic adjustment on January 1, 1975, would be 5.7 percent. After that, it was assumed that the rate of CPI increase consistent with a 2.5 percent GNP deflator increase would be 2.7 percent.

Projections for outlays on the railroad retirement system were based on data obtained from the Commission on Railroad Retirement adjusted to the same inflation assumptions. The system will have to be altered drastically within the next few years since it is on the verge of bankruptcy.[1] The form of the new system cannot be predicted, and the projections here assume that benefits under current law are raised concomitant with social security.

Projected civil service retirement outlays are based on data obtained from the Civil Service Commission. These data were adjusted for the inflation assumptions used in this study.

Policy Issues

Old Age, Survivors, and Disability Insurance. Probably no government program is more popular than the OASDI portion of social security. Congress has responded to this popularity by expanding the generosity and coverage of the system throughout its history, but at no time have the improvements been more rapid than over the last six years. In the summer of 1972 Congress voted a record-breaking increase in benefits of 20 percent. This comes on top of a 13 percent increase in 1967, a 15 percent increase in 1969, and a 10 percent increase in 1972. In other words, individual benefits rose more than 70 percent over a period of about five years. In contrast, between

---

[1] *The Railroad Retirement System: Its Coming Crisis*, Report to the President and Congress by the Commission on Railroad Retirement, June 30, 1972.

1967 and 1972, the consumer price index (CPI) rose 25.3 percent while average weekly earnings in the private nonagricultural sector rose 33.3 percent. For the first time, the 1972 legislation provided that benefits would henceforth be automatically adjusted for changes in the CPI. Adjustments are made each year that the CPI has risen 3 percent or more since the last automatic, or general, increase in benefits. The automatic increases will be financed by upward adjustments in the social security tax base, and adjustments will equal the average rate of growth of the wages of social security taxpayers.

Although social security benefits have been rising very much more rapidly than the living standards of the working population, it would be erroneous to give the impression that the aged are now living in luxury. About one-half of social security recipients have no other source of income and the average old age and survivors pension will be about $1,800 in fiscal 1974.[2] In other words, the rapid rise in benefits has been from a low level for much of the retired population.

The rapid rise in benefits has, of course, come at enormous cost. Over the decade from calendar 1964 to calendar 1974, the maximum payroll tax payable by an employed individual has risen more than three and one-half times. For someone working at a wage below the maximum tax base throughout the period, the tax rate has increased almost 50 percent. In fiscal 1970, OASDI revenues became more important than corporate tax revenues for the first time, whereas at the beginning of the 1960s they were only slightly more than one-half as important.

In the face of this very burdensome tax increase, it is interesting that the continued expansion of the social security system has not provoked more opposition on the part of younger workers. At first sight, the tax appears to be highly regressive because it applies only to earnings below a maximum tax base which will be $12,000 in 1974. Consequently, a person earning $24,000 per year will pay only one-half the tax rate of one earning $12,000 or below. Of course, it is dangerous to assume that the person handing the tax money to the government actually bears the burden of the tax. In the case of the payroll tax, public discussion is confused by the fact that one-half is "paid" by the employer and one-half by the employee. Theoretically

---

[2] It should be noted that the average is held down by the fact that many recipients have been working under social security only part of their working life. Typically, these individuals also receive income from federal or state and local pensions. On the other hand, those subsisting solely on social security tend to be those with the lowest incomes throughout their lifetime, and therefore, they are at the low end of the benefit scale.

this is irrelevant in determining the ultimate burden of the tax and there is some controversy as to whether the whole tax is borne mainly by the employee in the form of a lower after-tax wage, by the employer in the form of a higher gross wage paid out of return to capital, or by the consumer in the form of higher prices for the products of covered industries.[3] The controversy is far from settled, but it seems probable that a very high proportion of the shares of the employee and employer are in fact borne by the employee in the form of lower wages. If this is true, the regressivity of the tax is heightened.

Opposition to this apparently inequitable burden is probably muted by the language surrounding the social security system. The tax is referred to as a "contribution" and is considered to be quite different from ordinary income or corporate taxes. (It is interesting to note that in the recent presidential campaign, the debate over whether "tax" increases would be necessary in the near future never mentioned significant payroll tax increases which were already scheduled by legislation.) The taxpayer is encouraged to believe that his contribution buys a certain insurance package, and in a sense this belief is well-founded. Under present law one must have paid the tax for a certain period of time before one is eligible for the whole range of benefits, and one's eventual benefits do bear a very rough relationship to one's total tax payments.

However, the system is not contributory in the sense that one's contributions are invested in an account which can then be used to buy an annuity upon retirement. Instead, the system works on a pay-as-you-go basis with money being transferred directly from the working taxpayer to the beneficiaries. There are trust funds, but they contain only a small fraction of the investment that would be required to fund the system's long-run liabilities. Their function is to act as a buffer, absorbing funds when tax receipts exceed benefit payments and providing funds when the reverse is true. In the long run, the revenue and benefit structure is now intended to provide a trust fund which becomes equal to one year's benefits and then grows through time at about the same rate as the growth in benefit outlays.

Many have suggested that the payroll tax be eliminated and replaced with an increase in income taxes to make the system less regressive. Some adhering to this view believe that the tax contribu-

---

[3] John Brittain, "The Incidence of Social Security Payroll Taxes," *American Economic Review*, March 1971, pp. 110-125. See comment by Martin Feldstein, *American Economic Review*, September 1972, pp. 735-738.

tion should be completely separated from the benefit side of the system, others that the tax contribution, however designed, should still play a role in determining benefits. The basic issue is whether the system should serve welfare goals or retain contributory features. This question is explored later in this chapter.

An interesting characteristic of the present transfer system is that it can pay a rate of return to its participants even though the bulk of a person's contributions are never invested in anything. This happens because, speaking very roughly, the system implies the following social contract. The working generation agrees to turn over a share of its wage earnings to the current retired generation in return for the promise that when the current working generation retires they will have a claim on a similar share of the wages of the people then working. However, as time goes on, the total wage bill in covered occupations grows so that each succeeding generation has a claim on a larger absolute amount of money than they actually contributed over their own working lifetime. The amount grows both because the working population grows and because each worker is richer as a result of economic growth. In fact, it can be shown mathematically that the rate of return to the social contract is roughly equal to the rate of growth of the labor force plus the rate of growth of wages per worker.[4] This assumes that the contribution remains a constant share of wages. The share has been rising rapidly through time and the rate of growth of the share must be added to the rate of growth of per capita wages and labor force in order to determine the rate of return to the retiree.

In fact, the share has risen so rapidly as the system has expanded that the rate of return on the contributions of a recent retiree is much higher than he could earn from a private pension fund. For example, for a typical worker retiring with his wife in 1973, the cumulated value of his and his employer's tax contributions and the discounted value of his expected benefits are equated by a rate of return of 12 percent. If he discounts his benefits at a rate between 7 and 8 percent, the rate of return on his contributions approximates 14 percent.[5] Furthermore, if he does not believe that he bears the whole burden of his employer's contribution, he perceives a much higher rate of return. It also must be remembered that the system does not provide a retirement annuity alone. The system also

---

[4] See Henry Aaron, "The Social Insurance Paradox," *Canadian Journal of Economics and Political Science*, August 1966, pp. 371-374.

[5] The assumptions underlying this computation can be obtained from the authors of this chapter.

provides protection for survivors in the event of death before retirement, a death benefit, and insurance in the event of disability. Given the enormous past rate of return to one who survives to retirement, it is little wonder that the system is so popular.

In the future, the return is unlikely to be so high because obviously the growth in the tax share can not continue for long at past rates without absorbing an enormous share of GNP. Indeed, a younger person examining the present benefit structure will perceive a rate of return lower than that historically available on common stock investments, if he expects the law to remain constant.[6]

To understand the political dynamics of the social security system, it is necessary to examine the attitude of a typical voter any time a proposed increase in taxes and benefits comes before Congress. Suppose that a 10 percent increase in both taxes and benefits is proposed. The rate of return accruing to a worker as a result of such an increase will be higher the nearer he is to retirement. In other words, the rate of return resulting from an increase will vary directly with age. Taking an oversimplified view of the matter, it can be concluded that, as long as the rate of return exceeds the discount rate for a majority of the voting population, politicians will find it profitable to continue to push for increases. Using an age distribution of the voting population and data on the tax and benefit structure for a typical worker, one could presumably approximate the strength of this incentive under existing law. This has not been done, but one can guess that there is still a strong incentive for future increases.

In any case, it is obvious that there have been strong political incentives for past increases. As a result, such increases have been rushed through Congress with only a perfunctory examination of the whole tax and benefit structure and, as a result, a number of serious inequities have been built into the system and perpetuated through the years.

In part, the inequities have grown because it has not been possible to decide to what extent the system should be purely contributory with benefits actuarially related to tax contributions, and to what extent it should fulfill a welfare goal by redistributing income toward the poor. As a result, the program has had mixed goals and since these goals are in obvious conflict it cannot possibly fulfill either goal equitably.

---

[6] John A. Brittain, "The Real Rate of Interest on Lifetime Contributions Toward Retirement Under Social Security," in Joint Economic Committee, *Old Age Income Assurance*, Part III (Washington, D. C.: U.S. Government Printing Office, 1967), pp. 1471-1479.

As noted before, the system is contributory in the sense that one must have been working in a covered occupation and paying payroll taxes for a certain period of time before one can be "fully insured." [7] Also, one's benefits are roughly related to average monthly earnings in covered occupations during one's working life.[8]

However, the relationship between contributions and benefits is not exact and here welfare considerations come into play. First, benefits are related to average monthly earnings (AME) by a progressive formula which implies that the higher the AME, the lower the ratio of benefits to tax payments. Second, not everyone qualifies for benefits on reaching age 65. If a person continues to work, he loses $1 of benefits for every $2 of earnings in excess of $2,100 a year. Since he must also pay a payroll tax while working in a covered occupation, the implicit tax rate is in excess of 50 percent over a large range of income. Note that this provision is in violation of the contributory philosophy of the plan, and it has little to do with a welfare goal. Only wage or self-employed income reduces benefits. There is no limit on the investment income that can be earned without loss of benefits.

Third, the system treats working couples in an inequitable manner. A dependent spouse receives 50 percent of the family's primary worker's benefits whether or not he or she has ever contributed to the system. If the dependent spouse has earned benefits in his or her own right in excess of this amount they can be claimed, but if he or she has not, any contributions that have been made to the system by the dependent spouse are essentially lost. As a result, working couples can receive lower benefits than a couple where only the man or woman worked even though they have the same AME. For example, given the current benefit schedule, a husband and wife each with an AME of $200 (for a total of $400) will receive benefits of $308.80 on retirement. If only the man or wife works and has an AME of $400, the monthly benefit will be about $350. Again, we have a situation which violates criteria of equity whether the system is judged according to a contributory or a welfare philosophy.

---

[7] The person must have earned more than $50 in each of 40 quarters.

[8] For a detailed description of the computation method and eligibility requirements for different benefits, see *Social Security Bulletin, Annual Statistical Supplement, 1969*, pp. 4-12. An excellent analysis of the whole system can be found in Joseph A. Pechman, Henry J. Aaron and Michael K. Taussig, *Social Security: Perspectives for Reform* (Washington, D. C.: The Brookings Institution, 1968).

The Social Security Advisory Council examined the problems posed by working couples and explored various changes in law which would rectify the inequities.[9] However, they advised against any change, since any equitable solution for couples would create inequities when couples were compared with two single beneficiaries. They also noted that any reasonable solution would be very costly.

In addition, there are many other inequities if social security is viewed as a contributory system. The self-employed gain a higher rate of return than the employed if the employer's share of the payroll tax is shifted to the worker. In addition, late entrants to the labor force and those receiving minimum benefits receive an especially high rate of return. It is believed by many that it is only the poor who are favored by the minimum benefit but, in fact, the population receiving the minimum benefit includes many former federal employees who worked in the private sector just long enough to qualify for the minimum benefit and who also receive a generous retirement income from the civil service pension fund.

Although, at first sight, the formula linking monthly benefits to a worker's AME seems to be highly progressive, that is, would seem to favor the poor heavily, Milton Friedman has argued that many other features of the system favor the rich and he believes that these may more than counteract the effect of the progressive benefit formula.[10] These features are as follows:

(1) Social security benefits are tax free. The implied tax saving is much more valuable to individuals in a high tax bracket, that is, with other income supplementing their benefits, than it is to those relying solely on social security. Moreover, the tax contribution made by employers is not included in taxable income and this feature is more valuable to those in a higher tax bracket.

(2) The self-employed pay a lower tax rate than those working for others. Since there are many high-income professionals in the former group, this may have a regressive effect on balance.

(3) Highly educated people tend to have shorter working lives and thus lower contribution levels. Since the lowest five years of earnings between ages twenty-one and sixty-five are eliminated in computing the AME and since some of these are likely

---

[9] *Reports of the 1971 Advisory Council on Social Security* (Washington, D. C.: U.S. Government Printing Office, 1971), pp. 41-43.

[10] Wilbur Cohen and Milton Friedman, *Social Security: Universal or Selective?* (Washington, D. C.: American Enterprise Institute, 1972).

to be zero years for the highly educated who are also likely to have higher incomes, the ratio of benefits to total contributions will be raised somewhat.

(4) Persons with high earnings tend to live longer and have wives who did not work.

Whether these and other features of the system more than counteract the progressive nature of the benefit formula is an empirical question that has not been studied in detail. However, until the matter has been studied we must consider the possibility that the whole system is regressive on balance.

Any major reform of the social security system is difficult to accomplish. If no present or potential beneficiary is allowed to lose as a result of reform, it then becomes enormously expensive. If reform is allowed to impose significant losses on particular groups, it is in a sense a violation of a social contract. The system has been sold for so long as a contributory system that it would be a violation of the people's trust to deprive them of the benefit levels that are promised by current law and that they thought they were buying with their tax contributions.

Therefore, reform must proceed very gradually, either by slowly improving the benefits of people who are now treated inequitably by the existing system, or by placing the new entrants to the labor force under a totally new structure of benefits.

In designing the goal toward which the system should move, it is, of course, necessary to decide whether the goal is an equitable contributory system or an equitable welfare system, for both aims cannot be served within the structure. There would be some merit in moving toward an equitable compulsory contributory system and then allowing the incomes of the aged poor to be supplemented by a new welfare system, perhaps based on a universal negative income-tax approach to both young and old.

The arguments for a compulsory contributory system are of two types. The first is that people should be forced to provide themselves with a minimum retirement income. Otherwise, there is the likelihood that irresponsible members of society will become wards of the state in their old age and a financial drain on the rest of the taxpayers who would feel morally bound to contribute something toward their upkeep. In deciding the appropriate level of forced saving, society faces a trade-off. As the share is raised, the likelihood of people becoming dependent on welfare in their old age is lowered, but the freedom of people to plan their retirement saving in a rational, flexible manner is restricted. For example, it may be rational not to save in those early working years when relative financial obligations are greatest, while saving more after one's household is formed and one's children are educated. Any compulsory system limits one's freedom to follow such a strategy. Consequently, the choice of an appropriate spot on the trade-off is likely to involve some probability that people will end up without enough retirement income and, therefore, the contributory system would have to be supplemented with a welfare system. In other words, the point of the compulsory system would only be to reduce the drain on the welfare system and not to eliminate it entirely.

The other argument for a compulsory system is very different in nature. As described earlier, a system of transfers can be arranged between generations that provides the retired generation with a rate of return equal to the rate of population growth plus the rate of economic growth. If this real rate of return exceeds that available on invested capital, then it is socially optimum for the government to arrange such a social contract because the rate of return exceeds that available from private pension plans. This sort of argument justifies a much more lavish plan than would be required simply to lower the drain on our welfare system. However, the argument depends crucially on the rate of population growth plus economic growth remaining above the rate of return on capital for a number of generations. Some economists suggest that this is impossible and that there is a natural tendency for the rate of return on capital to equal the sum of the rates of population and economic growth in the long run.[11] If this is true, there is little to choose between the social contract and a private pension plan. If it is not true, some may question any scheme that is so heavily dependent on population growth given the very low birth rates experienced in recent years.

Railroad and Civil Service Retirement. The federal railroad retirement system was established before the social security system and therefore historically the two systems have remained separate. However, the two systems have become more and more interrelated over their histories. Although benefits are computed differently, the nature of the insurance packages are similar and railroad retirees are guaranteed at least 110 percent of the level of social security benefits. In 1966 a supplemental annuity system was created for railroad workers to supplement retirement incomes.

---

[11] Earl A. Thompson, "Debt Instruments in Both Macroeconomic and Capital Theory," *American Economic Review*, December 1967, pp. 1196-1210.

Like social security, the railroad retirement system does not have a trust fund sufficient to cover future liabilities. Instead, it operates as a transfer system shifting funds from the working generation to those retired. Given the structure of benefits and revenues, the system is viable only if the working population is growing and, unfortunately, railroad employment has been steadily falling since the late 1940s. Hence, the railroad retirement system is in deep financial trouble. The problem is mitigated somewhat by the fact that OASDI makes transfers to the railroad retirement system equivalent to an amount necessary to put OASDI in the same financial position that it would have if there were no railroad retirement system. However, these transfers are not sufficient to save the system from bankruptcy, and if past benefit commitments are to be honored the system will have to find new sources of revenues.

The Railroad Retirement Commission has explored a large number of possible financing options [12] and these cannot be analyzed here. The basic issue is to what extent the general or OASDI taxpayer has an obligation to bail out the railroad retirement system and to what extent the burden should be borne by the industry, its workers, and the current beneficiaries of the system. This is a complex moral issue which cannot be resolved here.

The civil service retirement system provides retirement and death benefits to government employees. The retirement benefit is computed on the basis of the employee's highest three-year salary and his length of service. It is partly financed by contributions equivalent to 7 percent of salary by both the employee and the government. The civil service trust fund is not large enough to cover all liabilities; in other words, the system operates very much like social security, that is, on a pay-as-you-go basis. It receives additional payments from the Treasury equivalent to the interest that would be paid on Treasury annuities if the system was fully funded. It also receives regular appropriations from general revenues to cover the cost of changes in the benefit system.

Outlays under the system are growing rapidly and are projected to reach almost $10 billion in fiscal 1981. In other words, they are becoming a significant form of government expenditure equivalent to more than 10 percent of OASDI outlays.

The system has one peculiar feature. Benefits are adjusted upward with the CPI every time the latter rises 3 percent since the last adjustment. Each time a cost-of-living adjustment is made an additional 1 percent increase is awarded. In other words, the more

---

[12] *The Railroad Retirement System*, Chapter 10.

rapid the rate of inflation, the faster the benefits will be increased in real terms. This is a very strange arrangement, but it cannot be altered for existing employees because it is now part of the implicit contractual arrangement between them and the federal government. However, one cannot help wondering whether it is necessary to provide new employees with the same promise.

Public Assistance and Other Income Security

The 1974 Budget. As of January 1, 1974, the federal government will assume full responsibility for providing basic assistance for the aged, blind, and disabled under the Supplemental Security Income (SSI) programs. In addition, supplemental payments will be made to state governments (the "hold harmless" provision) so that their outlays need not rise above the 1972 level.

The federal government also provides, in the form of grants to state governments, about 52 percent of total program outlays for Aid to Families with Dependent Children (AFDC). Total benefits under the AFDC program are expected to reach $7.7 billion in 1974, with the federal share put at $4 billion.[13] Other welfare-public assistance programs supported by the federal government include the food stamp and child nutrition and school milk programs. Major changes to be made in this area of federal support are: (1) management reforms, which began in 1973, and proposed legislation to ensure that eligible beneficiaries receive only what they are entitled to, (2) higher "per capita" benefit levels for food stamps, and (3) integration of the milk subsidy program with other child-nutrition programs. Total federal outlays on public assistance by major category for 1974 are shown in Table 10-2.

The Budget Outlook, 1975-81. The budget outlook for public assistance for fiscal years 1975-81 is shown in Table 10-3. The projection of outlays for this category of federal activity is based on the following assumptions:

(1) Enactment by Congress of the administration-proposed legislation requiring more effective management of welfare benefits;

(2) no major program initiatives, in particular welfare reform, to take place during this period;

---

[13] *Fiscal 1974 Budget*, pp. 142-143.

Table 10-2

FEDERAL OUTLAYS FOR PUBLIC ASSISTANCE BY TYPE OF AID, FISCAL YEAR 1974

(unified budget, millions of dollars)

Program	Outlays
Supplemental security income [a]	2,208
Aid to Families with Dependent Children (AFDC)	
Present programs	5,528
Proposed legislation	−158
Food stamps	2,196
Other food and nutrition	787
Assistance to refugees	103
Total	10,664

[a] One-half fiscal year (legislation effective January 1, 1974).
Source: *Fiscal 1974 Budget*, p. 141.

(3) a gradual phase-down of the special milk subsidy for school children to eliminate duplication of other federal child food programs;

(4) a steady decline in the rate of growth of the number of food stamp and AFDC beneficiaries, while average benefit per recipient is assumed to grow at the same rate as prices.

As Table 10-3 indicates, a major source of growth in public assistance outlays can be attributed to the federal takeover of responsibility for aid to the adult categories. Benefit payments under the aged, blind, and disabled (SSI) category are estimated to be about $3.9 billion in 1975, reaching $5.4 billion by 1981, with an average rate of growth of 6 percent a year.

The federal share in the cost of AFDC, the largest component of public assistance, is also projected to rise during this period. However, the rate of growth in outlays will decline from about 10 percent between 1973-74 to about 5.5 percent by the end of the period. The decline in the rate of growth by AFDC outlays is based on a projected decline in the rate of growth of beneficiaries.

Social and Individual Services

Grants to States for Social Services. The federal government provides states and localities with matching grants to assist them in supplying

Table 10-3

PROJECTED BUDGET OUTLAYS ON PUBLIC ASSISTANCE BY TYPE, FISCAL YEARS 1975–81

(millions of dollars)

Program	1975	1976	1977	1978	1979	1980	1981
Supplemental security income							
Benefits	3,880	4,099	4,333	4,581	4,843	5,118	5,411
Other	529	550	571	593	616	640	665
Aid to families with dependent children (AFDC)							
Federal grants for AFDC	4,449	4,880	5,251	5,600	5,913	6,238	6,587
Federal grants for state and local administration	496	507	522	539	559	581	606
Food stamps	2,405	2,569	2,693	2,834	2,943	3,090	3,241
Other food and nutrition							
Child nutrition	768	787	806	827	847	869	890
Special milk	34	30	28	26	24	22	20
Assistance to refugees	90	50	25	0	0	0	0
Total	12,651	13,472	14,229	15,000	15,745	16,558	17,420

Source: LRBP estimates.

certain social services to families or individuals on welfare. Financed 75 percent by the federal government, social services cover almost any program that helps those on welfare get off welfare, or that helps prevent a return to welfare of those who have recently been on welfare, or that helps prevent those who might end up on welfare from doing so. These programs run the gamut from day care to "meals on wheels." [14] Because HEW had not attempted, until recently, to establish federal standards for eligibility of recipients or specify the kind of services to be provided, the federal government was faced in 1972 with state requests for $1.6 billion in social services funds—an increase of 230 percent over the level in 1971. For fiscal 1973 and 1974, the cost estimate was put at $4.7 billion and $5.2 billion, respectively. [15]

To halt the escalating costs of these programs, a limitation on grants for social services under public assistance programs was included in the State and Local Fiscal Assistance Act of 1972. The act puts a ceiling of $2.5 billion on federal matching grants for social services. The 1974 budget estimates federal outlays at $2.4 billion for 1973 and $1.9 billion for 1974.

Reaction to proposed federal restraints on the virtually "open-ended" social services programs was widespread and in some cases intense. Operators of day care centers and welfare mothers using them painted a dismal picture of the proposed cuts. On the other hand, critics of the social services programs argued that such huge sums cannot be accounted for, [16] have been misused by some states to draw additional funds from the federal government, and that such sums of money may, in effect, help perpetuate poor programs. [17]

Assuming that the administration's efforts toward management reforms are successful in keeping the ceiling on social services programs and that no action will be taken by Congress to restore all cuts proposed by the administration in these programs, the budget outlook in this category for 1975-81 is given in Table 10-4.

Other Services. Several other categorical grant programs are included under social and individual services. These include vocational re-

---

[14] *Wall Street Journal*, February 13, 1973.

[15] *Fiscal 1974 Budget, Appendix*, p. 442.

[16] Excerpts from memorandum to the President from HEW Secretary Elliot Richardson, reported by the *Washington Post*, August 9, 1972, p. A20.

[17] "Critics have testified that 'tricks' used by states include putting 75 percent of state money normally spent for social services back into the state's general fund, then using the remaining 25 percent as matching money to draw another 75 percent out of the federal treasury." Ibid.

Table 10-4

FEDERAL OUTLAYS FOR SOCIAL AND INDIVIDUAL SERVICES, FISCAL YEARS 1974–81

(millions of dollars)

Program	1974 [a]	1975	1976	1977	1978	1979	1980	1981
Grants to states for social services	1,891	1,900	1,900	1,900	1,900	1,900	1,900	1,900
Rehabilitation and other social services	984	1,009	1,034	1,060	1,086	1,113	1,141	1,170
Disaster relief	250	260	270	280	290	300	310	320
Allied services [b]	—	20	21	22	23	24	25	26
Other	196	216	237	261	287	316	347	382
Total	$3,321	$3,405	$3,462	$3,523	$3,586	$3,653	$3,723	$3,798

[a] *Fiscal 1974 Budget*, p. 141.
[b] Proposed legislation for budget authority.
Source: LRBP estimates.

habilitation, special needs of older Americans, and allied human services at the state and local level. The fiscal 1974 budget provides for outlays of about $1.4 billion on these services. The budget outlook for 1975-81 (shown in Table 10-4) assumes no major changes in these programs. It further assumes the termination of the social work training programs by the end of 1974.

Disaster Relief. Outlays for disaster relief are difficult to project. For example, in 1973 these outlays increased to 3.5 times their 1972 level, from $92 million in 1972 to $325 million due in particular to the heavy impact of tropical storm Agnes. The budget estimate for 1974 puts outlays at $250 million. Assuming no unusual concentration of major disasters during the projection period 1975-81, a gradual increase in those outlays of about $10 million a year is projected (Table 10-4).

Program Alternatives in Public Assistance

The discussion of program alternatives in this area is confined to welfare reform. For three successive years, the administration has proposed and the Congress has twice voted on major welfare reform proposals. In the fiscal 1974 budget the administration has dropped its previous proposal for welfare reform and there is no indication that any substitute proposal is definitely forthcoming.

As noted above, one part of the welfare reform proposal was, in fact, adopted. This is the Supplemental Security Income (SSI) program, which completely federalizes the former so-called adult categories under public assistance. Hence, the discussion here is further restricted in scope—only reform of the AFDC program (the family assistance program as it was called in the administration reform proposal) is considered. The present AFDC program is generally argued to have serious flaws. It discourages work effort by preventing recipients from appreciably increasing their income from work, and it discriminates against poor families where a male is present, providing an incentive for these families to break up so that the female and the children will be eligible for aid. Also, the present system discriminates against the working poor, because families where the adults work at low wages (1) may have only slightly more income than families receiving welfare but (2) are not eligible for welfare unless they backslide considerably in income to a point below the welfare eligibility level. Finally, the existing system allows for wide variation in benefit levels and eligibility standards in the various states.

Even with all these faults, welfare reform might have been achievable if it were not for the interaction of the AFDC cash assistance program and other programs in providing in-kind benefits to the poor—food stamps, subsidized housing, Medicaid, and the subsidized school lunch programs.[18] As Aaron notes,[19] a growing number of families receive benefits under two, three, or even more programs, as the following data show:

Program	Percent of recipients of AFDC benefiting from special program
Medicaid	99
Food stamps	53
Public housing	13
School lunch	59

The problem of work incentives within AFDC is aggravated by the existence of these other forms of income-conditioned assistance. Under existing law, AFDC recipients who work have their benefits reduced by a maximum of two-thirds of earnings over $360 a year ($30 a month). In addition, in some states they are reimbursed for work-related expenses, which may include income and payroll taxes, other mandatory deductions, transportation, child care, union dues, uniforms, et cetera. If the particular state chooses to define work-related expenses liberally, the AFDC earner may experience no reduction in her income, at least for modest earnings; she is "taxed" (has her benefits reduced) at a zero rate on her earnings.[20] At the other extreme, she may receive little in the way of reimbursement for work expenses, and she then pays a "tax" rate of 67 percent *plus* other expenses on her earnings, and also may have her take-home pay reduced further by expenses not covered. If the AFDC mother (with a family of four) is also a recipient of public housing, Medicaid, and food stamps, then, even with reimbursement for actual work expenses (including payroll taxes and income taxes), she faces theoretical implicit tax rates as high as 80 percent on her earnings,

---

[18] A very useful summary of this problem and the other issues discussed here is contained in Henry J. Aaron, *Why Is Welfare So Hard To Reform?* (Washington, D. C.: The Brookings Institution, 1973).

[19] Ibid., p. 6.

[20] Ibid., p. 9. Aaron cites an unpublished paper by W. Joseph Hefferman, Jr., to the effect that "some pro-client caseworkers take pride in generating enough expenses so that allowable income (used to reduce welfare payments) falls to zero."

plus absolute loss of Medicaid benefits when her earnings plus AFDC benefits push her total income past the state limit for this program.[21] Under H.R. 1, a family of four receiving cash benefits and participating in the additional programs would face a theoretical marginal tax rate on earnings as high as 130 percent, and not falling much below 90 percent for any earnings greater than $720 per year.[22]

These possibilities of confiscatory taxation under the administration's welfare reform proposal played a large role in its rejection by the Senate in 1972 (it passed the House in 1971 and 1972). This plan worsened the work disincentives already existing under AFDC. And the provision that beneficiaries must register for work or training would not have had any strong countereffect; it is hard to see how any work requirement that might *reduce* the beneficiary's income could be feasibly administered.

One obvious solution to the disincentive problem is to lower the marginal tax rate, both for families now eligible for AFDC and, under welfare reform, for families with men. The problems with doing so are twofold. First, given any structure of "basic benefits" (the benefit for families with zero earned income), to reduce the marginal tax rate on earned income raises the cost sharply. For example, the administration's previous plan with a $2,400 basic benefit for a family of four (with a $720 "disregard") costs roughly 50 percent more if the marginal tax rate is 50 percent rather than 67 percent; if the tax rate is lowered to 33⅓ percent, the cost is four times as much as with a 67 percent rate. Second, the "break-even" point—the income level at which a family receives no benefits—varies inversely with the marginal tax rate. For example, with a 67 percent tax rate families with up to $4,320 income would receive benefits; if the tax rate were 33⅓ percent, eligibility would broaden to include all families with up to $7,920 of income.

No completely satisfactory scheme has been devised which would provide "adequate" benefits with really meaningful work incentives (tax rates, say, as low as 30 percent) at low cost and without extending eligibility to a very large proportion of the population.[23] This, of course, is the basic dilemma of the negative income tax, regardless of the population it is applied to.[24] Without strong work incentives and limited eligibility, welfare reform has little

---

[21] Ibid., p. 33.

[22] Ibid., p. 39.

[23] Ibid., pp. 50-69.

[24] See the discussion in Christopher Green, *Negative Taxes and the Poverty Problem* (Washington, D. C.: The Brookings Institution, 1967), Chapter 9.

appeal to conservative politicians. Without high basic benefits, it falls from grace with liberals. Neither group can "win" without the other losing, at least as far as a standardized, national system of welfare is concerned. Hence the impasse that developed during each effort in this direction during the last three years.

However, there is probably much less *effective* work disincentive under AFDC than has been supposed. In fact, recent research suggests that effective tax rates confronting welfare recipients are below 50 percent even where they receive Medicaid, food stamps, and housing subsidies.[25] This being so, the first step in welfare reform might best be to seek some uniformity between states in the treatment of work expenses and the marginal tax rates for AFDC families, that is, inducing states which provide little allowance for work expenses to be more generous and perhaps gradually reducing the maximum tax rate on earned income down from the present 67 percent to some lower level. At the same time, AFDC, with all its faults, may provide the basic principle which can resolve the basic dilemma of welfare reform.

State and Regional Adjustments in Minimum Payment Levels

As pointed out above, lowering the benefit reduction or tax rate increases the cost of welfare reform. However, if the national minimum payment were adjusted by states and within states to take account of differences in the cost of living, this would partially offset the increased cost of a lower benefit reduction rate. Important differences exist among states in the cost of living, and Congress could adjust the minimum payment levels of a welfare reform package to allow for these state differences. At present, no satisfactory indices which measure these differences are published, although, in fact, indices are used to adjust welfare payments to welfare recipients, interstate and intrastate. If Congress instructed HEW to devise annual indices which measured state differences in the cost of living of welfare families, this could be done. Current cost-of-living indices are statistically imperfect, and indices suitable for welfare reform would be imperfect. What seems certain, however, is that they would enable adjustments to be made in minimum welfare payments by states which would be more equitable than a uniform national payment, as well as less costly, than if all recipients received the national minimum.

---

[25] Leonard J. Hausman, "Cumulative Tax Rates and the Process of Welfare Reform," as cited in Aaron, *Why Is Welfare So Hard To Reform?*, p. 35.

Suppose, for illustrative purposes, that per capita personal income by states was used as the basis for adjustment of minimum payment levels. As Table 10-5 shows, this would make possible about the same $3,000 payment level (with a 50 percent tax rate) to the eastern industrial states as proposed by Senator Abraham Ribicoff.[26] At the same time, it would maintain the payment level in southern states at about the $2,400 level prescribed under H.R. 1. This adjusted payment formula, based upon a $2,800 national minimum, would cost $1.5 billion less than the Ribicoff proposals for a $3,000 nationwide payment for each and every state, and also would reduce the number of working poor eligible for income supplements by $4 million.

There would be adequate payments in the South to discourage migration to the North. The following states would have a minimum around $2,400: Alabama, Arkansas, Georgia, Kentucky, Louisiana, North Carolina, South Carolina, Tennessee, and West Virginia. The minimum in Mississippi would be $2,252.

A payment level of $3,000 or more would be obtained under this scheme in the high-payment-level states—California, Connecticut, Delaware, Illinois, Massachusetts, Maryland, New Jersey, and New York. The minimum in Rhode Island would be $2,852, and in Maine, New Hampshire, and Vermont it would not be much over the $2,400 level (Table 10-5).

Thus, those who fear the impact of high welfare payments in the rural and less urbanized states would have less basis to object to a national adjusted payment level. As noted earlier, the $2,800 minimum adjusted to per capita income state by state would be less costly than a $3,000 national minimum proposed by Senator Ribicoff by at least $5 billion. It would, however, cost $3.1 billion more than the 1972 administration proposal (H.R. 1). Since the administration proposal for aid to families with dependent children was estimated to have a net cost of around $2 billion, this would mean the variable payments proposal would have a net cost in fiscal 1975 of about $5 billion. By fiscal 1978, costs should be somewhat lower as incomes rise.

Per capita income is, of course, a good measure of interstate differences in affluence, and probably of differences in *standards* of living. It is not, however, a good measure of interstate differences in the cost of living of welfare recipients.

---

[26] See reference in Edward Moscovitch, "Income Supplements: How High Should They Be?" Federal Reserve Bank of Boston, *New England Economic Review*, January/February 1971.

Table 10-5

AN ILLUSTRATIVE VARIABLE BASIC BENEFIT FOR WELFARE REFORM

State	Basic Benefit	State	Basic Benefit
Alabama	$2,356	Montana	$2,604
Alaska	3,097	Nebraska	2,726
Arizona	2,639	Nevada	3,020
Arkansas	2,350	New Hampshire	2,734
California	3,024	New Jersey	3,018
Colorado	2,767	New Mexico	2,485
Connecticut	3,142	New York	3,099
Delaware	2,953	North Carolina	2,490
District of Columbia	3,211	North Dakota	2,517
Florida	2,706	Ohio	2,836
Georgia	2,538	Oklahoma	2,579
Hawaii	2,838	Oregon	2,757
Idaho	2,492	Pennsylvania	2,799
Illinois	3,029	Rhode Island	2,852
Indiana	2,796	South Carolina	2,374
Iowa	2,736	South Dakota	3,577
Kansas	2,752	Tennessee	2,456
Kentucky	2,482	Texas	2,640
Louisiana	2,478	Utah	2,542
Maine	2,556	Vermont	2,657
Maryland	2,931	Virginia	2,656
Massachusetts	2,969	Washington	2,909
Michigan	2,904	West Virginia	2,411
Minnesota	2,767	Wisconsin	2,766
Mississippi	2,252	Wyoming	2,706
Missouri	2,733	NATIONAL AVERAGE	$2,800

Source: Unpublished data, New England Council, 1972.

Nevertheless, these calculations illustrate the principle. The Department of Health, Education, and Welfare should be instructed to develop suitable measures of the cost of living of welfare recipients and to set payment minimums in each state to reflect that state's cost-of-living index relative to the national average. This would provide more equitable payment levels and reduce the costs of providing added work incentives.

APPENDIX

Projection Assumptions Not Explained in Text

Veterans. During the past five years, the Veterans Administration's budget has increased by almost 20 percent annually. By fiscal 1973, VA outlays had reached a level of $11.7 billion, which made it the third most costly agency in the federal government. The impetus for this growth in outlays came primarily from the massive American involvement in Vietnam. The buildup for Southeast Asia created an additional 7 million veterans, bringing the total veteran population to 29 million.

As the American involvement in Vietnam has decreased, so have the pressures on the VA budget. Expenditures for fiscal 1974 show no increase over the level of fiscal 1973 and total outlays for veterans programs for the remainder of the decade should remain almost constant in real terms. This analysis projects an increase of only $2 billion from fiscal 1974 through fiscal 1981. This represents an average annual increase of only 2.9 percent, which is only slightly greater than the assumed inflation rate.

Outlays for veterans benefits and services are made in four categories: (1) income security, (2) education, training, and rehabilitation, (3) hospital and medical care, and (4) miscellaneous. Projections in these categories are based upon official VA estimates of the number of beneficiaries and assume that: benefits will rise with the cost of living, the United States will not become involved in another war, and the eligibility criteria for veterans benefits will not be altered substantially from those in existence in fiscal 1974.

Outlays for compensation and pensions will total $7.0 billion in fiscal 1974. Compensation for service-connected disabilities is being paid to 2.18 million veterans and .38 million survivors. The number drawing compensation should decline gradually throughout the remainder of the decade as the number of veterans from the world wars and Korea decrease and the number from Vietnam remains constant. By 1980 there will be 2.1 million veterans and .37 million survivors drawing $8.4 billion in benefits.

Pensions are presently being paid to 1.1 million survivors over 65. The number of persons eligible for these pensions will rise for the rest of the decade as World War II and Korean veterans or their survivors reach retirement age. By fiscal 1981, just over 3 million people will be drawing veterans pension benefits of $4.0 billion, and total expenditures for income security will be $8.7 billion. These projections assume that Congress will not pass the administration's proposed legislation that provides for the inclusion of wives' income in the determination of eligibility for veterans pensions and the elimination of duplication of federal burial benefits, and that the VA will not be able to implement its new rating schedules that relate compensation payments to actual earning impairment.

Benefits to veterans for education, training, and rehabilitation (commonly referred to as the G.I. Bill) will go to about 1.9 million veterans or their dependents in fiscal 1973, at a cost of about $2.6 billion. This will be the largest number of beneficiaries and the greatest outlay since the introduction of the Vietnam G.I. Bill in 1966.

However, beginning with fiscal 1974, the number of veterans taking advantage of these benefits should begin to decline by about 13 percent annually for the rest of the decade, while the number of their sons, daughters, wives, and widows taking advantage of the bill will increase only marginally. This decline will occur for two reasons. First, since there is an eight-year time limit on the use of the G.I. Bill, the eligibility period for persons made retroactively eligible in 1966 will expire in 1974. Second, the number of new veterans is decreasing rapidly as the size of the nation's armed forces shrinks (for example, the number of persons leaving military service in fiscal 1974 is projected to be 20 percent below the level of fiscal 1973).

Based upon this smaller number of eligible veterans and assuming that previous participation rates remain unchanged, the projections foresee the number of persons using the G.I. Bill dropping below 1 million by fiscal 1979 and falling to about 750,000 by the end of the decade. Assuming that the currently effective base rate of $220 is adjusted only to reflect the rise in the cost of living, outlays in this category should drop to $1.1 billion by fiscal 1981.

VA medical expenditures fall into four categories: (1) personnel, (2) operating, (3) research and administration, and (4) construction.

Total outlays in these four areas will amount to $2.8 billion in fiscal 1974.

The VA presently employs 161,208 people in its Department of Medicine and Surgery. This is 88.6 percent of the total VA employment. The number of personnel required in this area is primarily a function of the staff-to-patient ratio. At present this ratio is a congressionally mandated 1.49 to 1. Assuming that Congress will not change this ratio, the personnel projections become a function of the number of patients who will use VA facilities. Based upon a slightly increasing veteran population size, but a moderately declining prevalance rate of medical use, the number of patients using VA facilities is estimated to decline by an average of 1 percent annually throughout the second half of the decade; consequently a corresponding decline in medical personnel is projected. However, the saving from the reduction in personnel will be more than offset by cost-of-living and productivity increases for the personnel remaining.

Projections for operating costs are based upon the decline in the number of patients, but allow for increases in the cost of goods and services and assume that the Congress will pass the proposed legislation that will compel private insurers to reimburse the VA for the costs of medical care and treatment provided to veterans for nonservice-connected disabilities. If this is not passed, an additional $80 million must be added annually.

Research and administration costs are assumed to remain constant in real terms. Construction outlays assume completion of the $363 million of major and minor construction projects already authorized and initiation of future projects at the same rate as in the fiscal 1972-74 period. Total medical costs should rise to about $3.6 billion by fiscal 1981.

Miscellaneous costs (housing and administration) should amount to $.7 billion in fiscal year 1974. Projections for these areas assume that present housing programs will continue and that administrative costs will remain constant in real terms. By fiscal year 1981 these costs should be about $.9 billion.

International Affairs and Finance. Projections assume a rise in outlays from fiscal 1973 to fiscal 1975 due to subscriptions to international lending institutions. Outlays are roughly stable from fiscal 1975 to 1981, reflecting the assumptions that the major beneficiaries of food for peace will become self-supporting in wheat and that there will be no major disasters requiring large-scale food donations. Aid to Hanoi is not included in the projection.

Interest. The projection for this area assumes that gross interest paid grows only by the increase in interest received by the trust funds, on the assumption that the economy is at full employment and there is balance in the full employment budget.

General Government. Outlays for this category assume past trends in real outlays through 1975-81 and that inflation occurs at the 2.5 percent rate. The administration project of law-enforcement revenue sharing is incorporated and WMATA grants are assumed to follow the planned path.

General Revenue Sharing. Outlays through fiscal 1977 are based on amounts appropriated by the State and Local Fiscal Assistance Act of 1972. Growth after fiscal 1977 assumes the same absolute growth as in fiscal 1977.

SELECTED 1973 PUBLICATIONS

PUBLIC CLAIMS ON U.S. OUTPUT: Federal Budget Options in the Last Half of the Seventies by David J. Ott, Lawrence J. Korb, Thomas Gale Moore, Dave M. O'Neill, Attiat F. Ott, Rudolph G. Penner, and Thomas Vasquez finds that the 1974 federal budget program, if implemented, meets the administration's stated goal of a virtual balance between expenditures and "full employment" receipts in calendar year 1975 and would provide surpluses thereafter, rising from $9 billion in 1976 to $57 billion in 1980. On the other hand, the *appropriate* full employment surplus (or deficit) is not clear. Uncertainty about the rate of private savings and future surpluses in the overall accounts of the state and local sector makes it difficult to estimate the appropriate budget posture to bring about any target rate of unemployment with fiscal policy. Uncertainty about the perceived benefits from federal spending and the effect of the federal tax system on private savings clouds any estimate of the proper fiscal stance for purposes of resource allocation while monetary policy assumes the burden of stabilization policy.

This volume, the second report from the AEI Long Range Budget Projection Project, also considers program issues within each major area of the budget. The authors examine the rationale for existing programs and develop, in varying degrees of detail, the costs of other alternatives, asking such questions as: How well are existing programs in defense, agriculture, science, technology and industry, housing, education, manpower, health, and income security meeting their stated goals? What viable options exist to present (or proposed) programs, including curtailments or terminations?

$3.75

 American Enterprise Institute for Public Policy Research
1150 Seventeenth Street, N.W., Washington, D. C. 20036